Bee Rowlatt is a former showgirl turned BBC World Service journalist. A mother of three and would-be do-gooder, she can find keeping her career going while caring for her three daughters (and husband) pretty tough, even in leafy north London.

May Witwit is an Iraqi expert in Chaucer and sender of emails depicting kittens in fancy dress. She is prepared to face every hazard imaginable to make that all-important hairdresser's appointment.

Talking About Jane Austen in Baghdad

BEE ROWLATT AND MAY WITWIT

PENGUIN BOOKS

PENGUIN BOOKS

Published by the Penguin Group
Penguin Books Ltd, 80 Strand, London WC2R ORL, England
Penguin Group (USA) Inc., 375 Hudson Street, New York, New York 10014, USA
Penguin Group (Canada), 90 Eglinton Avenue East, Suite 700, Toronto, Ontario,
Canada M4P 2Y3 (a division of Pearson Penguin Canada Inc.)
Penguin Ireland, 25 St Stephen's Green, Dublin 2, Ireland
(a division of Penguin Books Ltd)
Penguin Group (Australia), 250 Camberwell Road, Camberwell,
Victoria 3124, Australia (a division of Pearson Australia Group Pty Ltd)
Penguin Books India Pvt Ltd, 11 Community Centre,
Panchsheel Park, New Delhi – 110 017, India
Penguin Group (NZ), 67 Apollo Drive, Rosedale, North Shore 0632,
New Zealand (a division of Pearson New Zealand Ltd)
Penguin Books (South Africa) (Pty) Ltd, 24 Sturdee Avenue,
Rosebank, Johannesburg 2196, South Africa

Penguin Books Ltd, Registered Offices: 80 Strand, London WC2R ORL, England

www.penguin.com

First published 2010
1

Typeset in 11/13pt Bembo by Palimpsest Book Production Limited, Grangemouth, Stirlingshire
Printed in England by Clays Ltd, St Ives plc

ISBN: 978-0-141-03853-7

www.greenpenguin.co.uk

Penguin Books is committed to a sustainable future
for our business, our readers and our planet.
The book in your hands is made from paper
certified by the Forest Stewardship Council.

To Ali: for his indispensable support

For Justin and the girls: every day you make my life better

Preface

This was never meant to be a book. But when you read it, you'll see how it had to become one, regardless of any embarrassment I might feel about its intimate contents.

I made contact with May in 2005, completely at random. She was just another person at the end of a phone line in my busy working day. I never imagined that we'd become friends, our worlds were so different. But as a relationship developed, the intimacies that we shared took on a huge momentum in my life.

Writing the emails became compulsive. I wanted to share the personal moments in my life with my friend, someone I came to call my sister, never thinking that anyone else would read them.

I can't help but feel a degree of horror now that the book is being published. The only consolation is that my private revelations are quite meagre next to May's story – and so, in tribute to her courage, here goes.

Bee Rowlatt

When I answered that phone call, Bee was a journalist through whom I wanted to expose my country's misery. I wanted the whole world to see the unreason and injustice of the decision to invade Iraq and shatter our lives – how the simplest daily chores became far-fetched objectives. I never realized at the time that my life would change through a friendship that exceeded race, age, time and place.

May Witwit

2005–2006

17.01.05

Hello

Dear May

Thank you for agreeing to be available for interview. As I said, I'm a producer for BBC World Service radio, on the news programme *The World*. I've been phoning around all week trying to make contact with various English-speaking Iraqis to interview in the run-up to the elections at the end of this month, so I was very happy to find you!

Would it be OK if I called you on Thursday? Most people I have spoken to say they are nervous about the elections and possible violence on the day. I'd love to hear your thoughts. Perhaps you could tell us about everyday life in Baghdad at the moment as well? Hearing you talk about trying to do your hair in a city of power cuts – ending up with it half curly and half straight – made me think that life must carry on behind the street fighting and explosions on the news. I can't imagine what it's like, and I'd love to hear from you about how you manage.

I wonder if you would mind telling me more about your family and your background. It's not easy for people over here to discover the voices of ordinary Iraqi people whose lives are tangled up in the big news stories. In any case I will email you again, so that I can keep up with your plans.

Take care.

Very best wishes

Bee

26.01.05

Hi, Bee

I received your email and was delighted – it has been ages since I've been in contact with anyone from Britain.

Since you asked, here is a little more about myself: I am the eldest of three, two girls and a boy. We were born in Iraq – in 1959, 1962 and 1964. My parents, both pharmacists, travelled in 1960 to the UK to complete their studies at Queen's University in Belfast. My parents taught at the College of Medicine and my father was soon promoted to become the head of the chemistry department. Being a devoted scientist he got cancer from working with carcinogenic chemicals. My mother did all she could, but he died just before Christmas 1970, in London.

After his death, my mother (only 33) decided to study for her PhD and was accepted at Chelsea College of Science and Technology in London. But she wasn't very comfortable there. We moved several times before we eventually settled in Dennistoun, in Scotland. After she got her PhD we moved back to Iraq, late in 1975.

Life here, as I told you, is a mini hell. As you know, I teach English literature at Baghdad University. I think it helps my students, because it transports them to another culture, another life, and another world. The world of Jane Austen is so far removed from our daily terror of bombs and violence.

I hope that all is well at your end of the world. Iraqis here want to vote, and are looking forward to the day of the elections because they really do believe that it will make a difference. I'm not that optimistic, but still I hope that it will turn out right.

Hope to hear from you soon.

Best wishes

May

10.02.05

Election day

Hello, May! It was good to hear from you again. Thanks for letting the programme contact you. I wasn't in that day, but I understand they were very happy. It looked like election day would be trouble. But the news on the actual day was quite inspiring; I couldn't believe how brave people were and that eight million voted. It always makes me think about people here, who are often too lazy or indifferent to vote. If only they knew what other people go through to do it!

Everything is fine here. In fact, I took some time off after the elections to catch up with normal life. It was good to have a break – the news can be hard to escape when you're up close to it all day. I have two small kids so I only work part-time now, but sometimes it's hard to switch off.

Here in the UK everyone's caught up in the earth-shaking news that Prince Charles is to marry his girlfriend Camilla. News reporters are wondering whether the British public approves or not (given the enduring fascination with Diana). I never know whether to be reassured by stories like this: you think, 'Well the world can't be so bad after all.' But then you think, 'Do people really care about THIS?' Of course, we all follow Iraq on the news. But it's hard to imagine ordinary people caught up in the scenes on TV. I sometimes try to imagine what life would be like if the conditions in Baghdad were suddenly imposed on London.

Spring is nearly starting here and there are a few buds poking out of the soil. It's still cold but it feels like spring is on its way.

How is your teaching going? Are your students coping with the 'regime change'? I wonder what things are like now, compared to before the invasion.

Hope you are well.

Bee

Before and after

Hello, Bee

Things seem no better after the elections, but we do hope that the situation will improve. It's not so easy to try and foresee things; it's a bit early and there are conflicts among the winners themselves. We'll have to wait and see.

I was thinking about your questions and the comparison between 'Now' and 'Then'. You ask what it's like to teach at an Iraqi university. So let me try to describe it for you: classes start at 8.30 and continue to around 1.30. Before the invasion we used to have evening classes but now it's no longer safe, and public transport is not available after dark. I don't take classes before 10 a.m. because I adore my morning rituals and love to take my time when showering and having breakfast and drying my hair (this is my most important part of the day). I hate to rush things or be in a hurry, no matter what. And if the situation requires hurrying (as it sometimes does) my whole day is ruined. Besides, my brain doesn't function properly till after 10 a.m.

Teaching at the College of Education for Women is quite different from my other teaching experiences when I taught mixed-sex classes. As you know, our society is sort of restricted when it comes to mixing between the sexes. Many families do not approve, and think letting male and female students sit next to each other is like pouring petrol on fire. But if parents are more open-minded, they will send their girls to mixed colleges.

Young women in our college are treated like girls, and the department will send for the father or guardian if a student is absent or does not wear proper uniform. Sometimes a student who is very oppressed at home comes to college all covered up and wearing no make-up. Once she is inside she changes her clothes in the bathroom, puts on heavy make-up, removes her head cover and pulls her hair down. This is done without the knowledge of the family, and of course the procedure is reversed when it's time to go home.

Teachers have greater freedom, but there are limitations. In the old days before the invasion, trousers weren't accepted. I remember when I had to meet the former president of the university to sign my appointment letter. The man looked at me and said, 'Please don't think that I am old-fashioned, but trousers are not really acceptable because you are going to set an example to the female students.' I smiled at him and said cheerfully that I wouldn't be wearing them again, explaining, 'They have just been tailored to fit me and I thought that, since I was meeting you, I should wear nice clothes.' He laughed and said, 'You remind me of a teacher at medical college.' And then he gave my mother's name! I looked surprised and told him she was my mother, and he chuckled, saying, 'Now I know whom you take after.' (He was later assassinated, shot dead in his clinic shortly after the invasion.)

Will have to run to make dinner now.

Love

May

18.02.05

RE: Before and after

Dear May

Sorry to hear about the university president. But it's amazing to hear about daily life at your college. Could it be as though time's going backwards for women in your country? In the West we tend to view Arab countries as oppressive towards women, but by the sound of your mum it can't have been all that bad before the invasion. Unless she was considered unusual in being educated and working as a pharmacist? After your dad died, was she able to be independent and make a comfortable living from her work?

I guess I'm partly interested in how it is for women in your country because my children are both girls. They are Eva, aged 3, and Zola, aged 2. Even at such a young age they are very different people. Having daughters has certainly made me think more about how societies treat women. It's one thing when you're bothered on your own behalf, but quite another when you worry about your own child and her prospects. I grew up thinking women could do anything and everything, but now it strikes me that if you have kids you realize you are constrained in one way or another. You have to sort of choose: shall I try to forge ahead with my career, or shall I try to be a perfect mother? (Or completely do my own head in trying to do both.)

So that's why I love to know about your mum, and your female students. Plus I'm basically a nosey person, so there you have it. I must dash now, but I hope that you're well and that you can drop me a line soon.

Love

Bee

21.02.05

RE: Before and after

Hello, Bee

As you guessed, my mother was quite unusual for an Iraqi woman. She worked after her graduation from the college of pharmacy in 1957, and has continued to work ever since. I remember she had no time to cook or do the usual household chores when I was growing up, so we had a servant/cook for quite a long time. When one servant left we would get another, and for those periods in between my mother would order a whole week's meals from a restaurant and put them in the deep freeze for us to heat up and eat! Most Iraqi women are very domestic, though. Housework here is regarded solely as a female duty that has to be carried out whether the woman wants to or not, and whether she works or not. I remember an old man asking me once whether I could bake bread or not, and when I said no, he eyed me worriedly, saying, 'Women who can't bake bread are not popular in the marriage market.' I had been married then for 17 years so I laughed and said, 'Yes, you're quite right. I'm really suffering from this defect.'

I think around two-thirds of women stay home to raise the family, but this is all changing now because of the high number of men that have been, or still are, killed and imprisoned. But unemployment has actually gone up since the US invasion. Ministries and administrations have been dissolved, leaving millions simply jobless.

I think I would describe our family as educated upper-middle class. Not filthy rich, but you could say we are well off. Not many people in this category remain now. Most of them emigrated between 1991 and 2003, during the embargo years, and the rest have fled the country since the US invasion. I can't say that they do not exist but they are a tiny and ineffective minority. Our old neighbours were mostly doctors, pharmacists, mayors, lawyers, army generals etc. Most of these people have either died or left the country, and the houses that once stood empty are now occupied, either by distant relatives or by people displaced from other neighbourhoods who are very different in their habits.

The truth is that most of those still in the country cannot afford the expense of emigrating and have failed to get jobs outside Iraq, despite the hundreds of applications they have filled out. There are some middle-class types that also stayed, hoping to benefit from the present situation. They have shut their minds and souls to all that is logical, modern and cultured. One colleague, for example, totally changed her principles and loyalty after the invasion. When confronted she simply said that she had been oppressed and help-less in the old days, while in reality she was one of the regime's most committed followers.

Time to go now. I hope you are well in London.

Love

May

22.06.05

Hello again

Hello, May! How are you?

I hope you're well. It seems like such a long time since the elections, and looking at the news over here nothing seems to be getting any better. The BBC is reporting a study that puts the civilian death toll since the invasion at around 25,000 – so shocking.

It's been a busy time here but I am having a good summer; we have a heatwave here in the UK and London looks so beautiful, it's shimmering. It's very hot outside and I can hear the rumbling sound of central London through our office windows. You will remember from your time in Scotland that we British people take the weather very seriously as a subject: any change in temperature is greeted with shock and amazement, even if it's only to be expected.

I loved reading about your family. Mine is a bit patchy and hard to describe; my mum's family is all dead apart from her sister in Canada. I know very little about the previous generations. I don't really describe myself by class – if someone else feels the need to then that's up to them. I grew up in a very small family unit. My father left when I was a baby so it was just my mum and older brother. I've since found out that we were pretty poor at the time, she was a part-time teacher while she brought us up and that was her only income. But my mum's very clever and we had no idea that we were skint. I can now boast about our whacky upbringing: Mum bringing home and cooking squashed roadkill (pheasants and rabbits), weird hippy clothes that we wore, and strange family holidays. Schoolfriends teased me for not having a TV in our house, but of course all these things are very trendy now. (My mum and her boyfriend Dave now own a shop in York and live very comfortably in a gorgeous house in the countryside, so it's safe to say they made it in the end!)

I have better financial security than my mum had as a young mother. My husband Justin is also a journalist but works on TV (= better paid) and so he's the breadwinner. When we first got together I was embarrassed by our financial arrangements. I stopped earning for a while when our first baby, Eva, was born. He was scrupulously careful to make me feel the income was shared, but even so I still remember the first time I bought a lipstick with 'his' money, and how strange it felt. Now I doubt my wages will ever match his so I have shed those early misgivings – consider it a housekeeper's/mother's/secretary's salary if you will, haha!

Even so I wouldn't want the girls to be spoilt and not know the value of money. When they're teenagers I'll expect them to earn their own just as I did. And although our neighbourhood is one of London's posh ones, which is all very nice, the girls have very little in the way of Stuff. You know – Barbie dolls, technology, trendy clothes and all that. A bit mean perhaps, but fortunately they're still too young to have realized it.

Well anyway, I thought I would just drop you a line and say hello. Let me know how you are!

Very best wishes

Bee

13.03.06

A loud Hiiiiiii from Iraq

Dear Bee

It's been a very long time since we emailed but, believe me, I do want to continue our acquaintance. The reason for my long absence is due to various reasons such as the continued electricity failure in the country, the horrible and bloody daily events we have to live through, mid-term examinations and the marking of tons of students' papers and, last but not least, the collapse of my old and crazy computer.

Do you want to know what I did to overcome some of the depressive circumstances? I got married. Our families objected from the very beginning, so no one came to the wedding. It was all over very quickly; a friend took us to the marriage office and was a witness to the marriage contract, and that's all. On the way back we bought a chocolate cake and some cans of Pepsi. I wore cream slacks and a leopard-print T-shirt with an Islamic cloak and head cover, he wore a pair of jeans and a shirt. The friend dropped us at my house, we went in and that was that. (It was so unlike my first wedding, although that wasn't all that much better. I've been married before, and then widowed. There is so much more to tell you, but it makes me unhappy so, for now, that is all I will say.)

We are really on our own. At least now I have someone to talk to during the long evenings of the curfew, a man to hide behind when the sound of bombs wakes me in the middle of the night, and to protect me when I have to face the horrors of the daily drive to work.

Please do get in touch. Looking forward to hearing from you soon.

May

14.03.06

A big cheer from London

MAY, I'm so delighted to hear from you! Thanks for writing; it really is a relief. Even though it's been such a long time, every bomb made me think of you, and I wondered if you were OK. It makes listening to the news from Iraq a very different experience.

Congratulations on your marriage! I'm sorry your family didn't agree and you couldn't celebrate it in the usual way. I imagine a traditional Iraqi wedding is quite something. But then the important part is who you choose, not how you do it. So I wish you both the very best.

I also have some news: I'm only going to be working for another month or so as I'm expecting another baby, due on 25th May. I'm getting quite nervous actually. I haven't found out if it's a girl or a boy, but because I already have two girls everyone keeps saying that I must be hoping for a boy. It's irritating, and makes me automatically reply that I want another girl. But the truth is, I really don't mind either way. I just wish it would hurry up as I absolutely hate being pregnant.

Yesterday the withdrawal of some British troops from Iraq sparked a wide debate here. Some are saying that the Iraqis want the troops to leave, but other people (including the government) argue that since the troops are there, they should at least try to finish the job before they leave – whatever the 'job' is. Should all the troops leave? Has anything got better since the invasion?

Well, I'd better go and get started on the day's work, digging around for stories and news angles and chasing things up. But again I must tell you how happy I am to hear that you are OK despite the circumstances. And CONGRATULATIONS on your marriage!

All the best

Bee

Daily life (with no hairdryer)

Dear Bee

You can't believe how thrilled I am to hear from you. It is a nice thing to talk to someone who is not actually living in the inferno.

I'll tell you something from our daily experiences and you can judge how it is. This morning I woke up at 4 a.m., not because I'm an early riser but because I want to take a shower and dry my hair before going to work. As I got out of the bathroom the electricity went off, and so did my dreams of washing and drying my hair. So I wore it in a ponytail, though it is quite short.

At nine my husband started the car and we discovered that we had very little petrol (enough if everything goes well — but in the current atmosphere you can't take any chances). And so we went looking for petrol (black market, of course). We filled the car up and headed for work. But the bridge was closed and no one was allowed to cross, so after all the rushing and waking up early I still couldn't get to work.

Do you know that I haven't been to a petrol station since the early days of the invasion? Since then, the black market has flourished everywhere and in every business. People openly stand on the high-street pavements selling the kerosene and gas bottles that we need but can't normally find anywhere else. These people are merely dealers for the ones we call 'whales', who are usually influential people with prominent posts. They keep themselves in the background but take all the cash. They use bribes (or other means) to take the kerosene and gas bottles supplied to the petrol stations and pass them to their dealers, who sell them. I buy the black market petrol sold on the street for two reasons. The first is that petrol stations are not safe; they are an easy target. Many people waiting in the long queues have been killed or injured. The second reason is that some of these stations mix water with the fuel to compensate for the quantity stolen and sold on the black market, and this of course ruins the engine.

Food shopping has also changed, and maybe for the better. Residential areas like ours usually lack sufficient shopping facilities but since the invasion and the arrival of so many displaced people, shops have sprung up out of nowhere and they are everywhere now. We have more than we really need, but we try to remain in the neighbourhood because it is much safer. On the days when there is a curfew we have no choice but to buy from them, no matter how bad the produce may be. I remember buying bread that turned out to be stale, crushed tomatoes etc., and all for the same price as fresh. However, I sometimes stop on my way back from college to buy bread and vegetables, because they are fresher in a nearby neighbourhood that I pass through when driving home.

As for college, I am teaching first-year students the subjects of human rights(!) and democracy (!!!). Not topics to which they relate naturally, as you may imagine. It is hard to know how best to teach them. I also teach third-year students the novels *The Scarlet Letter*, *Pride and Prejudice* and *Hard Times*.

You asked what will happen if all the troops pull out? Well, I think it is so unpredictable. What I think is that they shouldn't have come in the first place and shouldn't have listened to the opposition. Yeah the Old Man had his faults, but we were better off then than we are now. Iraq is now a land drowned in blood and chaos. At least before we were a fully sovereign and independent country. If the troops pull out, I suppose there will be more bloodshed. And we never know what Iran will do.

But, Bee, I tell you this. The Americans say Iraq needs them to mediate between our warring groups. I really do not agree. Iraqi society is mostly tribal and governed by tribal rules. Actually, my family is not really governed by them. This is partly because of my father dying young and my mother being an only child – we are, to some extent, on our own, without aunts and uncles to interfere in our lives and our beliefs. It is also because Baghdad is like a mosaic of different cultures and beliefs with Sunnis, Shi'ites and all the different types of Christians, Arabs, Kurds, Turcoman Armenians and others living in one city. All these groups seemed to live peacefully together until the US 'democracy' ignited all the differences that we see today . . .

I'm so glad that you are expecting your baby soon, and I wish you an easy and quick labour – and good health for you and the baby, which is more important than its sex.

Please write as often as you can.

Love

May

28.03.06

A poem

Hello there, May

I hope things haven't been too spoilt by the daily madness today. I thought of you last week as I was trying to contact a Baghdad-based poet; he'd written very poignantly about poetry and his hopes for the new Iraq. I finally got him on the phone, hoping to get an interview, but he was so upset, he wept and seemed half crazy. He kept changing his name and acting terrified. In the end I couldn't bear to ask him to do an interview. I just tried to make sympathetic comments as I listened, then felt dreadful and useless afterwards.

He made me think about your literature students: don't they find it hard to relate to literature when their lives are a daily struggle? How can you teach Jane Austen in Baghdad? How can they make sense of it? I imagine it could be a kind of escape for them. When I was at school I had a wonderful English teacher. One day she set us a task: we all had to learn a poem off by heart, to recite in front of the class. It could be any poem but a minimum of fourteen lines. The reason, she said, was in case any of us went to prison. We all laughed but I remember her reasoning: a poem can sustain you. I've never been to prison but I can still remember my poem.

It was 'Spring and Fall: To a Young Child' by Gerard Manley Hopkins. I enjoyed the sounds, especially 'worlds of wanwood leafmeal lie'. At the time the meaning was a bit obscure, but now I'm older I think I get more from it. You may know it but I'm sending you it anyway:

Margaret, are you grieving
Over Goldengrove unleaving?
Leaves, like the things of man, you
With your fresh thoughts care for, can you?
Ah! As the heart grows older
It will come to such sights colder
By and by, nor spare a sigh
Though worlds of wanwood leafmeal lie;
And yet you will weep and know why.
Now no matter, child, the name:
Sorrow's springs are the same.
Nor mouth had, no nor mind, expressed
What heart heard of, ghost guessed:
It is the blight man was born for,
It is Margaret you mourn for.

Other news: I have only one more week of work before I go off on maternity leave. I am a little (= extremely) scared of giving birth, but looking forward to the baby.

A funny thing: I told you my husband Justin is a journalist too, well his programme, *Newsnight*, has asked him to do an experiment, to be their 'Ethical Man'. This means we'll have to live an environmentally friendly lifestyle for a year while they film us trying to do it. I am quite good at environmental stuff like recycling, but Justin is terrible. The idea is to change each aspect of our family life: the way we travel, eat, run the house. They'll take away our family car etc. and film the whole thing. I don't know if you can watch films on your computer, but if you fancy a silly distraction we're on the *Newsnight* website. My friends are already teasing me a lot about it, as you can imagine.

Well, May, I'll drop you another line before I finish work next week. In the meantime, I hope it's going well for you and your new husband. I hope you are both very well.

Take care!

Bee

22.04.06

Before the baby comes

Hi, Bee

I read the poem and I applaud your memory of your schooldays. By the way, I saw your photo and your husband's Mr Ethical project on the internet and I think you look very nice.

I expect you are taking your leave now, and I wish you a safe delivery and good health for you and the baby.

I hope to hear from you soon. Wish you all the luck and happiness.

Love

May

11.05.06

Quick hello

Hi there, May – no baby news to report (due in two weeks; wish it would hurry up) but I just wanted to say that it's nice to be in touch with you and I hope we can continue to email while I'm on maternity leave.

Just a quick hello, and hope that you are well and taking care.

Bee

06.06.06

Elsa is here!

Another girl! Elsa Rowlatt arrived at 5.10 p.m. on Sunday 28th May.

We're doing fine; and getting lots of rest.

Love to everyone

Bee

04.07.06

RE: Elsa is here!

CONGRATULATIONS. SO HAPPY FOR YOU. SORRY COULDN'T WRITE SOONER. THE PHONE THAT MY EMAIL IS CONNECTED TO IS OUT OF ORDER. THESE ARE POST-WAR LUXURIES.

LOTS OF LOVE FOR YOU AND THE BABY.

MAY

RE: Elsa is here!

Dear Bee

Congratulations once again on the arrival of Elsa. You must be very happy but also exhausted. Raising three children must be very time- and health-consuming, but still, children give life its meaning. I wish things on my side were like in 'the good old bad old days', then I would have been able to send you a little gift. But, I'm sorry, it is quite impossible at present.

Life is different here now. People have stopped socializing and visits are kept as scarce as possible. Neighbours can spend time together, but going out of the area to visit is only done when abso- lutely necessary. I suppose this is true of us all, because at the end of each holiday I ask students about what they did in their free time. Answers are usually the same: they weren't even able to visit their grandparents on special feast days, and had to keep it to phone calls.

My nearest friend is about half an hour's walk away. We used to meet frequently until the concrete walls and barbed wire prevented easy access. Now we talk on our mobile phones only when necessary, just to make sure that she and her family are OK when a roadside bomb or car bomb goes off near their home, and vice versa. Mobile phones tend to be costly and our landlines were cut off shortly after the post-invasion government was established.

The only people I get to gossip with are my close colleagues at the university where we sit and discuss current issues over coffee. My mother, however, gossips with the neighbours who come to her pharmacy and we get all the news through her. So you see, Bee, you are my major outlet when I feel the need to talk. Other friends have emigrated and we have lost touch, although we are trying to reconnect via the internet. You can't imagine how many friends and families have separated since the invasion, and those remaining are mostly depressed or have lost their trust in other people.

Everything has changed here. Even weddings. Before the invasion weddings in Iraq were celebrated in the evenings. The celebration usually began when the couple arrived and the music and dancing would follow. If the people were modern in their outlook, the party would be mixed and men and women would dance together. If the families were conservative, the hall would be reserved for women only, and the bridegroom would be allowed in at the end.

Couples usually started their honeymoon at around midnight or later. They'd get into a decorated car and guests would follow them for as long as possible. I remember seeing people get out at the traffic lights and dance around from sheer joy while the light was red, then hurry back into their car when it turned green. Others would fire gunshots in the air (though prohibited by law) and people, including the married couple, would end up at the police station (but they were usually only fined and then set free).

Now the wedding parties begin early, and end just before dusk. The other day I saw a young woman wearing a party outfit and jewellery, about to attend a wedding. She looked ridiculous in the daytime, but I couldn't blame her. We all have to live with the fear of what might happen at any moment, and night-time is not safe. But it makes me sad that people cannot celebrate like they used to, or even mourn for that matter. Even burials and the times for accepting condolences have changed. Do you know that sometimes the family of the deceased have to take the corpse back home and then return the next day, or even bury their dead in a different cemetery, because of road closures and security alerts? I've heard that some even had to bury their dead temporarily near their homes until conditions relaxed.

As for us, things aren't getting any better. We don't know what to do with ourselves. We are not rich enough to emigrate, nor can we find a substitute. It is a stalemate.

Anyway, we are still breathing and I'm trying to write a paper on *A Tale of Two Cities*. This makes me even more depressed but I need to finish it as one of three papers to be promoted to Assistant Professor.

Please write; I miss civilization and peace.

LOVE

25.07.06

Tale of two cities

Oh May, I LOVED *A Tale of Two Cities*! It is full of horror, but love wins in the end! I read it as a young teenager and fell in love with Sidney Carton. I thought Lucy should have loved him and not the other guy.

You have your own reign of terror. If Dickens could only know that someone in your circumstances is studying that book, while we correspond between our own two cities.

I hope you get the promotion. I would love to be able to send you some books. Do you need anything? One of the programmes I work for occasionally sends a correspondent into Baghdad and I could try to get something brought in for you. It would take a while, though. Is there anything you would like, something that would cheer you up in these difficult times?

It's proper summer now. We had a break in France with the entire Rowlatt clan (my husband Justin's family is huge) and there was a heatwave; it was mad. Eva and Zola are on school holidays, and Elsa the new baby is very sweet. In fact I keep forgetting I've got a baby, she's so quiet. So this is a lovely summer for me even though the rest of the world seems to be boiling into a fury. Lebanon is horrible and I'm glad I'm not at work having to think about it.

OK, May, sending you lots of love, keep your spirits up and good luck with *A Tale of Two Cities*.

Bee XX

26.07.06

Some questions about the future

Dear Bee

I received your email and was really happy to see you having a nice time. It gives me some hope for a better world, where people can come and go where and when they wish. I'm also glad that little Elsa is a very nice and happy baby. At least she won't make you edgy and nervous from the continuous screaming and lack of sleep. As for us here, it is rather difficult to describe what we are going through. It is not just the lack of security but it is the lack of everything. Do you know, Bee, that I am 46 years old and still can't do what I want? What is worse now is the threat of losing our lives, just because we are university teachers. Some of my colleagues have been viciously murdered and others have received threats warning them that if they don't leave the country they will meet a similar fate.

I would love to leave and seek asylum somewhere, anywhere, but I don't know where and how. Simple migration requires a lot of money, which I don't have, because I've always worked to provide for my home. My first husband was always in debt. My second husband is a nice person, but is jobless because he is a Sunni and no Sunni can ever work with the various militias controlling Baghdad.

Bee, although we have only known each other via email, I feel that you understand me. I know that I'm probably asking too much, but can you please inquire whether I can get asylum or anything similar? I have to go; there is a power failure.

Love

May

xxx

RE: Some questions about the future

Dear May

I am going to try. I will contact some friends I have who work at the Refugee Council (a charity which helps asylum seekers and refugees) to find out what the best procedure is. I know it's not easy and that Britain has become much more strict. But I will look into it, and let you know.

Hang in there, May!

Love from

Bee

30.07.06

Aborted trip to Jordan

Dear Bee

I am really very grateful – thank you for your concern. Things here are getting worse every day. Imagine, I was supposed to go to Jordan for a couple of days, to hunt for a job and a way out of here. Since I cannot afford to go by plane, I decided to go by car. A lot of my friends warned me that there were gangs on the way and that I might get robbed, raped or killed, or maybe all three. But my stubborn head kept telling me not to worry and so I made reservations and contacted some friends. But what happened was just unbelievable.

The driver told me to be ready at six in the morning, so as to start the journey as soon as the curfew ended. At five he called to confirm and I told him that I was ready. I had food and cold drinks etc. My husband was scared of my going alone all the way there, while he had to stay on his own in Baghdad. The mere thought of my leaving made him ill. But going to a hospital nowadays is out of the question because medical facilities in Iraq are almost non-existent. The hospitals are mostly controlled by militias, so that any Sunni seeking treatment is likely to be killed by deliberate medical malpractice, such as being given the 'wrong' injection. He could not risk going.

But it seems that fate had already made its decision about my journey. The driver called again at 6.15 and said that he was sorry, he couldn't make it because some armed men had broken into his uncle's house and killed his 27-year-old cousin. I realized how dangerous it was. I cancelled the reservations and sat at home thinking.

Anyway, in the afternoon we went out to try to buy hair colour to hide my grey hair but could not find one single shop open – except two or three selling food, which is of course a mercy.

Can you believe my homeland has become so lawless and chaotic? I thank you again for your concern, and I do hope that we can meet one day. My love to you and the girls and a big kiss for Elsa; my regards to your husband.

XXX

15.08.06

Not good news

Hi there, May

I'm sorry, but the news about immigration and asylum is bad.

I contacted a friend who works for the Refugee Council, and he said that when the invasion first began in 2003 lots of Iraqis claimed asylum here. But now the government is not accepting any more, and some who have tried to claim asylum are being sent back home. I asked my friend what the best way to claim asylum is, and he said you have to prove that your life is in clear and direct danger if you return to Iraq. I told him that some of your colleagues have had death threats or even been murdered, and he said you should look for documentary evidence of this; newspaper reports might help.

It is really difficult to do, and furthermore those in the actual process of claiming asylum can be treated very badly – I volunteer for the Refugee Council as a careers adviser, and my current mentee told me that the interviews to claim her refugee status were totally traumatic. As career mentors we're not supposed ever to talk about why they became refugees. But it came up once in conversation, what she had gone through at British Immigration. She just put her face in her hands and was silent for a while, and then said it was indescribable (she came from Angola several years ago).

I feel bad giving you such negative news, May. If you can get any kind of documentary evidence of your danger, you must do so. Also keep a diary of events, with the dates. Could you go to live in Jordan? I wish I could do more to help, and if there's anything else I can do then you must let me know.

I wish I could get hold of better news to cheer you up a bit. Today is Zola's birthday (my middle daughter) and she is 4. We're all about to go to an outdoor theatre in the park, to see a children's play.

Take care, May.

All my best wishes

Bee XX

Hiiiiii and thank you

Hi, Bee

Thank you very much for everything and for explaining the asylum situation.

It is getting worse here. We are on the brink of a civil war. The warring parties are all fighting for government posts and authority. Everyday life is a difficult mission. You have to search for bread, vegetables, petrol, clean water. But even so, there are many people who are finding it even harder than us. There are no shops. The shopping area in our district is closed and people are using it to dump their rubbish because it is not being collected. I've been keeping the black plastic bags in the garden but the hot weather rotted them quickly and the smell became unbearable so my husband took them and dumped them, just as other people were doing. Bee, when he went there he was shocked to discover that not only was rubbish being dumped there but also unidentified corpses. There were about four bodies dumped among the rubbish bags.

Please don't stop writing, because your emails give me hope that there still are good people in the world.

Love and kisses

May X

31.08.06

Another tale of two cities

May!

I can't begin to imagine your daily life, the backdrop of violence and then trying to get stuff done. How about your paper on *A Tale of Two Cities*; how is it going?

Summer is ending here. The leaves on the trees are just starting to go yellow; the smell of the air changes. It's very beautiful but it makes me feel a bit sad and nostalgic. My girls are back at school next week, so that will mean I'll have some time free to plan my next moves. Elsa is only three months old now but I know I will want to do some part-time work when she's about six months.

Take care of yourself and remember someone is thinking of you and wishing for your safety.

Bee XX

31.08.06

Fountain!

Hi, Bee

Got your email and was so happy. It was like a fountain in the middle of a desert.

I'm happy that you're thinking of going back to work because that is really your biggest asset in life. Kids grow up, husbands might become a pain in the neck (or anywhere else for that matter); but your work is your true life.

As for our life here, I can tell you that we have learned to solve all kinds of problems. We've solved the problem of electricity by buying private generators and also by linking up to a huge street generator (also privately owned) because our small ones cannot go on all day and night. You can't imagine the cost of all this. Almost 60 per cent of my income goes on fuel.

As for my work on Dickens, I've collected all the stuff I need and written a first draft. But it seems futile, and I keep asking myself, 'What is the point of work and education if the illiterate or semi-illiterate gain control over everything and kill the learned?' The other day a professor of linguistics was shot dead at the College of

Arts. He was a man devoted to his work, and I don't think that he had any political views or anything, but still this did not save him.

Bee, I have applied for a job at the UN and will have to take an exam sometime in October. I don't know if I will be accepted. Being an Iraqi is an obstacle in terms of getting any job with an international organization, or a visa to any country.

Anyway, that's all for now. Kiss the girls for me, and my love to you.

May

03.09.06

Gift for you

MAY, hello. I've been thinking about you a lot recently and I was very excited. I wasn't going to tell you, but I thought I had found a way to get a gift to you – a couple of nice books – because an old friend of mine visited us today and he's been working as a cameraman for CNN, embedded with the US military in Baghdad. I thought you could meet up. But he thought it was so horrific out there that he says he is never going back. (Even though they paid him TWO THOUSAND dollars a day, can you believe?)

Yes, you are right about the importance of careers. My father left when I was 2 and my brother was 5, and he never gave my mum a single penny from that day on. And so she did absolutely everything herself, and never stopped working. Indeed, I think we modern women really define ourselves by our careers – perhaps almost too much. I have always loved my job and thought I was lucky to have it. But even so, I sometimes feel I would like to try something new.

OK, May – I hope you had a nice weekend.

Love

B XX

11.09.06

Power failures and fish and chips

Hi, Bee

This is the third attempt to write an email to you. Every time the power fails my old computer breaks down. My husband took it to be repaired and it came back OK, but we didn't have an internet connection for three days.

We are back at college, and the re-sit exams are on. You can't imagine how frustrating it is to read the poor English of our students, but considering the current situation they cannot really be blamed.

The other day two more professors were killed. More shopkeepers in our area have been slain – and I mean that (their heads were cut off). I don't know what will happen to us all. I hope things will ease, but I doubt it.

Love and kisses to you, dear.

May XX

PS How much does a portion of takeaway fish and chips cost now, and an ice cream? Back when I lived in the UK it cost 90p for the first and 6p for the second.

PPS A joke: WHAT DO SEA MONSTERS EAT?? FISH AND SHIPS.

21.09.06

Fish and chips

Hello, May

Fish (large cod) and chips (medium) are now £4.95 at my local chippy. I sometimes get them if we're all really tired. I love it. And an ice cream from the ice-cream van costs around 60p, but with the girls we usually get a Mini Milk – they're tiny little ones but they're delicious and they only cost 30p.

I've been trying to think of a joke to send you, but I'm terrible at jokes and can never remember the ones I like.

Term's started and I am somehow suddenly on the Parents' Association at the girls' school. I'm not quite sure how it happened, I was basically pounced upon by a scary mum and so I said yes. Lots of meetings, fund-raising, chasing parents around and so on. We have to do it for two years. Hmm.

And I've also been in touch with my colleagues at the BBC, just to remind them I'm still here and when I'm thinking of going back (probably around Christmas time). May, listen: I've been asking around about who is going into Baghdad from the BBC next. One of Justin's colleagues is going over soon, and although they have to stay inside the International Zone, they work with Iraqis who come in and out of the zone. Is there any way I could get a present to you? I have two books I wanted to send you, but would you be offended if I sent a small amount of money too? US dollars perhaps, I don't know what would be best. Or, if not, is there something I could send to help your students perhaps? Well, in any case, let me know if I can proceed with that plan, and what is the best way.

Wishing you a bright day

Bee

23.09.06

Ramadan

Dear Bee

Can't tell you how happy I am to hear from you. Feeling happy, or at least satisfied, gives us inner strength and helps us overcome anything.

Today is the first day of the fasting month for Moslems. In this month people are supposed to fast from dawn to dusk (they literally eat nothing). Families gather at sundown with all kinds of lovely food to break their fast. Before the invasion people used to invite friends, but now it is just families. At sundown the streets of Baghdad are empty and you can drive fast and go anywhere in a few minutes, because everyone is inside eating. Yet most people are not grumpy, despite the hunger, because they know that this is the month of forgiveness and it makes people generous and kind.

Anyway on this occasion we were visited by the National Guard who carried out a house search. I haven't told you that I live next to the family home, where my mother and brother live (our neighbourhood is a quiet residential district with large houses erected on substantial plots, so there was enough space for me to build a small house in the garage area). My husband and I were visited, but my brother had filled in a form saying that he was the owner of the house. I've just been informed that the people who fill in such forms may be killed, and I'm scared stiff.

Some good news: we are painting our bedroom. It is a hectic job and we're tired, but it is really worth it. It looks beautiful. My husband says that he is painting it for me, to remove all the bitter memories of the past.

As for the books and the gift you want to send me, I'm really grateful. You don't have to go to any trouble. I'm already very happy with your friendship. You can of course send anything you like through your colleagues but it would have to reach me (even at the university) via an Iraqi because it would otherwise be very dangerous for both sides. We might both be killed.

Anyhow, I can send you my mobile number and your colleagues can contact me. I would be very happy because I also want to send you something to remember me by. I have to go now because I need to fix food for my fasting husband (who is quite chubby and adores food, so the first day of fasting is hard for him).

LOVE AND KISSES TO YOU AND FAMILY

MAY

25.09.06

The wonder of Marmite

Hello, May

How are you doing with the fasting? I don't think I could do it. I can't live without toast – hot buttered toast and Marmite. Maybe you remember Marmite? It's something I always try to give to foreigners as an experiment; mostly they recoil in fear. But we are brought up on the stuff in this country.

I always start the day really healthily; eating lots of fruits and porridge with the girls before they go to school. But then in the evening when I'm relaxing I love ice cream, chocolate, that sort of thing. And wine. There's a Turkish shop round the corner where they sell baklava; when you bite into it all the honey squeezes out. I love food, and luckily Justin is a brilliant cook – he does all the cooking. What is Iraqi food like?

Am heading out to the shops now. Hope your husband does OK with the fasting.

Love

Bee XXX

Food and Librans

Dear Bee

Our cuisine, though tasty, is very unhealthy. It is rich in fat, and is made up of a lot of everything: meat, poultry, rice, vegetables, sweets. You tend to gain weight because it is accompanied by laziness, especially since the invasion as it's become quite hazardous to take walks or go shopping. With the curfews and troubles people run to the shops and buy almost everything in them. We tend to do the same and mostly fill the house with cigarettes, cans of Coke, dry beans, cheese, jam, potatoes, cooking oil and flour because these to me are the most important items. I had a trim figure before the war, but now I'm really fat because there are no walks, no social life. The only exercise I get is giving lectures two or three times a week, and limited physical activity!

We have baklava mostly in winter, and it is a must in Ramadan. As for fasting, I don't fast because I'm a heavy smoker and a tea addict, so fasting becomes an ordeal.

Today is a Saturday and we've been stuck in the house because of a curfew since yesterday. It ends tomorrow at six in the morning, which is fortunate because it will be the first day of the first semester. We have to go to the university to see the timetable and check on things. If there are students I will have to give a lecture on social and living conditions in the Victorian Age, and something about America's Puritans etc.

You can imagine it is very hard for our students to capture the essence of things, due to cultural differences. They read the novel and then envelop it with Arabic traditional solutions. For example when I talk to them about Hester Prynne in *The Scarlet Letter*, they just can't understand why her husband didn't kill the two lovers instead of seeking indirect revenge. Or they invent their own endings, such as divorcing Hester and killing Dimmesdale. (I'm saving this in case the power goes. Bye.)

Hi again. I saved it just in time. We rent a line from a bureau a few metres away, but the terminal was cut off because the owner received a threat telling him to close his shop. We were left with no internet line until yesterday afternoon.

Anyway. It's hard to imagine but things are getting worse. Yesterday my husband came home terrified because someone had been killed right in front of him. The man – not yet dead – rose and started running blindly till he collapsed in the middle of the street. This was in addition to 23 other bodies found in the neighbourhood.

I went to college but there were no students, and so I decided to stay off work till Monday. Good news: we finished painting the bedroom and put all the furniture back.

By the way, when is your birthday? Are you a Libran? If you are then let me surprise you that I am also a Libran and was born on 10th October.

LOVE

May

05.10.06

I'm a Libran too!

May, you'll never guess what, my birthday is 15th October, just after yours! So I will raise a toast to you when I am celebrating. (Do you drink alcohol, by the way? We British are very indulgent drinkers. But now I remember you saying your first husband had a drink problem, so I imagine that would be enough to put you off for life.)

Well, I'm so happy to hear from you as I was in a really bad mood. I had a dream that Zola (my middle daughter) drowned, so I felt sick when I woke up. Then over breakfast I got in a mood with Justin, because he is running around being important and successful while I just have to do the bloody laundry and small day-to-day things that nobody has any regard for. He gets back late, all full of his brilliant job and I've just had enough of it. He's not actually a show-off but I resent the inequality in the impact the children have had on our lives, i.e. no impact on his career whatsoever. Obviously I don't regret the children at all because I love them so much; I just don't like the either/or dilemma between family and career. I know I'll feel better when I start doing my job again – I feel in a bit of a limbo.

But your email does put things into perspective. What a strange side effect of the curfew and insecurity that people are getting fat. You must get so bored when there is a curfew.

I was startled by your students' feelings about Hester Prynne. I did that book as part of my first degree and I loved it – so much so, that when I was pregnant with my first daughter I wanted to call her Pearl, after Hester's wild daughter. But Justin said no way; it reminded him of Formica tables (by that I think he meant old waitresses in cafés with cheap plastic furniture), haha!

I'm meeting up with a friend later for a swim in Hampstead Heath Ladies' Pond. It's a hidden-away large pond surrounded by dense bushes and trees. I think of it as an earthly paradise. In the summer it gets crowded but now that it's autumn only a few people keep going. There's a bare wooden hut where we get changed, then a big ladder sinks down into the dark water and you just have to plunge right in. It will be cold but it feels amazing afterwards, and the water smells so pure, like rain.

At the entrance there is a large sign saying NO MEN ALLOWED, which makes me laugh, as sexual discrimination is illegal in Britain (and also racial discrimination, and as of this week there is new legislation making it illegal to discriminate against someone on the grounds of age too).

OK, I have to go now – take care of yourself.

Lots of love and hugs

Bee XXX

PS Guess what, I have sent off a little parcel to you! It contains three books: one that I thought you would like (*Life of Charles Dickens*), another that I love (Blake) and another book (*Short Stories of Nathaniel Hawthorne*) that I bought second-hand in Glasgow. You will see inside my old name before I got married: Bee Späth, it's a German name. There are also a couple of pictures that Eva and Zola drew for you, and $200 in an envelope for you, and another $50 in an envelope for the 'fixer', that is, whoever can help to get it to you. Andrew North is the BBC correspondent there and an old colleague of mine. He'll call you to arrange it.

PPS What shape are your weekends over there? It sounds odd to me that your academic term would start on a Sunday.

6.10.06

Women's talk

Dear Bee

Thank you very much for taking the trouble to send me presents. I will try to send you something to remind you of me.

It is only natural to feel like that about husbands. I've always felt that I never got what I really deserve because of the creation of those creatures called Men, but they are something that we cannot do without for various reasons. In my country it is a man's world, no matter how hard you work and whatever degrees you obtain, still they are a teeny-weeny bit above us. I always thought men lacked consideration and were cruel creatures, until I was loaned a book called *Men Are from Mars, Women Are from Venus*. Then I realized that they tend to think in a different way (we might call it twisted or practical or whatever).

A few months after I was widowed by my first husband I got used to making my own decisions and I loved the freedom, but life began to get harder and harder: shopping, paying bills, getting fuel and even driving around. I had several offers, but was really scared to commit again. They were all very rich and highly educated but I always had this sense of their being selfish and self-obsessed. One night, and after nine months of widowhood (just before this war started), the phone rang at 3 a.m. I was terrified and lifted the speaker expecting to hear something awful, but to my surprise there was a stranger on the other end. All he wanted was to talk. He had dialled the number randomly. I told him off and put the fear of God into him, as you might say, but he did not give up. The phone kept ringing and ringing all night. I gave up and asked him what he wanted, and he said that he had always dreamed of meeting his soulmate by chance or fate. I told him that it was rather late and perhaps we could talk some other time. I thought that he was drunk and that everything would be over.

But he called the next afternoon. He told me all about himself and I found out that he was young. I told him that I was older than him, and he asked if we could just be friends and nothing more. I agreed and we talked regularly for about three months. I told him that I usually went to bed by midnight and was not ready to extend that deadline for any reason. He was very polite – by midnight he would remind me that it was my bedtime and put the phone down.

After three months, the war started and all the phones were cut off. I lost contact with him because he lived in another city, and I forgot all about him.

That's enough for today; I will tell you what happened in another email.

Good news. I got my hair cut and had what we call mesh; like blonde highlights. We finished the painting and then I did an overall clean, which included emptying cupboards, polishing metal and silver things, and cleaning the fans and the windows.

Love

May

PS Iraq's weekend used to be Friday, when families had their meals together, watched TV or entertained. The invasion added Saturday as another weekend day and so we now have two days in our weekend. But I describe Fridays as Frightdays because we are usually under curfew and there are often problems somewhere in the country. For some families it is Fightdays, since all are in the house due to the curfew and family quarrels tend to break out!

For Ali and me all our days are the same. We spend the weekends watching TV and eating more than five meals a day (without really being hungry) and reading tarot cards just to pass the time and ease our depression. But at least Saturdays are a bit better because there is movement in the streets and the shops open. Now I MUST go.

X

14.10.06

Birthday treats

MAY!!

I've had a lovely week but how fast it flew by. How was your birthday? I hope you had a good day.

I was fascinated by the story of your friend on the phone. How mysterious. I wonder what he is doing now, or if he is still alive. And when did you meet your new husband?

I've never read *Men Are from Mars, Women Are from Venus*. I suppose it's worth realizing how different we are. But then again, it doesn't have to be an excuse: 'I'm from Mars, so of course I don't know how to work the washing machine!' Haha.

I'm getting ready for my own birthday celebrations this evening (although it's actually tomorrow); a bunch of us are going out to a bowling place with live music. Yesterday I treated myself to a manicure and a pedicure, both in bright red, and I keep noticing them and smiling.

Busy week in the news: a former government minister made a comment about Moslem women in his constituency, saying that if they come to talk to him, he asks them to consider removing their facial veil. The media have gone mad about it; everyone's now talking about Moslem women covering their faces etc. I think it's rather a reflection of people's fear of Moslems in general because of world events and terrorism. The comment was supported by right-wing people and tabloid newspapers, but also many liberal people joined in, saying that wearing the veil oppresses women.

Must people get so upset? I was brought up with no religion whatsoever, and educated in the secular state system. Then I did 'A' Levels at a Quaker school. Although I didn't believe in God, I was impressed by their values (basically tolerance and pacifism) and have thought about it a lot since. To me it seems amazing that, after so many centuries, medieval things like religious persecution still persist. I know this is naive, but I don't think it's irrational. Unless every generation actively deletes what came before it. Maybe we don't progress at all but are merely subject to entropy. I am a bit of a teenage Hamlet today, aren't I? 'And yet, to me, what is this quintessence of dust?'

I realized that if something happened to you, May, I would never be able to find out. Your emails would just stop and I would never know why. It makes me feel horribly sad. I always think of you every time I hear about casualties in Iraq (almost daily). And yet if we walked past each other in the street we wouldn't even know.

War is the ugliest thing in the world. Oh May, I do hope that things will get better in Iraq and your life can be normal.

Take care.

Bee XXX

15.10.06

Happy birthday

Dear Bee

HAPPY BIRTHDAY AND MANY HAPPY RETURNS.

So happy to hear from you. I wrote an email telling you all about Moslem women but unfortunately it was swallowed up by the computer. What I wanted to tell you was that Moslem women do not have to cover their faces. They have to cover their bodies and most probably their hair, but NOT their faces, feet and hands. Mind you, this has been the costume of Middle Eastern women since as far back as early Christianity. This is clearly reflected in the pictures of the Holy Virgin.

What I do not understand, and what gets on my nerves, is the way in which extremists add their own rules and regulations. These people are doing more harm than they realize. Islam was never, ever a religion of violence, nor was it a religion that harboured hatred towards other religions. On the contrary, Moslems are required to treat people of other religions nicely, and to protect them in places where Moslems represent the majority. But those extremists have deviated from the course.

As for the story of the person I met on the phone, I last told you that the war had broken out and so I forgot all about him. Then, after 16 months, the phones were repaired, and you wouldn't believe it: the first person who called me was him. I was amazed to hear from him again, and he told me that he used to call my number every day at all hours to check.

I was so happy to hear from him. And we started to talk again. But this time we talked for hours and hours, and we became so close that we started having breakfasts, lunches and suppers together (on the phone). After four months I thought that it was time to meet this person face to face, and we set a date for our meeting, but then I chickened out because I lacked self-confidence. I thought that I was much older, and he couldn't possibly love me if he saw me. I did not realize that I had told him where I worked, and he had come to see me without me knowing.

That's all for now. I will tell you more later. I have to run to prepare dinner.

LOVE XXX to you and family.

May

03.11.06

It's a mess

Bee, dearest

Sorry for not writing for such a long time. I knew you'd be worried, but I just couldn't put my bum on a seat and write. My thoughts are all in a mess. Can you believe that we only go to the university once a week, and there are still no students to teach? They just don't come any more. We are living in a state similar to house arrest; we are literally imprisoned in our homes. It is so depressing.

My husband just can't go out anywhere, even to buy bread, without taking me with him, because a man on his own is an easy target for all the different militias. Our financial matters are very bad and my monthly salary isn't enough any more; it can't keep us for 10 days no matter how hard we try. We've cut down on all the 'luxuries' like meat, vegetables, haircuts, new clothes etc. But still it isn't working. I suppose we are better off than many Iraqis because we have no children to support and I have a regular salary. The self-employed and workers on a daily wage suffer the most.

I got a reply from the UN saying that I have not been selected, so that's that. I know that I am bothering you with all this news but at least you'll know that I am still ticking. How are the girls? Please give big hugs and kisses for each one of them. I wish I could see them some day.

You know I'm deprived of all my nephews and my niece, because my family are against my marriage. The same applies to my husband's family; they have disinherited him for marrying me. So you see, we are quite alone in this world. Although I live next door to my brother I can't hug his children, because they obey their father. The only person who talks to us is my mother, and I learn all their news from her.

What is keeping you busy? Please sit and write to me. Your emails give me psychological energy.

Love you always.

May XXXXX

03.11.06

Families

Dear May

I don't know how you manage it. Thank God you are OK, though.

I can't understand why your family and your husband's family have disconnected themselves from you. Is it for religious reasons, or because you were married before? Family feuds are so sad. My German side of the family (my mother's English but my father is German) is riven with feuding. I would consider my life a failure if my daughters all hated each other when they got old.

My older brother Wenz and I are quite different personality-wise, but at least we talk on the phone and see each other a few times a year (he lives up in Yorkshire). The girls just love him; they climb all over him and he never gets cross with them. My relationship with my mum is very close – I think she is a hero and I adore her. Occasionally she irritates me but I also miss her as she's in Yorkshire too, so we don't see her often enough.

Apart from your mum, do you have any other family you're close to, or were they all too angry about your marriage? May, you're like Emily Brontë – alone in a wilderness, with a rich interior life but no way of escape.

Well, I will try to tell you something to cheer you up. You know the Ladies' Pond up on Hampstead Heath I have mentioned? I went with two friends to do our last swim of the year, on 1st NOVEMBER! It was soooo cold, May. We had on bikinis and big woolly hats in the water! We were shrieking hysterically, partly from laughter but partly out of panic. The water was around 13 degrees, which isn't actually all that bad, but it was a very windy day.

I have to go now but I hope your day improves and you have a good weekend.

All my love

Bee XXXX

08.11.06

Andrew called

Hi, Bee

Today Andrew called. I asked him if I could send a driver to pick up the parcel, and take something to deliver to you. And the driver has just called saying that he received it!

Love XXX

May

08.11.06

Saddam's verdict

May

What did you think of the Saddam verdict? I don't agree with the death penalty, however bad the criminal. I think it puts the judicial system on the same level as the original offence. Have you seen what's happening in the mid-term elections in the US? It's very exciting. The tide seems to be turning against Bush.

It's getting really cold now and I'm wrapped up in a large fluffy white scarf my sister Hannah got me for my birthday. (She's actually a half-sister: same father, different mother. She grew up in Germany but has moved to the UK and we see each other a bit more, kind of a new discovery.)

I should really go out and get some stuff done.

Hope you're well.

Bee XXXX

Your present has arrived

Bee

Thank you so much for everything. I was truly happy and grateful. As for the children, their drawings brought tears to my eyes. I felt as though I was really their aunty.

You asked me about the S.H. verdict. Well, I'm against death sentences apart from in cases of rape and murder. But this death sentence is not proper. You know I finally realized that maybe his cruelty was designed to prevent the country from reaching this point. You can't imagine what it is like now.

People are killed because of their names – there are names which are preferred by Sunnis and others by Shi'ites. People are killed merely for being named Omar or Ali (names that identify them as belonging to the wrong faction).

Those who have control now are worse than he was. Do you believe that the winter has come, and it's cold and we have no electricity or fuel for the heaters? (By March it will be warm, and then by early May it will be 40 degrees centigrade and by July it exceeds 50.) Such extremes in this country. Last night I was shivering and my nose started running and I couldn't do a thing. I held Hawthorne's book, and started reading to keep my mind off things, but I only managed one short story and couldn't go on. So I went to bed and wore socks and covered myself with a duvet and two blankets. People who are doing this to civilians deserve a darker sentence than that of S.H.

I never knew that Hawthorne had written such lovely short stories. As the students have not yet started I won't have time to teach them *The Scarlet Letter*. I think I'll probably teach them the short stories instead. As for Dickens, I will probably teach them something shorter – that is, if they show up at all.

Bee, I asked Andrew to call me as soon as he comes to Baghdad. What is your dress size, and what is your shoe size? There are some things that carry the fragrance of the East which I would like you to have. I have them at home. I will also be sending you a copy of my thesis: 'The Theme of Love in Chaucer's *Canterbury Tales*'.

I have to go and make lunch. We are under curfew because it is Friday, or Frightday . . .

LOVE AND KISSES TO YOU AND THE GIRLS.

MAY

10.11.06

Christmas Fair and pancakes

HURRAY! May, I'm so glad the things reached you. Sometimes I feel like you're on a separate planet. But you are not! I'm glad you liked the girls' pictures. In particular, my eldest girl Eva really thought about you a lot, and asked me questions. I didn't want to scare her by telling her too much about the violence (she is only 5 and she gets scared easily).

How exciting that you can send me something too. I am around a dress size 12, and my feet are big – a size 7 or 40 in European sizes. I was upset at having got quite fat after Elsa was born, but finally it's going, and I am now almost back to normal. It helps that yesterday I was ill, in bed all day with some terrible vomiting bug. Today I'm much better, and noticed with glee that I had lost weight. But I celebrated by making pancakes and eating them with butter and sugar.

I have to go, we're organizing the Christmas Fair at school, it is the big fund-raising event of the year. I'm now running the Parents' Association (PA) along with Marie, who was the scary mum who got me into this whole thing in the first place. Turns out she's a star. I hope we make loads of money. It's a really excellent state school. Anyway, I have a meeting in an hour and haven't sorted anything out.

Will write again soon. Loads of love to you, and stay warm!

B XXXXX

10.11.06

Puritans

Hi, Bee

Do you see how funny it is that people who are worlds apart can become so close?

The term has just started and around half the students showed up! I felt restored and energized as I stood talking endlessly about the Puritans at an introductory lecture, and I was deliriously happy. I realized how much I like teaching.

But things soon went wrong when 150 employees were kidnapped from the Ministry of Education, and the minister announced that studies will be stopped until further notice.

I bought you a sexy nightdress, which I hope you'll like and will please Justin too. I also got you a pair of Indian-style shoes, and I want to go to a certain shop to get you something that can be called an Arab costume, but I'm waiting for the area to cool down a bit. You know, Bee, that I'm beginning to miss your emails so much. I open mine every night just to check if you've sent any.

I mentioned before that it was 'Frightday' but nothing bad took place, thank God. My mother had lunch with us, and she and Ali (my husband) helped the gardener doing her garden. She's planting new roses and other plants, and she has also made a little path for her to come and visit us.

You know, I want to tell you about my life and the problems that face my second marriage. Bee, I married the man whom I met on the phone.

I made all kinds of tests for the posh ones, and they all failed. He was the only one who stood by me when my car broke down, when the water tank had holes and water started dripping from the roof.

The problems lie in many things. On my family's part: the fact that he is younger than me, that they do not know his family, and also that his family have objected to our marriage. It is a bit like a Jane Austen novel: here in Iraq it is all about the marriage of families. But I have never in my whole life obeyed the social rules. On his family's part: I am older than him, previously married, and I come from a Shi'ite background, which they loathe.

We decided to get married and 'whatever will be, will be'. We were, and luckily still are, in love. Bee, you know, his father has told him that he can never come back to them, ever (the man means it) and he will have no family, and he'll also disinherit him (and God, they are rich). And can you believe it? He chose to live with me. Our relationship is not just that of two lovers. No, it is like a mother–son relationship somehow, if you leave out the intimate side. I don't know if his being younger is such a big deal. We need each other for many different reasons. And if it ends someday, it will be just like any other marriage — nice while it lasted.

I told you that I'm the eldest child of two PhDs (pharmacists). My sister is also a pharmacist and my brother is a PhD engineer, as is my brother-in-law. And my sister-in-law is a pharmacist. So you see, for them I'm the black sheep of the family.

Write soon because I wait for your emails.

LOVE XXXX MAY

22.11.06

I'm back

Dearest May

Sorry it's been ages. Right now I'm getting a cold and feel achy and horrible, that itchy throat feeling, but I am curled up on the sofa drinking honey and lemon and watching a dreadful but compelling thing on TV called *I'm a Celebrity . . . Get Me out of Here!* where 10 celebrities are sent into the Australian jungle and forced to eat maggots and do weird challenges, while the public votes on who should be evicted and who should stay in.

It's nice to have my brain entirely disengaged. I should actually be reading a book (*The Go-Between* by L. P. Hartley, never heard of it before) because I've just joined a book group and this is my first one. I really should try to think about it and have something to say in time for next week. Book groups suddenly popped up all over the place here a few years ago. I quite like the notion – it's a sort of female solidarity thing as well as reading books that you might not normally choose.

The reason I couldn't write last week is that we went down to Dorset for a break. In winter the landscape is very bare and bleak, with a huge sky. Sometimes a thick grey mist rolls in and you can't see anything at all. I just love it there, May, and so do the girls. Eva first went there when she was just two weeks old, and she took her first steps there.

The bad thing about Dorset (it's on the south coast of England) is the people. They are so dour, maybe from resenting the Londoners breezing down to their holiday homes. I can't blame them for that. But it's not just the locals, it's the other Londoners. They pretend they're not Londoners at all, but authentic country folk. You get excruciating moments such as being at a remote pub, hearing people talk and knowing they're from London, yet everyone ignores each other, as if to show that they were there first.

Anyway, May, it's getting late and I'm dying to go to bed. Think how important you are in your students' lives. It's a wonderful job you do, May.

Loads of love

Bee XXX

25.11.06

Bloodbath

Bee, at last you're back. You can't imagine how much I missed your emails. I don't know what to tell you. My country is flooded by a bloodbath. Death is everywhere, and it was right in front of me on Thursday as we almost got killed by those who call themselves a police force (but are actually militias). They shot at us as we came out of the office where we were trying to obtain an official translation of our wedding certificate. I became hysterical and the car was badly damaged. I can't describe the situation but it was like the gates of hell have been flung open.

I can't tell you how thankful I am for the money you sent; it helped greatly in buying fuel, which is only available on the black market. Now I am quite warm, thanks to you.

Anyway, we have been under curfew for the past three days, and despite that people are getting massacred and even burned alive. Bee, I am scared and don't know what to do. We tried selling the car to escape to Jordan but no one is buying anything nowadays. I wrote to a friend in a Gulf state for a job, and am still waiting for the answer.

I received no comment from you about my story with Ali. What do you think?

Give my kisses to Zola and Eva and the little angel Elsa, and tell them that I hope to see them one day. That is, if I survive all this riot. Also my love to you and your husband.

May XXXX

26.11.06

Love is all you need

Dearest May

Thank God you're OK in the middle of all that. As for the story of you and Ali, and what I think? Well, I think it is just lovely. The only reason I didn't make any comment is that I don't find the age difference shocking. Like the Beatles said, 'All you need is love!' And it's a delightfully unusual way that you two found it. The only problem I can see is the families getting so upset; that's very unfortunate. Perhaps for them it's a question of appearances?

My mum had one or two boyfriends after she and my father split up, before she found the right man. They have been together ever since, over 25 years now. They are from different social backgrounds. My mum is elegant, educated and articulate, whereas Dave (her man) was a builder when they met, from working-class parents, and he is a man of few words. But he is very kind, and totally reliable.

Years ago my mum said something wonderful that I have never forgotten. She said, 'Every day, he makes my life better.' I was single at the time, and thought, 'Oh God, what if I never feel like that about a man?' I think she had just had enough of clever, show-off men. So there you have it: I think that you must appreciate love wherever you find it, and if someone else doesn't approve then that's a sign of their own limitations.

Once you wrote to me that careers are the most important thing in our lives, but I don't agree, May. I think that having someone to love, who also loves you, is the most important thing. Justin's mum (a formidable achiever, very successful, now semi-retired) once said something I was surprised to hear. She said at the end of your career you finally realize that no one from work cares or matters as much as your family. Even in a very influential job like yours, where your students probably adore you.

Of course, jobs make us what we are on a day-to-day basis, and I have to admit that when I'm not working it affects my self-esteem. Like at the moment when, at the end of the day, I have done a load of laundry, made nice food for everyone, looked after Elsa and tidied up endlessly and no one is going to be impressed by that. Whereas when I'm at work and I'm chasing important interviewees, or arguing with my editor, it is something I might then have a bit of a boast about, to Justin or my friends.

BUT, all this being true, I know many women (fewer men, don't know why, workplace sexism?) whose lives are so consumed by work that they have no love life or home at all. Just to sit down after your long day and talk about things with someone who cares what you say and feel, May, that is a thing that all the professions, degrees, success and status in the world cannot bring.

So look after your lovely Ali!

Justin just called me; he is now on his way back home, and tonight we'll have some sausages and a nice bottle of wine. The girls are in bed but reading, and Elsa is fast asleep in her cot.

Blessed peaceful moment.

All my love

Bee XXXX

PS May, can I try to send you some more money; would it help? How much do you need? I'd really do anything to help you, and I'm sure you'd do the same for me if our positions were reversed. So don't be shy about asking, and I will do what I can.

28.11.06

My Iraqi destiny

Dear Bee

I am really thankful for your concern and offer to send money to me to help me out of the country. But after giving it a lot of thought my husband and I have decided to stay and face our destiny. You see, we cannot take any chances. You have probably heard what is happening to Iraqis in the neighbouring countries. They are being humiliated, and many have spent all their money on rent and food and have failed to get jobs.

As for the importance of family life, Bee, I absolutely agree with you. What I meant about the importance of a career was that a person should always be armed for the unexpected. My ideas probably come from the hardships I went through in my first marriage (I was only 17 with eight SCE/'O' Levels from Scotland). This wasn't much, but when my late husband indirectly forced me to abandon my studies at the College of Science, I wasn't unduly concerned. I had hopes of living happily ever after; he was an engineer, which in my view, at the time, meant he would be able to provide a decent life for me and our children.

But I was a fool. Years just went by and at the age of 21 I realized that I had to do something. I couldn't go back to any college because I'd been expelled for non-attendance, so I studied in a petroleum institute for a three-year diploma in material management. I graduated with an average of 96 per cent. My late husband, who was influential in the institute at that time, secretly connived with the dean so that I wouldn't be employed, even though I was the best student in my year. I felt so sad at the time but I couldn't do a thing about it.

All that time I suffered from maltreatment because of his drinking habit. My mother did help me financially, but with every penny I received she reminded me of my bad choice of husband, which was just like stabbing me in the heart. Oh Bee, I was abused and battered and all sorts of things. Now when I think back I always wonder why I suffered so much without taking positive action. But I think it was because I feared returning to my family home, and facing society as a divorced woman.

Two years had passed after my graduation when a friend of mine (a journalist) said there were vacancies for translators at the Iraqi news agency. They wanted people who could think in English when translating news items. I passed the examination easily and was trained by very efficient translators, and I was so happy to have my own income. But still I suffered; my husband spent our rent money on drink, which made me despair.

On my thirtieth birthday I did not celebrate. I just sat all alone and thought deeply about my life. Then I made the three most important decisions of my life: 1) to build a small house 2) to divorce my husband, and 3) to complete my studies. You can imagine that divorce is frowned upon in Iraq and other Arab countries. Divorced women are mostly blamed and their morals are often questioned, no matter what kind of a 'Zombie' they have been married to. But at 30, all I thought of was that we only live once and I was not prepared to spend what was left of my life this way.

OK love, that's all for now. I will tell you more in another email. Warm regards to Justin, and all my love for you, dear friend.

May

XXXX

06.12.06

Getting festive

May, well done for making those decisions. I had no idea your previous life was so hard; you endured so much and it moves me to hear about what you have come through, only to suffer this horrible war.

I hope hearing about life outside Iraq helps to take your mind off things. You remember that book group I joined? I went last night. I only knew one person there and she was the one who invited me to join. We were seven women and it was very charming; they were very funny and friendly. We had dinner and then talked about the book, *The Go-Between*. I loved it, so sad. I asked for the next book to be one by Thomas Hardy but some people groaned, 'Oh please, no. Not *Jude the Obscure*.' To which I had to agree. The last time I read *Jude* I felt sick for about three days. Perhaps *Return of the Native*. I wish that you could be here to join in the conversation with the others at the book group. I think you would like them.

I was walking along today, and as I went I wondered what you were doing at the same time. Then I started wondering what your street is like. Our street is elegant at one end, with white houses and gracious tall windows, while we live at the small end. The houses at my end are 1920s Art Deco style and not very big, and there's quite a lot of council housing mixed in. It has good trees, especially a twisted copper beech tree that I love. Sometimes I pause under it. It grows in front of a house where the sculptor Henry Moore used to live.

In the big houses the Christmas decorations are all quite tasteful and modest. In the smaller houses the lights are more colourful and festive, then some of the council houses are completely decked out in lights, tinsel and plastic Father Christmases and reindeer. I'm on the tinsel end of the scale personally; what's the point in trying to be tasteful when it's all so exciting for the kids? Like a lot of London, it's well mixed. There are all sorts.

So I wander up and down this street several times a day with any combination of the children. No bombs, no armies or militia groups. The scariest thing you might see is a couple of kids racing on stolen scooters, or very occasionally drug dealers taking over the phone box.

Lots of love to you

Bee XXX

PS GUESS WHAT? The Christmas Fair broke all previous records. We made £4,000 for the school! I hope it was fun – I was too stressed to notice.

PPS Eva's joke. Q: What does a bear wear? A: Hair!

07.12.06

Hi, Bee

Hi, Bee

I liked the joke. It is amazing the amount you have raised for school, which means a lot of hard work. It must be lovely now in the UK with all the Christmas decorations all over the shops and town centres. I wish I could see all that again. I remember the last time was in 1981, when we visited Glasgow and Coventry. It was a dream. Then there were sales in all the shops such as Littlewoods, Marks and Spencer, Selfridges and a shop which I thought was fascinating called What Every Woman Wants.

Anyway, you asked about our street. Well, it is a very, very wide two-sided street, with a middle area in which plants and short palm trees are planted. Houses are not near one another. For example, to reach the house opposite I have to walk past our garage, which is 16 metres long, and then another 6 metres to reach the pavement on my side of the street. Then I cross to the wide middle area with the plants. I cross to the other side and the pavement, and then there is still about 20 metres before I reach their gate. So you see, it is quite a distance. And the same applies to next door, although the distance is not as far because I built my house nearer to them.

Our area was once one of the posh ones in Baghdad. But it has been rather damaged by events . . .

Not much to celebrate at the moment in Baghdad. We've received threats describing Shi'ites as dirty dogs and telling them to evacuate the district and leave their homes. I have an email copy that is in

Arabic. I also have a list of the names of the university teachers who have been killed or kidnapped. One of my colleagues is on the list. He was in the room next to mine, and we shared a love of animals. He used to bring me poems about all sorts of pets, and we enjoyed reading them together. I still have the copies that he gave me.

A threat has reached university teachers and students – which I also have a copy of, but in Arabic – warning them to stop attending lectures or be classified as enemies and as followers of the Shi'ites of Iran. The warning, or rather the threat, says that all who do attend the university are known and will be pursued, even to their homes, and killed in their beds. On the other hand, the prime minister threatens to sack anyone who does not go to work. So for God's sake, what are we supposed to do?

Bee, the things I prepared for you are ready. They are simple things that I managed to gather. I couldn't go to the shop that sells the Arabic outfit and am very sorry. In the package you will find two silver rings for you and Zola. There is also a silver-plated necklace for Eva, and amber cufflinks for Justin. There is also a necklace for you, a wooden box with the map of Iraq on it, a nightdress, a pair of Indian slippers and a draft copy of my MA thesis. I am also sending a sexy black headscarf, which some (not very devout!) Moslem women wear. I will also get you this sweet thing you like, the baklava, so you can have it at Christmas. That is, of course, if I can find Andrew again.

Have to go now . . . May XXXXX

08.12.06

Christmas sparkle

MAY, oooh I can't wait to get your gifts of exotic things.

Yes, Christmas is very nearly here now; there are sparkly lights all over the place. We've been playing Christmas music and the girls go mad with excitement. This morning was the Christmas show at school and the girls sang their hearts out. I could see them opening their mouths as wide as they could and really singing with all their concentration. It brought tears to my eyes.

When Eva went to bed the other night she asked me, 'How old is God?' So I tried to put on a thoughtful face and said, 'Probably quite old.' She asked if I believed in him and I said, 'No, not really, but lots of other people do.' She said that she had decided to believe in God. She looked quite pleased with herself. Their school is secular with a wide ethnic mix of children so I don't know how she arrived at her belief. Maybe it is because of Christmas. I want to protect her magic and her innocence of the world by letting her believe in anything she wants.

I still remember as a child being convinced that all animals could speak, but that they chose not to. How do we lose these ideas? Do they fade away or suddenly stop? Christmas in particular reminds me of the intensity of childhood. It's almost agony when you are waiting for Christmas day and every moment is laden with symbolic importance.

On a horrible note, May, I think you have to get out of Baghdad. I think it will get a lot worse. I truly have a deep horror that one day your emails will just stop and I won't know what happened to you. It's too awful. What if you stayed in Iraq, but went to a calmer place than Baghdad?

By the way, how long were you in Glasgow for? Did I tell you I did my first degree at Glasgow University, and am still very fond of the place?

Take care, May.

Lots of love

Bee XXX

Growing up in Glasgow

Hi, Bee

At last I talked to Andy. I will be sending him the things within a couple of days because the driver who collects the stuff will not be free for another two days. We exchanged emails and now we can communicate more easily.

I'm sending you some documents and a newspaper clipping that talks about the death of one of the people who helped me survive all the misery of my previous marriage. I feel so sorry for him, but no one can reverse time. I'm writing to you with the sound of bombs and guns roaring all over the area. It seems that members of al-Mahdi militias are trying to gain control over our district.

As for your questions regarding my stay in the UK, well, in 1971 (after my father's death) my mother took us to Glasgow to study for her PhD, and she obtained her degree from Strathclyde University. Before settling in Glasgow I attended two state schools in London. The first was in Shepherd's Bush but I can't remember the name (because I didn't know much English at the time) and the second school was called Mayfield. We lived in Wandsworth SW18, very near to Wandsworth Common. After nine months in London we moved to Glasgow. At first we lived in a place called Barhead near some other place called Paisley. I also attended school there, but only for a very short time because we moved to Glasgow itself, where I sat my 'O' Levels.

I wonder, Bee, would this information help me get to England? I so wish it could. As for the reason that I cannot go out of the capital, well, we are a mixed family, which makes it difficult. I can't go to a Sunni area because my family is Shi'ite, but on the other hand I can't go to a Shi'ite area because my mother and husband and also my sister-in-law are Sunnis. So you see, I'm hated by both groups.

Did you receive the cards I sent you and the girls via email? I hope you like them.

Love you.

May XXXX

15.12.06

How annoying are men?

Morning, May!

Oh God, last night Justin did the most annoying thing ever. We went to a quite posh dinner party at his cousin Xand's house, full of people I have never met before. The conversation turned to plastic surgery and things like breast implants and face lifts and so on. Justin was sitting a few people away, and he turned and boomed, 'Oh Bee, you've had that face thing done, haven't you!?' by which he meant that I did a face pack with my friend Amy a few weeks ago. All cosmetic stuff is a mystery to him, I suppose.

So I clumsily denied it and there was a strained silence while everyone naturally assumed that I must indeed have had surgery. After a pause one of the men turned to Justin and cheerily said, 'Well, you're in trouble later on, aren't you!' and everyone laughed, 'Oh, hahaha!' and I was boiling! How can men be so stupid sometimes?

Take care, dear May.

Bee XXX

Annoying men

Hello to you, Bee

Yes, dear. Men are annoying because they can be so thoughtless about what women regard as sensitive subjects. A similar thing happened to me. Once, when my late husband was just back from Libya with some dollars, I thought that maybe I could pamper myself by going to a dermatologist because I had greasy skin and the hot sun caused some dark blotches.

He gave me the money for the first time, but when my second appointment was due he totally refused. In the evening we went to his mother's and all his sisters were there, and do you know what he said? 'Mother, your daughter-in-law wants to have cosmetic surgery. I think she is passing through her second adolescence.' Everyone laughed at me and started giving advice about the risks of such surgery, and reassuring me that I was nice looking etc. You can imagine how I felt at the time.

Don't think too much of it. This is how nature designed them. Just tell him calmly that you were annoyed and that you'd expect to be hurt by anybody, but never by him. Maybe this will make him more understanding.

Still haven't been to work for the past two weeks. I am scared of the threats but I must go in tomorrow, first because they called me and second because I have to get my salary. I was preparing a lecture on democracy last night, and thought how funny it was when I read about legitimate governments. The article says if legitimacy fails then it will turn into chaos. And that is exactly what we have.

Give the girls a big hug and a kiss from Aunt May, regards to Justin and lots of love for you.

May XX

19.12.06

Frosty hello

Hi, May

Your former in-laws sound horrific. Thankfully Justin isn't cruel, just a bit daft sometimes, so I wasn't really upset for long. And although he has a huge family and it's quite overwhelming, at least they are all nice individually.

I hope you got into work safely. I am going to a work party tonight. I haven't seen lots of my colleagues for a long time; I can't wait to go off into that separate world again. I get a bit nervous having been out of it for a while. I try not to do the unforgivable thing of yakking on about my kids in a professional environment. (I've noticed how if a man has a screensaver of his baby on his computer it's 'Aahh, so cute!' but with a woman somehow less so.)

Tomorrow is the last day of school before the Christmas holidays so you can imagine the excitement that is building up. Yesterday I wandered around Camden and did a bit of shopping to get some sparkly things for the girls and a sweet little fluffy dress for Elsa.

It is suddenly extremely cold and frosty outside, and it's very beautiful. In the back garden I have a few bird-feeding devices hanging on the apple tree, and from where I'm sitting I can see several small birds eating the peanuts. Isn't it wonderful to have changing seasons?

See you later, May. Take care.

All my love

Bee XX

21.12.06

Brrrrrrrrrrrrrrrrrrrrrrr . . .

A very frosty hello to you too!

Bee, you are right that the changing seasons are beautiful, but here in Baghdad we have such extremes that require us to be properly armed against them. But what can we do? Now it is freezing cold, but with electricity scarce it is almost impossible to have hot water for a shower, let alone washing clothes. Cleanliness and hygiene have become a luxury. I don't mind boiling the kettle to wash the dishes but I will never accept washing clothes without a washing machine. The other day the most dreadful thing happened – the electricity came on and I put the dirty clothes in the machine but, as usual, I was fooled. Just as I started the program and stood back to watch the machine fill with water, the electricity went off. I can't use the generator to work the washing machine because it takes up so much electricity, so the clothes remained locked in there for three days! I had to empty it and rewash all the clothes, adding disinfectants to get rid of the bad smell.

Anyway, today is one of those celebrated days when we have been blessed with electricity after three days with nothing. I was so excited about the idea of a hot shower to warm myself up that I hurried to switch on the boiler, waited for an hour for it to heat up, then turned on the water motor and went into the bathroom, singing happily to myself. I mixed the water to the right temperature and stood under the heavenly spray. But, before I could blink, I was lashed with boiling water – the electricity had gone off, cutting the water motor and leaving me with only the hot water. Six times the water went hot and cold and I had to get out to fix things. By the time I'd dried myself and run to the hairdryer, the power had gone. It seems that democracy is contagious. The electricity current may have thought it was part of democracy to come and go as it pleases!

Happy Christmas to you and Justin and the lovely girls.

Love

Mayxxx

25.12.06

A big hug to you on Christmas day

MAAAAAAAAAYYYYYYYYY!

Right now I am wearing your black headscarf, the necklace and your lovely ring, and I just can't believe it. I feel so moved. We opened your huge bag of things last of all, after all the other presents. Justin's mum and dad were here too and they thought it was amazing when they heard the story of my friendship with you. (You should have seen Justin's dad's face when I pulled out the leopard-print nightie and tiny knickers, haha!) Justin's cufflinks are a wonderful gift; what an honour it is to have some things from you and your family. I'll write a long letter about today soon but I just had to tell you about all this. And I can't wait to read your thesis. B XXXXXXX

27.12.06

Post-Christmas hello

Hi again, May

Christmas day was so lovely. Justin's lovely dad secretly built the girls a huge wooden doll's house in his workshop (he stayed up all night finishing it), and we got tiny furniture and things to go in it. The girls were suitably impressed. It brought back memories of my doll's house when I was little; I made a library of miniature books but the house was occupied by small animals.

So on Christmas morning we had a big breakfast then went out for a walk over the Heath, ending in a SWIM in the pond! Yes, it was freezing but extremely funny. Lots of people do it as a festive tradition and it's a great atmosphere. After that we came home, lit a big fire and opened up all the presents. As I told you, we opened yours last as I was most excited about them. I've told everyone so much about you, and so we were dying to see what you'd sent.

Yesterday, Boxing day, we took the girls for a long walk on the Heath but had a big argument halfway round (about nothing, like all the worst ones). My friend Talia has pointed out that every time we have a huge row it is precisely a month since the last one, and it's always when I have PMT. She is right, much as I hate to admit it. I am so bloated, May. Oh my goodness, those baklava you sent are delicious; I've tried not to eat too many. I'm managing to save the bottom layer for New Year's Eve.

I can't tell you how nice it is to read your thesis and the letter that was attached. You're right, it's as though you are much more real. All those gifts were in your house and now they are in my house, as if to prove that we don't live in separate worlds. I felt like some Baghdad air may have seeped out from the packaging; from your home into mine.

Anyway, I have sent you some more dollars and some photos of me and the girls, and some pictures and messages from them to you. Eva in particular keeps asking about you.

Actually, May, you have become famous among all my friends. I have talked about you such a lot and now we all worry about you.

I hope you're OK, May. Do write me a letter as I want to know what you've been doing. Are you OK?

Lots of love

B XX

27.12.06

The extremists are here

Hi, Bee

I knew you'd be worried. But we've had no internet connection for the past few days. We are physically OK. But our area has been occupied by the Islamic extremists. We don't know what to do.

Ali was out buying cigarettes and bread the other day when a stranger shouted at him that smoking was sinful and that he had to put his cigarette out. Then this person shouted in a loud voice that any woman seen without a head cover or with make-up on would be beheaded. Of course, this applies to me as I don't put a scarf on and I do wear make-up and drive to work, but I will not bow to this bullying. I will not let them turn me into a big wobbly bin bag, no matter what. What can one expect from people who interfere and even try to impose the type of toilets a man should install in his home? These extremists insist that people do not use western toilets (because they think these are not clean enough to be used by a Moslem). The eastern type have no seats; they are just white porcelain holes in the ground. A person has to crouch in order to use them, and the water flush comes through a metal or plastic tube connected to a small tank hung high on the wall.

I expect the next few days will be pregnant with events. We feel a mixture of fear, anticipation and anxiety. News reports say that S.H. has been handed over to the Iraqi authorities. This doesn't sound good, but we'll have to wait and see. Watching TV and waiting is all we do now, since we can't even go outside. OK, my love, I will have to go now. Happy New Year in advance, dear Bee.

May xxx

RE: The extremists are here

May, now I'm even more worried about you. I hate the extremists, I hate them, I don't want them near you. I've been glued to the news and I can't believe what I'm seeing. Please just send me a few short lines to tell me you're still there.

Worried

B XXX

2007

The Old Man is dead

Dearest friend

Happy New Year to you and all the family. I'm sorry I couldn't write over the past few days because they've been quite extraordinary. We are in a state of shock. You must have heard about the execution. We were awakened by the sound of helicopters flying at low altitude at 5 a.m. We've just been switching from one TV channel to the other.

Now that the Old Man is dead, I expect it will get worse. You probably didn't know that the day of his execution was a Moslem feast and greatly honoured by Moslems all over the world. On such a day Moslems butcher or slaughter sheep and cows, or whatever animal may be eaten (not pigs), and distribute the meat to the poor and needy. So the Old Man was butchered in a symbolic way.

This timing is not in the new government's favour. It changed his image in the eyes of the people from that of a dictator and a brutal killer into a martyr who was sacrificed, and a scapegoat for the occupiers and their collaborators. But to tell you the truth, I was impressed by his unprecedented courage in meeting his death.

Gunfire is rumbling all over the area. The militias have come to occupy our district again, and the residents have gone out to defend it. The villas in our area are considered a very tasty meal for the looters, and also for the militias, because many of the residents were well off before the war. Now there are many newcomers, mostly Islamic extremists and I expect a lot of violence to come.

Bee. Please, please, please advise me what I should do. As for Ali, and all the other men in the district who are Sunnis, they are afraid to go out because of the brutal militias and Islamic extremists. So we both have good reason to fear for our lives. We are terrified and have decided we should try to get out and seek asylum. What do we need? The only evidence Ali has is his passport, which has expired and which he can't renew at present.

By the way, if you do not get emails from me for two months, write to my friend Maysoon. I will forward you her email. She will know what has happened to me.

Will always love you.

XXXXXXX May

02.01.07

Be careful, May

May. I urge you to try to get another passport for Ali. And is yours still valid? There is a law centre nearby that offers confidential legal advice and I will phone them to see what they think.

I did of course know that they killed Saddam on the festival of Eid, and I agree that it is significant. There is a video recording of his death that shows his last moments (I haven't seen it and I don't want to) and I think it is utterly squalid on all sides. And in this case it will not help. From the reports I have seen, it seems that although there were cele-brations in some areas, people are unhappy – either because they still supported him, or because they hated him and wanted him to stand trial for so many other crimes. So apparently no one is satisfied.

Anyway, I think it will get a lot worse just as you say, and I am so worried about you. The last part of your message made me feel quite sick; I can't bear it. I don't think you can stay there. I dread having to email your friend.

Start thinking about the asylum route, May, and try to collect as much evidence as you possibly can. And I know it's an insult to an intelligent woman, but for God's sake, May, just stay inside and try to hide from the madmen.

All my love

Bee XXX

03.01.07

Other thoughts . . .

I was just thinking, May. How come your family didn't mind when your mum and dad married, if he was Sunni and she is Shi'ite? Was it easier back then, or was it OK as long as you were from a similar social background?

And also, you never told me the next bit of the story, after you and Ali spent months on the phone and planned to meet but you were too afraid. Then he found you at your work, so what happened next?

Justin and I met one rainy night in the Dog and Duck, a pub on Frith Street in Soho. It was Tuesday 8th February 2000. I was recently single and having a ball. I'd just landed a great new job; I was living in a lovely small house; I felt very attractive and excited about my life. Everything was just right. When I first met Justin (through a mutual friend) I liked him immediately because he argued with me. I love arguing and will argue about pretty much anything. So we challenged each other, and that was exciting. We carried on drinking at a few other pubs and ended up at a very late-night Soho café, drinking coffee.

I remember that I kissed him right there in the café, quite surprising as I have never kissed anyone so quickly before. We shared a taxi home and he tried to come to my house, but he was drunk and slobbish so I said no. The next day he got my email address from the mutual friend, and we began flirty emails at work (at this time Justin was the north of England correspondent for a TV news programme so he lived up north in Leeds, but still used to come to London a lot) but it wasn't serious. He came every weekend and we got close, but I was rather in denial and insisted to all my friends that he was NOT my boyfriend. My mum began to tease me about him and I'd get cross. I didn't even hold his hand in public as it would compromise my independence.

That spring I was sent to the US to work in Boston for a month and I missed him. By the summer I was gradually having to admit that I did like him, a lot. We planned a holiday in Corsica. Oh May, it was and still is the most romantic holiday I have ever had. Corsica is for us like a honeymoon (our actual honeymoon was wretched). While we were there I had a dream one night that we got married. It made me feel extremely strange and sort of electrified. Didn't tell him about it of course.

THEN suddenly in October my period was a bit late, so I did a pregnancy test one day at work, thinking I'd put my mind at rest. It was just before I had an editorial meeting on a conference call with my colleagues in Boston. But the test came out positive. I was in shock. Imagine me trying to say things about world politics to clever people in Boston, while my whole mind flew into a panic as I stared at the small blue line on the plastic pregnancy test!

My first thought was to get an abortion. I'd had one before (when I was 18) and seeing as I had never once thought about babies, and didn't even like them all that much, and my career was so important, it seemed obvious. I called Justin straight away. He was reporting on some story up in Northumberland (other end of the country) and I squeaked in a deranged voice YOU HAVE TO COME HERE NOW. I didn't tell him why. He later said he guessed I was either pregnant or that something had happened to my mum.

He got the next train to London and I met him off his train at King's Cross station. I was green in the face, sick with worry, and felt somehow ready for a fight. But he was perfect; he said all the right things. He said he really wanted a baby with me, but that he would do anything to support me, whatever I chose to do. More than that, he said, 'I will never leave you, whatever happens.' That floored me. That's the background he comes from. My background is different, if I think about it I had never really trusted men before.

We didn't say any more for a little while as that weekend we had planned to go away for my birthday. I had always wanted to see the works of Gustav Klimt in real life, and there was a big exhibition of his paintings in Vienna, so we had already booked to go. The Vienna weekend was amazing, with golden autumn leaves floating in the pale sun and Klimt's beautiful sensual paintings. We ate posh food, walked a lot, and NOT ONCE did we mention the pregnancy. (Isn't that weird? But remember, we'd only met just eight months before!)

Well. We got back to London on the Monday and the following morning I went to work, and he caught the train back up to his work in Leeds. But he boarded a train that was to become famous: the Hatfield crash. The train was derailed and ripped open, four people were killed on the spot, and many more injured. Justin was there broadcasting all day (every journalist's dream, being in the middle of a crisis) but in between the interviews he was calling me up in tears, in shock about the accident and very shaken. He was live on all channels filing throughout the day, and everyone at work kept calling me going, 'Bee! Bee! Your boyfriend is on TV!' ('Yes, I KNOW!')

It was horrible, but at that moment I realized how deeply I loved him, and that life is fragile, precious and short. It changed my feelings about being pregnant too. It really changed me. (And now that's Eva, who is 5½ and whose wobbly front tooth came out today in her bowl of pasta.)

Anyway, that's enough for today. Take care, May.

All my love and hugs

Bee XXX

03.01.07

My life

Dearest Bee

Thank God you wrote to me. Today I feel so depressed, I don't know what has come over me, and hearing your beautiful story lifted my spirits.

You reminded me in your email of an important point – my parents' marriage. My grandmother on my mum's side objected strongly to the issue not only because my father belonged to a different faith, but also because he came from a different background. My father belonged to a class of landowners and traders, whereas my mother belonged to a class of educated people and government employees. My grandfather was broadminded and did not object, saying that there are no real differences between the two faiths and that as long as there is affection between spouses they are bound to be happy. My father was madly in love with my mother so his family couldn't object too much or they would have lost him (they were wise). They got married, as I was informed by my mother, in miserable circumstances and my granny refused to meet her son-in-law for six months. After that they were reconciled, and the two became best friends.

But for me it is different. Ali's family did not only object to my Shi'ite background. His people are extremely prejudiced, and there is a kind of tradition that almost no one dares to break. It is this: their men must marry from inside the same family or, at the very worst, from inside the same province. His cousin, for example, fell in love with a Sunni from an area about 30 kilometres away, and the poor woman and her children have not yet been accepted. That was about fifteen years ago.

Though Ali's family is well off, their behaviour is tribal, and they believe that fathers rule to the end of their lives. Mothers and sisters are over-protected (to the point of suffocation for people like me). Their women are only allowed to study and attend colleges that are for women, and they are not allowed to talk or mix with the opposite sex. On the other hand, they get as much pocket money and jewellery and other luxuries as they want. (I could never dream of living like that.)

Apparently one of Ali's sisters told him that even if I wasn't a widow and much older, I would still be rejected for being an educated, free woman. She was scared I would create problems in their family as other women would want to imitate me. She is probably right. I suffered a lot at the beginning of our marriage because Ali thought that all the housework is a woman's job. But I made it clear that I wouldn't be a traditional wife, and I refused to do any chores at all, until the house became filthy. Finally he said, 'Let's do it together, love. I know you are not used to such a lifestyle.' The same happened with the types of food he preferred – the tribal grilled fish and meat dishes with rice and a lot of fat or grease (YUK, YUK).

I still have problems adjusting to his habits, but for now we don't address them as it's simply too dangerous for me to go out. He is happy at present because I am imprisoned in the house but, believe me, when the time comes to go out and meet people as I used to do, I assure you a lot of problems will crop up. It is on my mind all the time but it is too early to worry about all that now.

Sometimes he shocks me with his views. Would you believe it if I told you that he, or rather we, don't talk to my mother now? All because she introduced him to a person from the same region as him as 'my son-in-law, MAY'S husband'. The mention of my name drove him crazy, and I had to spend the whole night trying to make him understand that there was nothing wrong with that.

But he refused to understand, saying that the man was from a region where it was a disgrace to mention a woman's name.

The next day we were supposed to have gasoline brought to us (for my mother, my brother and us). I tried to talk to my mother about what had happened and ask her to be careful the next time, and she became angry. When they communicated about the gasoline they were tense and he was, I suppose, a bit stiff or rude (I don't really know). She became mad and refused to give us our share. This made ME angry and I stopped talking to her. And that's that.

Oh Bee, I'm under so much pressure and I don't know what to do. Sometimes I think of just running away, but this isn't fair to him or to my reputation. Next time I will tell you the rest of the love story. See you then.

Love you.

XXXX May

PS I think your story with Justin is fantastic.

03.01.07

RE: My life

AAARGH, May. Sounds like a lot of trouble you have taken on, but I am sure that he also fell in love with you because of your intelligence and strength of character, so he has to embrace these even though they are culturally alien to him, doesn't he? I don't know how you cope. Are you friends with your mum again?

Anyway, I'm in the middle of packing. We are all catching the midday train up to my mum's today, so I have loads to do. I can't wait; the girls adore my mum and she spoils them, so it's a real holiday for them. It's also lovely as she lives in a big house in nice countryside (although her two dogs are a bit smelly and my mum's partner Dave feeds them from the table, yuk). I will call that law centre and phone you very soon.

Bee XX

06.01.07

Where are you?

Dearest Bee

Are you OK? Did your trip to your mother's go well? Are the girls OK?? Do drop me a line: I worry when I don't hear from you.

LOVE YOU ALL.

XXXX May

06.01.07

Back from York

May, don't worry about me. You see, I'm simply indestructible (!). Quite apart from the fact that you are the one who is living in a war zone, while I've been having a lovely and uncomplicated time up in the Yorkshire countryside.

The girls love it there so much. It's possible to do almost nothing for a whole day. My mum loves birds and there are bird-feeding devices all over the place, so everywhere you look there are different kinds of wild birds fluttering about and eating up the seeds. It's colder up north but smells much fresher and cleaner than here in London, and at night the skies are wonderful.

I have to go because Elsa is in a whiny mood and can't seem to be happy today. I've checked and it's not her teeth but I don't know what's bothering her. Anyway, just wanted to let you know I'm fine. Hope you are too.

Lots of hugs

Bee XX

06.01.07

WELCOME BACK

Dearest Bee

Welcome back. I'm glad you enjoyed your stay with your mum. By the way, I love dogs and had one for 13 years. She was a black Hungarian Puli. Her name was Mina and she used to sleep in the same bed with us. But she didn't eat at the table because I think it is unhealthy.

Last night I became a nervous wreck and poor Ali didn't know why. At first he became angry, then when he found out about my fears for the future and my disgust over the execution of S.H. and how I just couldn't understand the brutality of the whole thing he calmed me down. He even cried and said, 'I never thought you were so delicate in your emotions.' It was funny really, I was treated like a 3-year-old toddler who was scared of the unknown. (Between you and me it was very nice to be a child even for one night.) HA . . . HA . . . HA.

Back to the story. I told you that I chickened out and was scared to meet him, but that he came and saw me in the college without introducing himself. He said that he kept watching me while I was giving some directions to a student. Then he said that he came a second time, and I was in my room alone smoking and looking up something in the dictionary. Of course he never told me at the time; I only found out after we got married.

On our first date I picked him up at a place near my home. I was surprised he recognized me, but he just said it was because my car was something different and red. Anyway we went to a café and I was so shy, as if I was a teenager going out on her first date. It was actually like that because I've been married for as long as I can remember. Of course I knew a lot of men, but they were just friends and colleagues, and no more.

I couldn't even look at him properly, and all the time I was saying to myself, 'What am I doing here? Have I gone crazy? What about my reputation? What if someone sees me?' etc. I didn't even realize that he is more than six feet tall. I thought that he was short and fat.

Our meeting lasted for four hours. He was so gentle and so nice but I had decided to call it off. He was younger than I am, and that's that. The meeting ended and I returned home and he went back to his province. On arrival he called me, and said nice things about me that I never even thought possible. He sounded worried that I might not accept him, and we talked on the phone till dawn. The next meeting was after another two days. I kept thinking to myself 'What is it that attracts this man, and makes him travel all the way to Baghdad despite the risks?'

I just couldn't believe that love was his motivator. My previous life taught me a very hard lesson about love, and I had reached the conclusion that it only existed in books and fairy tales and those naive Mills and Boon novels. Even Chaucer decided in his *Canterbury Tales* that all forms of love, except divine, are based on mutual interests and sexual desire. So why does this man insist on loving me???

Time went by and our meetings became more frequent. I even took him to meet my mum, and she liked him very much but insisted that his family come and ask for my hand formally. This continued until it was too dangerous for him to come to Baghdad.

We couldn't see each other for four months. After that, I decided to go to Jordan to try to get a job and escape everything, but it didn't work out. I went again after a few months and still failed to get anything. On the way to Jordan everything diminished except his face. I called him and gave him my new number. He kept calling me regularly in Amman. I couldn't bear being away, and missed talking to him for hours on end.

While in Jordan the second time, I tried to phone him (I recall it was a Thursday) and he didn't answer. I got worried and called again and again, until his brother answered and told me he was too sick to move. I don't know what came over me; I felt as if my soul was on fire. I immediately made reservations and was on my way to Baghdad the next morning. On my arrival, he told me that he had wanted to follow me to Jordan and that his father had attacked him and broken a vase on his head. He was also denied food, and his money, which he kept in the family safe. He begged me to put an end to our misery because he could no longer stand the situation. He asked me to define my position, and said that if I really loved him I should act.

I sat down and evaluated my life. I discovered that I was nothing but a lonely person who just wasted time by going out with friends when they needed time off from their busy family lives. I realized that all this might come to an end for any reason. As for my family, they couldn't care less how I coped on my own. All they did was criticize my lifestyle and my friends. They were too busy with their own lives. I remembered when I needed someone to accompany me to hospital, they were too busy going to a wedding. It was only my mum who came with me.

I told my brother and sister about Ali, and they disapproved as usual. Then I realized that I should not waste my life trying to gain their approval, or anyone's for that matter. It is my life and if it's good I'll be happy, if it's bad then no one will shoulder the responsibility but me.

Oh, I remembered something else. You know that my country is a man's world and there are things that women cannot possibly do. During that period my car broke down, just before my last trip to Amman. I begged my brother to fix it for me, and he did nothing. At this point I called Ali and told him that I accepted his proposal of marriage, and would bear all the consequences and family conflicts that I assumed would take place.

He came to Baghdad and we got married. It was a surprise to everybody, even ourselves.

Love you . . . May XXXX

08.01.07

The stories of our lives, continued

May, I love that story. I've read it a few times now. You are a brave person; I admire you. You have faced such odds, and taken decisions alone and unsupported.

In my case I am lucky to say that I've had nothing but support and love from my mother all my life. I had no father (he lives in Germany) and I don't know if that's why, but I did go a bit mad as a teenager. I idolized my absent father and was horrible to my mum. I went away to be a dancer — yes, I was a showgirl! Glitter, large plumes, high heels, all that. I had trained in ballet for many years and done all the exams, and then when school ended, instead of going straight to university I came down to London and did all these weird auditions. In the end I got a job with a dance troupe at a theatre out in the Canary Islands.

I was 19. I stepped off the plane with no idea of what I was letting myself in for. I didn't even speak a word of Spanish. Knowing what I know now, I wouldn't encourage my daughters to be professional dancers. They all had low self-esteem even though they were beautiful, and many were anorexic. There was a bullying atmosphere, and the captain was a revolting pig. Once in rehearsals he forced me to go through a dance holding big ashtrays in my hands (on my own, in front of the whole company). He hated my 'balletic' arms. He even shoved me once when we were onstage.

But I was looked after by a kind dancer called Debbie. She was old for a showgirl (in fact she was only 24 or 25, but that seemed old at the time!) and we called her Aunty Debbie. I could tell you so many adventures from that time, it was my coming of age and also a period of personal glory for me; I felt I had created my own independent life. I read Elizabeth Barrett Browning's *Aurora Leigh* and felt that I too was a woman stamping her mark in foreign climes! It was gruelling but also a triumph. I still dream about it, and when I wake I feel a strong nostalgia.

After the year of dancing I started at Glasgow University. Only two years later I couldn't bear the endless dark weather and sideways rain (remember that?) and I ran away again, this time even further, to Colombia. It was supposed to be a 'year out' from my studies but it became two years as I loved the place so much. I had a completely charmed life. I don't know if you've read any magical realism or Gabriel García Márquez, but let me tell you magical realism is just everyday life in Colombia: delirious beauty, generosity and violence.

I returned (again, reluctantly) to finish my degree at Glasgow and after that I started working at the BBC. I've been there ever since, apart from time off having the babies. But even then I did a Masters in political economy, as I was worried that my head would become babyfied and I'd only talk about nappies.

May, there's one thing that really bothers me about your emails. I don't want to sound insensitive, but I just can't believe the stories you tell me of how parents treat their children. Did Ali's dad really attack him? How is it possible for someone to love their baby and nurture them as they grow up, only to reject them like that? I can't believe it, that the bonds or laws of society/religion overrule those of familial love so completely. I am incapable of doing anything other than just loving my children, I don't care what they do. If Eva wanted to marry a murderer I hope I would at least try to understand her point of view.

I am shocked by your family, and by Ali's even more so. They should learn a lesson from the Montagues and the Capulets. I hope you don't mind me saying that.

I wonder what it would have been like if you had stayed here, and never gone back to Iraq . . . We might have met . . . Idle thoughts . . .

Good night, dear May!

Love and hugs, Bee XX

10.01.07

Legal situation

May, are you OK? I'm worried about you with Baghdad in chaos like this. And I hope I haven't offended you with my comments on family relations in Iraq?

I have just spoken to a lawyer about the possibility of coming here and it is very bad. First of all you definitely cannot apply for asylum from Iraq, you have to do it here. But it is illegal to come here without it. Which forces anyone who is seeking asylum to break the law straight away. Most are held in detention centres while their applications are considered.

The lawyer told me that few Iraqis are coming here and, of those, many are being rejected. She has just dealt with an Iraqi whose case was rejected and he was sent back home again. The reason given by the courts was that, although Baghdad is dangerous, the man should have sought refuge somewhere safer within Iraq. This is called 'internal flight' and should be the first option for a refugee.

If you can prove to the court that you are being persecuted by the state (showing documentary evidence) this will support your application. I asked her what if you are being persecuted not by the state but by paramilitary organizations? She said that in that case you would have to prove that the state has failed to protect you from that persecution, either because it didn't want to or was unable to. When I pointed out that a failure of the state to protect you from persecution would mean you would probably already be dead, she said she was just telling me the law as it stands.

May, I have never broken the law before, but I insist that if you really need to come here I will try to help you and Ali live here, illegally if you have to, until something else works out for you. So just keep that as an option.

Write to me soon May – I'm missing you.

Love

Bee XXXX

10.01.07

The attacks are getting worse

Dearest Bee

Thank you so much for the effort and worry. Bee, it is getting worse. The government, which your lawyer says should protect the people, is filled with militias. Those in cooperation with the occupying forces will attack Sunni and mixed areas under the pretext of cleansing areas. I have made some contacts about acquiring new passports for Ali and me. I was informed that they cost $1,000. I managed most of the money but I am not sure if this will be of any use. I would gladly leave as soon as possible but it will take at least a month to get the new passports. Then I don't know what is going to happen.

As for the advice that we should go to other provinces, it is just the same wherever you go. As I told you, they are after university teachers and Sunnis. And if I was to be accepted in a Shi'ite area Ali would be rejected and vice versa.

I enjoyed reading your story. I think we Librans are the same all over the world. We just can't be easily satisfied. We have to try and try and once we find what we think is best we settle down quietly for some time.

No, dear Bee, I was not offended by your comments, which are quite true. I will leave them for another email. You can't imagine how close you are to my heart. But we have had no petrol for the generator and we've been without water, electricity and fuel for the heaters for the past week.

Ali and I began to feel there might be hope on the horizon. We had decided to sit and wait for our fate. But with the small chance of an escape, hope flourished once again and we jumped up with joy and tears of happiness poured from our eyes. Oh Bee, I just can't believe that it will ever be possible to get out of this inferno.

I will be handing in the papers necessary for the new passports on Tuesday (I hope) and I have been told that it will take a month (with the bribe) to get them. I have managed to collect some newspapers that talk about militia operations and I also have a few documents stored in my email about my murdered colleagues, giving their names.

So Bee, do you think that when the passports are done we should leave for Damascus to try to get a plane from there? (There are no direct flights from here.) Or what? Unfortunately, Iraqis are seen as a plague wherever they go.

May XX

14.01.07

Got your present from Andrew

Dearest Bee

I received your letter and the girls' drawings, as well as the money, and I thank you very much. The driver picked them up from Andrew's yesterday and brought them to me this afternoon.

First of all, the photos are absolutely gorgeous and I love them. I've put them in frames and placed them on a book cabinet in the living room. The girls look very beautiful and intelligent and you are absolutely gorgeous.

I specially liked Zola's magical animal and Eva's Xmas greetings. As for the chocolate, it is lovely. I hurried and made some Turkish coffee to go with it. Oh Bee, thank you. I have this feeling that we are family already. You know, I feel as if you are my younger sister abroad and the girls are just part of me. I read your letter and held it close to my heart and said maybe some day we will all meet.

Ali was very sick last night and I couldn't sleep well. Although he kept telling me to go back to sleep, I was so worried about him. I think he had food poisoning because he brought home frozen chicken liver (I hate it) and asked me to cook it for him. I didn't eat it and so I'm OK. You know, I can't trust the stores here any more because there is no electricity and of course they don't keep the generators on all the time as fuel is expensive and scarce, and so frozen food is no longer safe to eat.

I woke up this morning with one idea on my mind, and that was to get my hair cut. Ali went mad when I told him that I was going on my own, and so I wore a scarf on my head and no make-up, and drove to the hairdresser's. The last time, he drove me there. We almost got killed by the militias and had to hide in a shop next to the hairdresser's and it was awful. So I was brave today and went out on my own. Thank God nothing happened, and I got back safe and sound.

I should be going to college tomorrow because my students have an exam. I'll also be going on my own because it is more dangerous for Ali as a Sunni man to drive.

I'll go now.

Love, kisses and hugs to you all

May XXX

16.01.07

Hi, Bee

Dearest Bee

I went to university yesterday. It was calm all the way there, but trouble started on my way home. I noticed that there were a lot of armoured cars in our area, then a gunman pointed out to me that I should speed up and so I did.

You'll never believe what happened, Bee. As soon as I drove the car into our garage, several gunshots went off. I hurried inside and within about 10 minutes the area had turned into a battlefield. It was terrifying and went on for two and a half hours, then all went quiet. Everything stopped working. The electricity went off AGAIN. Oh by the way, our water tank already has two holes in it from a previous battle.

This morning I had to go to work because there was another exam, and also I had promised to deliver the documents for the passports. I drove about 500 metres only to discover two bodies lying in the street. Can you imagine? I went hysterical and returned home immediately and called the department, asking them to examine the students without me. I sent the questions by text message.

How are you and the family? I miss your emails.

Love and kisses

XXX May

17.01.07

Hello

MAY! Hello, dearest

It doesn't really sound safe to go out. I don't blame you for doing it as otherwise I'm sure you'll go mad. But I wish you didn't have to.

I have more bad news – my friend who knows an immigration lawyer got information from her, and it is terrible. Basically you have almost no chance of doing it legally. She said this strictly in confidence. You have to decide if you could cope with being illegal here. It may be better, even though you would only be able to do horrible jobs, than being in Baghdad and fearing for your life.

I was talking about it to Justin and he wondered whether it might be easier to get into another Arab country, like maybe Egypt. He said we would try to help you out financially if you did this. I told him what you said about it being intolerable in Jordan as Iraqis are not welcome. Really, you have to just consider it a survival strategy.

Again I stress that we will still help you if you want to come illegally but read the lawyer's email – I'll forward it to you – and see what you think.

I'll write again soon.

All my love

Bee XXX

A FRIEND INDEED

Dearest Bee

I really can't thank you enough for all your care and help. I am sorry that it has turned out this way but I believe that everything is related to fate. We can never really escape it even if we wanted to. Ali also sends his deep thanks and gratitude. You know, we were just talking about you last night, and he said, 'A real sister would not care to do what Bee did and help us like that,' and I think he is absolutely right.

Anyway, we have paid this man for the passports and they won't be ready till maybe the end of February or early March, which means quite a long time (if we survive the new strategy). During this time we will make inquiries about all the Arab countries to find out which one is the most accommodating.

Bee, I will always cherish your offer to help us come illegally but I will not do this even if all else falls. I DO NOT want you to break the law for any reason. Besides, life would be hard in the UK. I let my imagination run and the film I saw was not very romantic.

I still have some of that chocolate bar you sent me so I'll go and make a cup of coffee to drink with it.

How are the girls? I really loved their work. As for the adorable Elsa, I think she looks like a child out of a magazine or an ad. Please thank Justin for me and tell him that I appreciate his concern so much.

I'll go now.

Love & hugs to you all

May XX

17.01.07

RE: A FRIEND INDEED

Dearest May. I just read your email and burst into tears.

Each day small moments from your emails occur to me as I'm doing things, walking down the road or whatever, and I remember a funny thing you have said or described. But then this is set among such horror and disgusting fear – the idea of you seeing dead bodies in the street, being fired upon – it's like a different planet to me. I can cope with the idea of never meeting you, but not the idea of your emails just ceasing.

I have the appalling feeling of having raised your and Ali's expectations only then to dash them again. I won't give up, May. And now that I've told my friends about you I'm not the only person thinking of how to help you.

But even if you end up in a neighbouring country we could come and see you, or send you money. But for now I think you are right to focus on what you can find closer to home, try to get a job in Oman or Qatar, from there it may be easier.

I'm too emotional right now to tell you a funny story about yesterday but I'll try to write to you tomorrow.

Take care, dearest May.

Bee XXX

19.01.07

Hi, Bee

Dearest Bee

Couldn't answer right away for we still have no electricity. Bee, it is funny that the closest relationships I've made came either via phone like Ali or via email like you. Isn't that amazing? I think it is because we tend to show our real selves without any reservations.

The man doing the passports called last night and said to meet him tomorrow morning at a place near our area. We will be going but, between us, I'm not very relaxed about it. He looks like a militia-man, and I'm scared that he may have a gang who will try to hurt Ali. But we have no choice. Both of us have to be present to sign some papers.

Oh, I forgot to tell you. I showed Ali the photos and he has a special liking for Zola. He thinks she is adorable in a very distinctive way. I'll go now to make some lunch.

Love & kisses to you all

May XXX

19.01.07

Hi!

Oh God, May. The passport man sounds bad. Write to me as soon as you get back so I don't worry about you.

Ali is right to spot Zola. She has an unusual charm and people often fall in love with her very quickly. Eva is thin and wiry with a constant energy that can be maddening (she manages to spill my tea just by being in the same room), but she is a classic beauty. Listen to me boasting about my gorgeous girls, haha! Oh, I've never been one for false modesty . . . !

You will laugh at this; on Tuesday I had the most dreadful evening. I had invited a bunch of the girls' friends round after school, on what they call a play date. I had made individual little pies and puddings for dinner, planned to make bead necklaces with them, and I felt pleased with myself that it was all nicely worked out and I was Supermum. But it all went wrong.

Eva had three friends coming, and Zola had two, but then the phone rang 10 minutes after we'd got in from school and it was the mother of another girl I'd invited, BUT FORGOTTEN TO COLLECT FROM SCHOOL. The little girl was still there! Can you imagine what her mum thought of me? I apologized profusely and ran to school and picked her up (she was fine) but that got me all flustered. Then the other problem was that one of the kids' mums stayed. Usually mums drop their kids on play dates, and gratefully rush off to do some shopping or just relax. And naturally we all know that we only do it so that we get the same favour back in return. It's sort of an unspoken rule.

But no, this mum stayed and stood there in my kitchen, talking away about famous people that she'd had lunch with, while to my increasing agitation the girls all rampaged off upstairs. Because I wasn't giving them my complete attention, it all spun totally out of control. They broke Eva's bed by bouncing on it. There were two huge fights, and by the time the parents came back at 6 p.m. to collect, everyone was sweating and crying and frenzied. Especially the poor girl I'd left behind at school to start with – her mum arrived to find her screaming in the hall. The sofa was tipped over, cushions and dressing-up clothes all strewn about, chairs upside down.

After many more long minutes of kids running shouting upstairs and trying to hide, the parents finally took them all home. Suddenly they all were gone. I collapsed on the sofa with a glass of wine. In the silence my ears seemed to be ringing. I was all sweaty and bright red and my chest was tight. I imagined the parents going home and saying, 'Jesus, I'm not sending my child to that house again!' The phone rang and it was Justin. I tried to tell him what had just happened but I was still half laughing and half having a heart attack.

That's all for now, May. Do write as soon as you can – I feel very unhappy about that passport man.

All my love as always . . .

Bee XXX

20.01.07

Your voice

May! It was magic to hear your voice on the phone yesterday. That's the first time we've spoken since I called you that first morning to try to arrange an interview, must be two years ago now.

Small yucky story. I took the girls to ballet on Friday and as Zola was standing in the queue to go in, I spotted a small brown thing running in her hair – it was a louse! Poor Zola, I'd heard about nits at school and a few of her friends have had them, but once I started combing her hair with a special comb, loads of them came out. I was squashing them! It made me itch all over. So now I have to comb her constantly, and annihilate them with sheer persistence. It reminded me of when I was little; we all got them at school and I thought it was so exciting, I loved being combed by my mum for ages.

Anyway, some quick news. A friend sent me details of a campaigning charity that is trying to rescue Iraqi academics called CARA, and I spoke to a man there called Professor John Akker. May, I really think they may be able to help – they have fellowship schemes designed to help people in your position. Perhaps there is a way of getting you out legally. Of course you mustn't get your hopes up, but he says he's going to find out more on your behalf. He also said that most Iraqi academics are going to Syria or Jordan. You might need to prove why that isn't an option for you. He asked for a CV from you. Can you send one to me, and I'll send him it.

I'm going to call him again when we have all that in place.

All my love

B XXX

PS Mobile phones are a miracle! I have to resist the temptation to text you every time I think of you.

20.01.07

CARA

Dearest Bee

I couldn't believe that I was actually talking to you in person. I can't describe how happy I was last night. I couldn't sleep for a while and sat thinking about you. You actually heard Ali's voice and I heard Justin's. Ali says that you probably thought that I was cold – but no, dearest friend, I work and talk in slow motion. I am so happy we have phone contact now; it was so nice sending you a text message and knowing right away where you were and what you were doing.

Sorry I couldn't write before, but besides lack of electricity, we had an awful day yesterday. Ali was in a very depressed mood. Would you believe it? He was in tears. Life has become so difficult and he feels so helpless. In the old days we wouldn't have needed to find someone to get the passports, Ali would have just done it by phone. Anyway, all is well now. The man turned out to be greedy, but not militia, and asked for more money. My bargaining gift failed and I will have to give him extra. Beggars can't be choosers. We need his talents! Oh, how I'd love to give him some dictation. I'm sure he'd fail a spelling test.

Bee, do you think that this campaign for Iraqi academics can really do anything to help? Did you receive my CV? I typed it yesterday for you.

By the way, how much does a modest family need per week to be able to survive in England? You know, Bee, if I ever go to another country, or if things calm down here, I would love you all to visit me and I think we would have a great time. I wish Iraq was peaceful. I would have taken you to see all the historical ruins and antiquities of the ancient civilizations and I'm positive you would have a superb time. Maybe we can do it sometime in the near future. Oh, I am being over-optimistic probably – but who knows?

Love

May xxx

20.01.07

Me again

Oh Bee, I was so excited about the asylum news I forgot to tell you the lice business reminded me of when I was young. My mother sat me on the terrace and kept combing and combing my hair. She never said it was lice to me; she said it was dandruff. I don't know why she did that, because when my sister got them she told her quite openly.

Did I tell you that up until yesterday the house was filled with garbage bags? We didn't know what to do with them because the dustman still fears coming to our area, and the whole neighbourhood is floating with rubbish. I didn't want to just throw them outside because of the stray cats. Then the solution came to us when we saw an empty piece of land where rubbish had already accumulated, and so we went home and brought the black bags and threw them on top of the rest.

I'll be going to work tomorrow (I hope). I miss work and seeing people.

Time to go. I love you, Bee.

May XXX

23.01.07

. . . the kitchen is mine again!

Dearest May

I hope Ali feels better today. He was wrong to say you sounded cold on the phone – and he must know better than anyone, because he fell in love with you on the phone! And I can imagine why; your voice is so rich. I notice voices because I work in radio.

Yesterday was funny. The camera crew arrived early for some more filming. The place was suddenly overrun with people shouting into their phones and leaving half-drunk cups of tea everywhere. Early on a huge crane turned up for some aerial shots of the house; it was a caged-in platform that lifted up into the air, going nearly 50 metres up. (A huge effort to go to, just to get fancy external shots of our not-very-interesting house, but never mind.) Justin and I got a go on it before they started filming. It was so high that we were above the birds, and looking way down on all the roofs and tiny gardens far below. The surrounding streets and houses made a sort of quilt-like pattern. As everything got smaller and smaller below I felt a strange affection for it, like I was looking down on a toy land.

I should have told you, I did receive your CV and I've sent it to Professor Akker at CARA. He put me in touch with a key person there called Kate Robertson, and I spoke to her about you. She is the one who works on the fellowship scheme and she has your CV now, so let's see what she says.

Bye for now, dearest May. I hope the sun shines on you today!

All my love

Bee XXXX

23.01.07

Hi, dearest

Ali is much better now. Thank you. And there may be some good news for us – they say the Americans will come to our area. I think this will make it a bit safer, because the militias will no longer be able to come and carry out any violence.

There were a lot of explosions today, but my route to work was empty and I managed to get there in 15 minutes, which is great, and I drove there on my own. You know, Bee, that's important to me. It made me feel strong and capable. And I enjoyed buying things, which I haven't done for ages, at the small college shop. It sells shampoo, make-up, perfume and even a few clothes. I went there after my lecture and bought myself some make-up and shampoo. It felt like luxury.

These emails about my voice make me think. Ali complains that I do not scream. Our talk on the phone reminded him of our first talk after the war was over. Although I was so happy to hear his voice – as I was when I heard yours – in both cases I failed to scream. I tried telling him about the extraction of my thyroid gland, which prevents screaming, but he doesn't understand this impairment. Anyway, you both know that I love you and so that's that.

We have one week to go before the mid-term holidays and I'm not sure if I'll go in next Monday, because I've finished *The Scarlet Letter* and will start *Hard Times* next semester. Time to go and make some dinner for my chubby baby.

I'll try to write tomorrow. Love you so much.

May XXXX

EXCITEMENT!

Dearest May!

It is about to go totally mad with work, May. They've asked me to make my own short film about ethical investment as part of Justin's Ethical Man project. It'll be full-time over the next couple of weeks. I'm at work now in the huge buzzing office and it's just so exciting to be back and full of ideas. I feel so fabulous in smart clothes and heels, instead of the usual mum clothes.

I'm so excited that I found it hard to sleep last night and THEN in the middle of the night Zola was sick three times, her bed was in a total mess, there was even sick on the wall. Meanwhile poor Eva developed a very high temperature and rattling cough. And Elsa had a sticky infected eye. So this morning I got up to total mayhem and the inevitable guilt of leaving all my ill children in the care of someone else (luckily our au pair Martina is really kind, but even so it's a bad feeling). I cleared up and rushed out of the house, totally stressed and with that sour smell still haunting me.

But I must confess that it's rather a pleasure to be away from it all and in a different environment. I can't write any more today. I'll write more if I get a moment tomorrow.

Lots of love and hugs always

B XX

Busy Bee

My lovely and wonderful (Busy) Bee. I'm so happy that you are back to work. Life always smiles upon people who work. As for the children, there will be plenty of time to care and play and love them after work and, believe me, being away from them for some time during the day will make you and the children more loving to each other.

Life here is still the same. No activities, no outings, no students because of the mid-term holidays. As for our chances of leaving Iraq, relations with other Arab countries are deteriorating and Iraqis are no longer accepted in Egypt unless they go as investors with large amounts of capital (at least $50,000), which is crazy. Bee, do you know how much I've missed your emails over the last few days? I realize that you are a vital member of my family and my life. Ali and I always talk about you and wonder what you are doing at this time of day, or how you are getting on with your work etc. Always remember that I love you my (now very busy) Bee and wish you all the success in your life.

May XXX

PS The violence is worse and we had another four university teachers killed during the week. I wish that all this would stop, one way or another.

09.02.07

Bright Friday morning

Good morning, dear peach!

Sorry it's been a while. It's been so hectic. But I have found out some more from Kate at CARA. They try to find placements for Iraqi academics at universities here in the UK. She says she's looking into it but it will take time, if they can do it at all.

With it still getting more dangerous all the time maybe we should keep trying all options, including the tourist visa route?

This morning with Elsa in my bed I found that her first ever little tooth is just starting to come through! You can feel it with your finger, and only just see it. Little thing, being ill has made her quite skinny and she isn't as sunny as usual. I feel bad about having left her all this time, but then I'll be back to normal next week.

Have to dash now – we are going to start editing.

All my love. Hope you are well today; how are you?

Bee XX

12.02.07

Hi, lovely friend

Dearest Bee

I know you must be worried, but I have no credit in my mobile to answer right away. I don't feel well and am very, very depressed. Even the internet connection is so bad (it takes an hour just to send an email).

I love you.

May XXX

12.02.07

RE: Hi, lovely friend

Oh, thank God you are there, May. I was beginning to wonder what had happened to you; the images from Baghdad over the weekend are horrific. It worries me that you feel so down. Is there anything I can do?

Back home it has turned to chaos while I've been away at work. Elsa was ill and then cut her first new tooth on Friday. Eva was very ill too, but she's better now. Then yesterday Zola got chicken pox. I keep telling her not to scratch. I'm sure Elsa and Eva will catch it too. But at least after today I won't be working, and we're all going up to my mum's soon. Haven't seen her for ages.

Got to go.

Love to you

B XX

13.02.07

Get well, my poor girls

LOVELY FRIEND

FIRST THINGS FIRST: HOW ARE THE POOR LOVELY GIRLS? Oh, you can't imagine how I would like to be bitten by Elsa's tooth! I keep remembering it now and then. Your girls, and of course you on top of all, are like the light at the end of a dark tunnel. You represent all the nice things I escape to, away from the bloody massacre surrounding me. And how is your mum?

Bee, yesterday was a close shave. Ali almost got killed by a sniper. Oh Bee, I couldn't hold myself together; I was in tears checking every part of him. I am terrified and now I want to get out no matter what. I am serious – to hell with the house and furniture and all the earthly rubbish we kid ourselves is important. As soon as the passports are ready we will be leaving. We cannot wait any longer. I can't describe how disturbed I am with what is going on. I am on antidepressants, but nothing seems to do the job.

Write to me.

Love

May XX

Sorry, it's been AGES

My dear friend, are you OK? I have been so worried about you and I hope things are getting better. We've finally got through a half-term holiday of illness and the trip to Yorkshire and all.

I just had an email from Andy too. Have you heard from him lately? He was very interested in your story when I met him the other evening. He asked a lot about you and said it was sad that he couldn't meet you because of the danger that would bring to you.

You asked about my mum. I think she was a bit tired and stressed in general, but also there may have been a bit of . . . mmm, how can I put it? Not being impressed by all the attention I got during filming. She isn't the sort of person to give lots of praise, and maybe she thought I'd get big-headed about it. And it's about to get worse – tomorrow there is a *Panorama* documentary about us on prime-time TV; it's in the papers etc. I don't tell her when we're on the radio or TV any more. After this month it all calms down again and things will be back to normal.

OK, May, I have to get Elsa's dinner ready now as she's quite impatient about food these days.

Lots of love to you and Ali always

Bee XXX

04.03.07

Love you always

Dearest friend

Getting our passports fixed has been an awful task and I don't trust the militiaman who is helping us at all. Suddenly he asked me to arrange another cheque to pay another fee and was very tense about the Americans finding out. We agreed to meet on a main road near our district at 11 a.m. (I couldn't take Ali with me because it was too risky for him.) At 10.45 I received a call from him and he said, 'Hurry, you have to come now,' but I got held up in a traffic jam because the Americans were searching the area – this is what really scared him. Finally I reached him and gave him the papers. He asked for an extra $200, but I said I wouldn't pay him until I was satisfied with the passports. I was so nervous I thought I might collapse. Now I have to wait for 10 days for them to be ready.

I went to college this morning and the situation seemed OK but there were dozens of checkpoints on the way, which made the traffic rather slow. I heard several explosions while teaching but I acted as if I had heard nothing. The students murmured each time that it was an explosion but I did not pay attention. As for their mobiles, I ordered (yes, I did) that they be turned off before entering my class. And so I managed to give a proper lecture.

You know, your mother seems a bit like mine, and your Elsa is just like Ali (hahaha). Your kindness always reminds me of a Shake-speare verse (I think), which says:

She that is thy friend indeed,
She will help thee in thy need:
If thou sorrow, she will weep;
If thou wake she cannot sleep . . .

You really are a true and honourable person, Bee. I love you so much.

Love to the girls, Justin and all the people who are nice like you

May XXX

06.03.07

Well done, May!

MAY, well done! How tough you were, even if you didn't feel it. But I don't understand (is this really stupid?), how come a militiaman is in a position to get you a passport? I thought that the militias were engaged in street warfare, not trying to squeeze money out of civilians.

It's lovely today. The spring is coming; I have washing hanging out to dry, a sight I really love. (I know it's a somewhat domestic pleasure but it's a job that pleases me – I think the smell of clean clothes on the line reminds me of my mum.)

All my love as always, and STAY STRONG.

Bee XX

06.03.07

Oh Bee, it was a close shave

Dearest friend Bee

Today was the worst of all. In the morning Ali and I had a terrible row. He didn't want me to go to work but I insisted that I must go because I had appointments with students whom I supervise. I drove out of the district and found, to my horror, that the security measures were on high alert. They stopped me several times and asked for my documents, whether the car was mine or not, and I had to keep presenting my ID.

At college I went to the hall to give my lecture, which is situated above the students' cafeteria. I walked in, greeted the students and started talking right away. Then I heard screams downstairs, and the sound of breaking glass, but I continued because I have decided to keep teaching till the last minute before we leave the country. I always tell myself that it is not fair to desert the students, who face similar dangers. They have taken the trouble to come to college so it is only fair that I perform my duty the best I can.

As I finished I was told that a sniper's bullet had gone through the glass of the cafeteria. I realized that the bullet could easily have penetrated a metre or two higher and hit me, or one of the girls. When I'd finished my second lecture (and this ironically was first-year human rights) I collected my stuff and went to the car park and drove out of the college. I drove for a while, then there was shooting and an explosion and everything went crazy. I closed the car window and listened to a song, trying to fool myself that there was actually nothing to fear.

I saw things that I can't describe. (Later I heard on the news that people who were going on a religious sort of marathon were attacked and shot.) Anyway, I reached my district only to find that it was closed by 'our army'. I tried another route, and another, but they were all closed. Eventually I remembered a way to get through, though it was a very long detour.

To cut a long story short, I finally entered our area. It was peaceful – I didn't see anything but armoured cars here and there – and as I passed the last one, they shot at me. I am sure of it, because I was the only car in the street, but they missed and I'm alive and well and had lamb chops for lunch and drank a ton of tea. Thank God.

You asked about the militiamen. Well, Bee, they are members of the militias but they also work at government offices (especially the Ministry of the Interior, where passports are issued) and they are quite influential. As I told you, the Shi'ite government of today is made up of militiamen, and this is the serious problem facing my country.

Oh Bee, I can't wait to get out.

Love to all of you with warm hugs and kisses

May XXX

07.03.07

You are amazing

I can't believe the things you tell me. You and Ali must still both be in shock. Sometimes I feel like my emails, and indeed my life, are so silly, so trivial in comparison. I write about hanging out my washing, and you are being shot at.

You must be extra careful for the next few days. Do you know where you will go for the tourist visa? Speak to Andy. We have to get you out as soon as possible; I just don't know what I'd do if you got killed. It would really break my heart.

Once you have your passports you can both get out of Iraq. Go somewhere with a British embassy, and try to get the visa. Where will you go – Jordan or Syria? Make sure you ask Andy what he thinks is best; he might know more about it. I have the documents you need from me. Tell me how I can fax them to you safely.

There are three photocopies:

1. my passport

2. bank statements showing we can support you during your visit

3. letter explaining our relationship and the nature of your visit.

For your part you must prove that you plan to return – having a two-way ticket might suffice.

We'll make it work somehow, May.

All my love and hugs

B XXX

10.03.07

I'm worried, Bee

Dear Bee

One of the things that attracted my attention was that when applicants present all their documents, including those of the host, they want evidence proving that the applicant is returning back home within six months at the most. (The examples given are a letter from work saying that you are on leave, or papers proving that you have business or some private enterprise.)

Then after that they say that it all depends on whether the visa officer is convinced that a person is really going on a visit. This brings another question to mind. Are they so simple or so ignorant as to think that a person from a war region is likely to be going on holiday at a time that is neither the holiday season nor normal in any way?

Today I had a horrific shock. As I went to college there was a black placard mourning one of our students; she was shot by the Americans on her way home. I was so sad because she was one of the brightest students and recently married.

WHAT DO YOU ADVISE ME TO DO, BEE?? HELP, I'M GOING MAD.

Love you always

XXXXX

11.03.07

I'm worried too

Dearest May

I've been feeling tired and a bit down lately. Maybe it's PMT. I do find it very hard to know what to say to you sometimes – I feel quite useless. But we must find a way through.

I love you, May.

Bee XXX

24.03.07

Stay or go?

Dearest Bee

I am torn, but I think I must stay until July. If I leave before the end of the academic year I will lose my job, which means I can't return home and will become a wretched beggar. We could both go to Syria and put in the visa application for a later date, then I could come back to Baghdad to work and Ali could stay there where it's safer.

Kisses to all of you

May XXX

PS Did you see the UN Secretary General's face when he was rocked by one of the endless explosions that go on every day? He looked so scared. Maybe this will make the UN people speed up their measures towards finding a solution.

25.03.07

I'm on top of the world today!

Dearest

At last I am taking a step forward. The passports are here. I called the British Embassy in Damascus and talked to the visa section. I told them that I need a visitor's visa for July and that I am a university professor. And I am so busy that I need to know how long it will take and how long I have to stay in Syria to obtain the visa (imagine).

Before all this the woman who answered asked who the visa was for, and I replied, 'For my husband and myself.' She said, being Iraqis, we'd have to come in person to apply because they need to take our fingerprints and an iris picture, or something like that. I told her I have an invitation and a very close friend is sponsoring my visit, but she said I have to bring all these with me.

Oh Bee, I can't describe how I felt – it was like flying in the air, sitting at the top of a hill. Or more probably like a child opening the long-awaited Christmas surprises, because I was singing and dancing around the house with my awful voice. But what the heck? I was so happy and that's what matters. Bee, I am now smoking a big cigar and it looks so funny but it tastes very good, and Ali is sitting next to me smoking one himself. He sends you, Justin and the girls all his love.

How is everyone? Are the girls OK? Give them my hugs and kisses plus ONE very special kiss and hug to Eva for being so considerate and interested in my welfare.

Don't take long to send me one of your heart-warming emails.

May XXX

27.03.07

RE: I'm on top of the world today!

MAY, I just love the image of you singing and smoking a cigar. So you could be leaving in July! When will you go to Damascus to get the visa? How long do you think it will take? Do you have everything you need to get it? It feels like we're one step closer to getting you out, but I wish you could leave Iraq sooner.

It was a crazy weekend of rushing around and a lot of socializing; I feel tired now. But an amazing thing has happened. Last year Eva wrote a short story for a competition run by Daunt Books, a famous local bookshop. (Well, she spoke it out loud and I transcribed it.)

Anyway, on Friday a letter came for Eva in the post. She opened it, with her serious face and her eyes all big. It was to say that she has won! Over 400 children entered. And her category is up to 9 years old (she's only 5). It will be published in a book, and she gets to go to a poetry masterclass with the fantastic poet Adrian Mitchell.

Elsa too has been busy. She can now crawl around at top speed, and can pull herself up. She goes straight for the rubbish bin and pulls stuff out. Yesterday I found her with a load of onion skins in her mouth. This morning I took her for a bike ride on the back of my bike; she has a little seat and wears a small helmet. Everyone smiles at her. Zola has developed a talent for miniature books. She sticks them together and writes in an indecipherable language and draws complicated pictures. She is quite secretive and hides her small things in little bags or socks, and puts them under her pillow or down the back of the sofa. I find Zola's stuff, bundled up like a ritual offering, in the weirdest places.

Love to you and Ali

Bee XXX

28.03.07

The plan for Syria

Dearest Bee

I've arranged with the college to be away 15th April to 1st May so that Ali and I can go to Damascus. After that I will have to come back to Baghdad, but Ali will stay in Syria until we leave in July (I hope) because it is becoming far too dangerous for him here. I will go to see him in Damascus as much as possible. But if I get the UK visa I will then go, even if the college doesn't give me the leave.

May x

30.03.07

At work

Hello there, lovely May

At last things are moving – it feels good. Well done! You've been so active. Shame it's still quite far away, but I can understand your timing.

I'm back in World Service in the middle of a buzzing office with shouting people all around, a lot of familiar faces and some new ones too. Got in at 5.45 this morning – oh my God, not nice, I'm just not a morning person. Well anyway we get an hour or so to 'read in' and then there's a planning meeting where we all contribute our ideas. Sometimes you can get new stories on the air, but if it's a busy news day like today it's more a case of reacting to circum-stances and thinking of new angles on the subject, moving it on. Top story is the British sailors held hostage in Iran. People here are talking about war with Iran! Can anyone still have the stomach for war after Iraq?

I have to go – am trying to persuade some Catholics to talk about the Pope on Monday. (Although by then I will be frolicking around on the great Yorkshire moors!)

All my love and take care

B X

04.04.07

DOOMSDAY

Dearest friend

Today was one of the scariest days of my life. I woke up in the morning and started to get ready for work. I put the generator on after my morning shower, and started to dry my hair. Ali was asleep. Then there was this loud banging on the front door. I called out, asking who it was, and they answered, 'Open up – it's the army.'

I woke Ali up and he went downstairs, and as soon as they came in they started searching the house. I came down, buttoning up, and asked what they were looking for. They said they wanted the rest of the weapons, and we both screamed, 'What weapons?' The officer said, 'The ones you've hidden for your neighbours.'

We were terrified. Then Ali asked the officer to explain and he told us that they had found arms, bombs and high explosives next door. We told him that we knew nothing about them, and he could search as much as he liked. The soldiers searched a little bit then the officer ordered them to withdraw. We were also searched on Sunday, when they messed the place up. Today they didn't take long, and the officer seemed convinced that we knew nothing.

Then some American troops banged on the outside gate. They told us to open the windows because there was a great big bomb that they couldn't move and they were going to detonate it on-site. They also asked us to bring the women and children next door into our house. We don't know them. They moved into the district about eight months ago, after the previous neighbour was shot and killed outside a nearby shop.

Anyway, they detonated the bomb. My mother has three broken windows and my brother has one, but funnily I don't have any, though I am the one closest to the bomb.

All I hope is that we make it to Damascus.

xxx

13.04.07

We're out!

Dearest

We made it. We have arrived safe (but not sound) in Damascus. I cannot describe my feelings. I am relieved to get out of hell, and a bit homesick and afraid of the unknown. Our journey lasted almost 12 hours. We arrived exhausted. Some friendly Iraqis helped us find a tiny flat with what I call shabby furniture, but they say it's not bad for here. The Syrians are generally friendly, but not so friendly when it comes to money. Imagine this: they took $1,200 for two months' rent, while they wrote in the contract only $100 per month. But food is not that expensive, so we'll be OK.

The thing is, I don't know how long we can last like this. Oh dearest, I'm so scared. It is not a good feeling to have no one you know in a foreign country. But this is war, I suppose. (As agreed, I will ask the embassy for a visa and let you know the details.)

OK, love, time to go. Kiss the girls for me.

XXXX

20.04.07

A second hello from Damascus

Dearest Bee

My mood is much better now. We've been out for some long walks, and the country is nice and the weather is good. People are very noisy here and the flat we rented is situated in a shopping area. Shops here do not close until very late and people fill the streets all the time. But, as I said, they're friendly and not depressed like us Iraqis. Over the last decade in Iraq it has become very rare to see people being friendly to strangers. There's always an element of distrust enveloping all human contact. Here, at last, we can taste the beauty of peace and walk in the streets without fear of robbers, killers and all the other hazards that I've told you of.

Bee, please send me more emails from now on, because I'm going to need you so much. In Syria we are all alone, and if I go back to Iraq I'll be on my own. The idea terrifies me but I don't show it to Ali, because he will simply return with me and will definitely be killed.

I did not tell you how I got him out of the hands of the army when they burst into our house back in Baghdad. The officer asked for Ali's ID. I know that men from Ali's Sunni background are taken away, and they do not come back. So I just brought out the club membership ID which has my family name on it, and Ali's name as husband of the member. The officer asked for proper IDs and I just said they'd been taken to get our new passports done. Thankfully the officer was convinced. But who knows what could happen next time?

I must go now.

May XXXX

20.04.07

Hello at last

Hello there, May

Sorry about my short response to your text this evening. There is a time from about 5 p.m. to 7.30 p.m. which is like rush hour. When your text came asking why I hadn't written to you, Elsa was crying, Eva and Zola were fighting in the garden, and I was trying to get their dinner ready.

Eva and Zola are back at school now so things are settling down. They're both very happy. I didn't tell you, but we had a bad experience a couple of weeks ago when we were up in Yorkshire. We were in the middle of nowhere, climbing around with the kids when Zola fell off an eight-foot wall (that's two metres high); she fell off it and landed on her back. It made a sickening noise which I will never forget as long as I live. I ran to her as she lay on the ground, thinking about first-aid training, broken spines and necks and how you mustn't move the casualty. It was a nightmare. As I got to her side I screamed, 'Zola, can you hear me?' She opened her mouth and let out a massive scream, so I scooped her up in my arms and lifted her. As I did she was sick all over me and herself, and then her face went grey. We carried her to the car, drove to a village pub and called an ambulance.

She was still grey, but breathing. I was holding her and I began to shake and cry. Strangely the thought in my mind was how Zola has just been 'promoted' by her ballet teacher to the next class up. Anyway, the paramedics arrived and checked her all over for spinal injuries, internal bleeding, concussion etc., only to find that our little Zola was fine. Indeed, within two minutes of this she ran off to get an ice cream with the other kids, as I stood there still shaking. May, I felt that we came so close to losing her. I felt a sick gratitude that she was OK, and so many mixed feelings about how it could have been. That night I woke in the middle of the night and kept reliving every second in my head. In the end I had to go and see her, and check her sleeping body just to make sure she was still OK.

I know that you face this kind of closeness to death and destruction all the time in Baghdad, but for me it was new.

I'm glad that you have got out to Syria, May. I think some normality and rest will be good for you. It is brave of you to take this step. I remember Andy saying a refugee must be prepared to lose everything. I guess you have reached that point, because you have already left. I wonder what will become of your home when you leave it behind. Will you want to return one day? What do you think you will do if/when you get to London? Justin and I can try to help you with your accommodation for up to six months, but you will have to do some work to support yourselves. Ali will have to learn English. Have you thought all of this through?

You would have laughed if you'd seen me trying to fax the letter of invitation and documents to you. I had to keep walking past my editor to reach the fax machine, so I timed it whenever he was on the phone. I'd rustle the documents in with some newspapers and wander about like I was doing something else, then get to the fax and furiously type in the numbers again and try to send it properly. Then I'd nonchalantly saunter off in the other direction.

Right then, dearest May, enjoy the freedoms of Damascus and have a lovely next few weeks.

Lots of love

Bee XX

21.04.07

HELP

Dearest friend. I read your email and something between the lines has made me feel that it will be so hard. Bee, I am so grateful for all your help and your offer to accommodate us. But Bee, do you think we can support ourselves in a matter of months? Then do you think I could get a proper job? If you have time to answer me, please do. My final decision depends on you.

Love

May XXXX

Not nice

Hi, dearest

I think that you haven't really thought enough about what it is to be an asylum seeker. You ask me would you get 'a proper job in a matter of months' and say your decision depends on what I tell you. The blunt reality is that it would be very hard. A legal case can take up to a year or even two or three, during which time it is illegal to work. You would find illegal work easily enough, but it would not be what you are used to. Ali would probably not find anything unless he can speak English. You could be separated. Maybe you should think about staying in Syria or another Arabic-speaking country, so that at least both of you can support each other?

May, you can't ask me to make the decision for you. I can only point out the various options and try to help with whatever you choose. It *is* possible that you could win asylum quickly and find a nice job here. But there really are other not so good possibilities too, and I hate it that I have to tell you that.

All my love

Bee XX

22.04.07

RE: Not nice

Bee Bee Bee, my lovely friend

I know what you are saying is absolutely true. You are also quite right that it is not what I'm used to, but please don't think that I am a spoilt brat. I just can't describe to you the horrible psychological imbalance we are going through, especially since we came to Syria.

It is a mixture of fright, homesickness and nostalgia for familiar things, plus fear of the unknown.

Bee, you are my friend and I am used to opening up my heart to you and telling you whatever comes into my mind. My email was an outcry of inner fear and I guess that worried you and you probably hated me for it. Anyway, I am really sorry for getting you so mad at me. But really, we are very lost.

Today I went to the embassy and applied for the visa. They took our passports and forms and said they would contact us in 10 days, as the papers have to go to Amman and back, so we won't know the outcome until then.

You ask about finding jobs here. Well, the highest salary an Iraqi can get is $100 per month, but rent is $600, so Ali has been looking too. It is bearable for the Syrians because their rents are much much lower than ours. I've told you the landlords take advantage of our misery.

NOW, let's leave all this and talk about your journey to the Moors. Poor Zola must have given you the fright of your life. I don't blame you for feeling so terrified as it is not easy to think even for one moment of the possibility (God forbid) of losing someone so precious. Thank God it turned out well. I have missed your emails. I can't wait for the time to get a real bite from Elsa. Do you know, I have started for the first time in my life to actually look at stores where baby things are displayed, and I always think of her.

OK love, I must go now and I repeat that I am sorry for driving you nuts with my fears and worries. And that's probably why I also keep pestering you with my messages.

Love you always

May XXXXX

Emotional weekend

Hello, dearest

Don't worry, it's OK to talk about your worries. It's only frustration at the circumstances that makes me so angry.

I know you can't write so much now as you have to find an internet café and it's not easy, but there are a hundred things I wish I knew about your daily life. In your Baghdad emails you used to tell me about making lamb for dinner, but in Damascus do you even have a kitchen or somewhere to make tea? What is the space like where you are living?

It's small rituals that make us human, like making tea. For me it signifies a moment of my own in the chaos of motherhood. I do it in a particular way and there is The Perfect Cup, when it's hot but not boiling, you breathe down and it gently steams your face. (God forbid you get distracted, and when you get there it's gone cold.) But for a refugee it must take on an even greater symbolism, having one's own space quite literally.

Well, I am thinking of you.

Yesterday was a big day. Eva had her award ceremony and book launch for that competition at Daunt Books. She got a bit shy when she collected her prize, and she looked so small compared to the other kids. But she was proud of herself and enjoyed the whole day. A sad thing also happened: our old cat Booker T. died. A neighbour came and knocked on the door, saying, 'There's a dead cat in the back alley.' Justin, Eva and Elsa were out. I went round the back to see, and Zola came with me. Booker T. was a good cat; I've had her since my sixteenth birthday and she was very old so I didn't feel too shocked about her dying. That is, until we found her body: she had no head. She was entirely decapitated and the head was nowhere to be found. There was just a hole. It looked so

unnatural and I began to sob and scream out, 'Where's her head?'
Zola saw the whole episode, which I regret.

Booker T. had a stately funeral. We buried her in the garden near
some forget-me-nots, with flowers and love letters placed in her
grave. It might seem excessive for a cat, but it was the girls' first
encounter with death and I thought we should dignify it. I think
they will remember yesterday for a long time. They are still talking
about it a lot. Justin says it was probably a fox that took her head
off and I hope that's true rather than some sick weirdo.

I have to go.

Love

Bee XX

29.04.07

LOVE FROM DAMASCUS

Hello, love

CONGRATULATIONS TO EVA PLUS A TRIPLE HUG
AND A BIG FAT KISS. I am really so happy and proud.

I thought of you a lot on Friday. It was Ali's birthday so we went
to a nice area just 20 km north of Damascus. Oh Bee, it was so
beautiful. There was a narrow river with trees and farms, and on
the banks of the river there were nice simple restaurants and we
took a lot of photos, one with me up a tree. I thought of you all
the time and wished you were with us to enjoy the beauty of the
place.

I am sorry about your cat. It was rather old but the way it died is so
ugly, and reminded me of death in my country. You know, Bee, a
lot of people die this way nowadays. I wonder how could it have
happened?

Have to go now.

Love

MAY XXX

03.05.07

Where is the visa??

Oh Bee, I am so worried. My time is running out and I must leave for Baghdad soon but still no sign of the visas. We are both so scared and nervous that we stay in the flat talking about what will happen to us, even though we are free to go out because it is safe here. I think we Iraqis have become rather complicated in our attitude to the world outside our homes. I have noticed (and this applies to many Iraqis) that we are too tired to establish new human relationships and contacts, plus we are too scared to do so. Trusting one another is no longer easy, and is becoming rare in our community. Iraqis have restricted friendships to people they know and trust from back home.

Anyway, Ali and I are blessed to have each other. As we have nothing to do we have turned into lazy bums (to be honest, I hate it deep down). We stay up late at night talking and watching TV, and so we don't wake up early. Bee, you know I think we are sick. We eat and cat all the time without being really hungry; we have lost interest in life and a secure future feels just a dream. I have even stopped wearing make-up, because I don't go out and so I've lost interest. Imagine me neglecting something I have enjoyed doing since I was 14?

I must go.

Love to those nieces of mine

May

09.05.07

May!

Hello, lovely May

Did you get an extension from your university? I hope you're feeling better. Is it still OK to be in Damascus? May, I know you feel down but it still feels good just to know that you're not in Iraq. But let me know what's going on.

Loads of love

B XX

10.05.07

NOT OK

NO, BEE, THINGS ARE NOT OK.

I AM IN A HORRIBLE MESS. I'VE TRIED CALLING THE BRITISH EMBASSY SEVERAL TIMES BUT ALL I CAN GET TO TALK TO IS THE LOCAL EMPLOYEES WHO SAY THEY DON'T KNOW A THING. I WANT MY PASSPORT BACK WITH OR WITHOUT A VISA BECAUSE I HAVE TO GO HOME OR LOSE MY JOB. I DON'T KNOW WHAT TO DO. THEY DON'T ALLOW PEOPLE TO SEE THE BRITISH STAFF. HEEEEEELLLLLPPPP.

17.05.07

Where are you?

What on earth happened, May? I got your text saying you're still in Damascus. I can't understand. What will happen to your university job back in Baghdad? Why did it take so long to get a rejection from the embassy? I hope you are both OK. Let me know what's happening as soon as you can.

It's been raining here for nearly two weeks and Elsa is driving me mad; she is so busy and active and wants to be outside. She's frustrated as she can't do the things she wants to do. She now pulls herself up on all the furniture and wobbles around before falling back down again. She also chews everything she can grab. This includes all the girls' artwork we have on the wall. Elsa pulls it down and eats it, and the girls get upset.

Write soon, May. I'm thinking of you and hope you'll be OK.

Bee XXX

17.05.07

The horror of the visa ordeal

Dear Bee

Oh Bee, let me first tell you about the visa disaster. The problem was not with the British people who work at the embassy, because you don't ever get to see any of them. The problem was with the locals. It was chaotic. After we were told it would take 10 days for the application to come back, I went to the embassy to find out the result but nobody had any answers and every time I asked, they said to wait — even though I explained that I needed my passport to return to Iraq. Eventually they called me in on Sunday morning, then cancelled the meeting. Again and again I was told to wait and I pleaded that it was a humanitarian issue. When I eventually went to collect the papers, a document from the vice-consul said she didn't believe that we weren't intending to work in the UK, that she didn't think we would leave within six months and that even though we had a sponsor she was not convinced because the invitation and the other documents were photocopied. I felt so humiliated.

To be honest, Bee, I'd rather be killed in Baghdad than become a beggar on the doorsteps of other countries. Especially when these countries are the ones who have shattered our lives, exploited our national wealth and put us through all this misery. I am sorry to say BUT this event has changed all my beliefs about Great Britain, which I have cherished in my heart since I was a child.

So we have no visas, but it is too dangerous for Ali to return to Baghdad. And it's not worth me returning now. I had already missed the deadline for my return to college so I called the department to ask for an extension. Thank God I was unwell for some time (I did not tell you) and was able to get a medical report recommending rest. The college will soon close for the summer vacation anyway, and they've been so considerate letting me stay here till the end of the holidays. If security in Baghdad does not improve then I can probably return a bit late. They will keep my job for me until the autumn. We have decided to stay in Damascus while it is too dangerous to return, and for as long as we have enough savings to live on. But Bee, it feels like a half-life here with nothing to do and nothing of our own.

I have to go now as my time is finishing at the internet café. Write to me soon.

XXXXXXXXXXXXXXXXXXXXXXXXXXXXX

PS If you want a copy of the embassy's letter I can fax it to you.

18.05.07

RE: The horror of the visa ordeal

Bastards. There is nothing worse than small-minded people invested with a bit of power; they become corrupted. I think you faced the worst of the worst. But at least you are persistent and resilient. I think that that is the reality of being a refugee, May. This is what I was so worried about. It would be just as bad in London. I've told you that I have worked with refugees; I know how bad it can be.

I have just got back from a day at work. I hate sitting still at a desk for hours. It makes my bum ache. I decided to throw a party, and have started planning a secret surprise birthday party for Justin. Last year he was 40, but he didn't want to have a big celebration, plus Elsa had just been born. He gets all grumpy about birthdays, whereas I absolutely love them. So this year I am taking over. It's been brilliant – I've sneakily tracked down lots of his mates and everyone is very excited.

I'm glad that you are able, at least, to stay with Ali in Damascus rather than return to Baghdad when it's so dangerous.

Take care for now, dear May.

Bee XXX

24.05.07

Life goes on in Damascus

Hi, Bee

Life is dreary here. Although we are fine in Damascus, it is useless to try and find a job. The maximum salary the Syrians pay whether you are a dentist, a professor or a dustman is no more than $100 a month. I think they do it on purpose to limit the number of Iraqis working in their country. I don't blame them, of course. But most Iraqis enter the country and spend their own money without burdening the Syrian economy. So I think it is they who benefit from our immigration, contrary to what is written in the press.

Ali has made lots of friends (Iraqis and Syrians) and he walks freely around the streets and enjoys the freedom of security. I've found some of my old students and some colleagues, although we don't socialize with them much, but we still go for long walks.

I hope that all is well with you.

MAY xxxx

25.05.07

Elsa's birthday: how wonderful

Dear Bee

I was thinking how it's Elsa's birthday soon. It is a shame that I can't be there. Do you know that my head of department tried to send someone to replace me and cover my absence but the students refused to have her? I hear that they told her they would only accept her on the condition that she tells them May is dead or is no longer coming back. Because, with 'Miss May', novel class is not just a lesson: it is a journey in a time machine (I always compare some of the Victorian traditions with the present day, because there is a great deal of similarity and this seems to make them like it more). I do miss my students, Bee. They are eager for life and they think that there is a future waiting for them. I hear from a colleague that they have just finished Book Two of *Hard Times* and are eager to find out if Louisa is going to marry Harthouse. Oh, they so love these things! Most of them are deprived of real experiences because of the strict Arab traditions, so they just dream away in their classes.

I am glad not to be in Baghdad. Now it is summer and around 42 degrees, just like a hot oven. And it will soon rise to 46–48 degrees in July and August. The security situation in Iraq is getting worse with every explosion and I hear the soldiers are getting more nervous, banning people from moving around, and waving their guns. I should be glad that Ali and I can walk safely here.

I will write to you again as soon as I can.

Love

MAY XXX

Still trying

Dear Bee

I miss you so much. I just couldn't help but send you a message. LIFE HAS TO GO ON, doesn't it? The journey has not yet come to an end.

Today I received an email from Kate Robertson of CARA, inquiring if I had made it to the UK. This was so very nice of her and I told her part of the story, but not all of it. I really do miss the heart-warming emails of my younger sister (you) but I know you are so very busy.

Tell me all about the surprise birthday party for Justin. And kiss the lovely little nieces of mine, especially the lovely four-tooth angel.

Time to go.

Love you always

May

02.06.07

Home alone

Hello, dear May

I feel awful not to have written in so long, but I think I have some good news. I spoke to Kate again and she said that she had heard from you. She has an idea that may provide a way to help – if you were to secure a place at an English university to study and teach, CARA could pay for the fees, but we would still need to find some way of covering your living expenses. But Ali could come too. It's still just an idea, but perhaps there is hope.

I am alone, but at least only for three nights (Justin's in Belfast). It's been a busy week. The nightmare of the Summer Fair is in full swing. Remember last year we did the Christmas Fair? It was incredibly hard work and I was demoralized by some of the mums' comments. One of them appears to be some kind of class warrior. She is a single mum living in a council flat (which doesn't concern me in the least, but she prefaces almost every comment with it, as if it adds weight to what she's about to say) and she battles against almost everything I suggest. She seems to disapprove of making money, even though it's our job to raise funds. The Parents' Association is a two-year job, and right now I wish I'd never agreed to it. I've become a social leper; people scatter when they see me coming in case I start nagging them to do stuff.

Still managing to keep Justin's surprise party a secret, and it's been funny getting all his friends in on it. I am enjoying the sneakiness.

Ah well, May, it's late again and I think I'd better start getting ready for bed, so that I don't sit up as late as last night. Big hugs to you, dearest. I hope you are feeling OK right now.

Love from

Bee

06.06.07

Missing a soulmate

Dearest friend

How nice to be talking again. I really miss you but have tried to hold back, as I realize that you are a young mother fighting hard to get everything done at the right time.

I hope all is fine. I am writing to share my happiness with you, my best friend: Kate has just written to me and said CARA will be able to help me for the coming four months, which means we can stay here in Damascus longer. Oh Bee, I am so excited! We can survive here for another four months. It is great and thanks, of course, to you, my dear friend — you really are an angel, or the good fairy. I love you so much, Bee. Ali also sends his love and thanks for all you've done for us.

It is so hot now in Damascus. Can you imagine? It is now 45 degrees centigrade — like a really hot oven. So much for escaping the heat of Baghdad.

Love you always, lots of hugs to you and the girls

May XXX

PS I can't write very often because I don't have a computer. I go to the internet café and sometimes it is very busy and I can't find a place. But I swear you are always on my mind and in the centre of my heart.

10.06.07

Hurray for CARA!

Hello, dear baked potato in the slow oven of Damascus.

I didn't know CARA had the resources to do this; I am so happy that they can help you to stay on there for longer. What a reprieve for you and Ali. I hope you feel you can relax and enjoy life away from the Baghdad horrors for a longer time.

The surprise party was great. I had all J's friends in on it, and one of them took him out for the day. I told Justin I was having some girlfriends round, so he would secretly want to escape. It took me all day to get it ready; at about 8 p.m. people started arriving and I hid them in the garden. Justin got back home at about 8.30 and everyone cheered when he came in. There was lots of dancing and the celebrations went on late. Very, very late. Right at the end Justin admitted to me that one of his friends had in fact let it slip (I now hate this man for ever) so he'd known all along that something was happening! Can't tell you how annoying that was. Doing a secret party is so much work, I don't think I'll ever do it again. But I'm glad I did it.

These next few weeks are going to be pretty mad, May, and I might not be able to write so often. There's Eva's birthday, Glastonbury Festival for the weekend, then the school Summer Fair, and the day after that we're leaving for our big summer holiday in Colombia. I just keep on frantically writing lists – and lists of lists – to get everything done.

Good night, May. Hope you can sleep in that crazy heat.

Take care

B XXX

27.06.07

Festival madness

How are you, May? I hope you're OK.

What a bizarre weekend. We went to Glastonbury. Normally that would be great news as it was a sold-out event and Justin was invited as a speaker (Ethical Man strikes again). But it rained and rained and rained, and then rained some more. The whole thing turned into a mudbath. We, like everyone else, were camping, and our tent was totally brown with mud inside and out. It got so bad we couldn't actually put Elsa down anywhere on the ground, not even while we were trying to eat. Her buggy sank into the mud over the wheels and was totally clogged up, and the mud went over the tops of the girls' wellington boots and they got upset, and then Eva got blisters.

Eva's blisters were the last straw, so I said it was time to leave. We left early on Saturday instead of on the Sunday, and then watched the rest of the festival on TV, thinking, 'Thank God we're not there any more!' Strangely enough the kids loved it, though (apart from the blisters); it was funny and unreal and they saw some very strange sights.

It is a point of meaningless pride to me that my mum took me to Glastonbury when I was only six. The date was 07.07.77 and all the hippies were going mad about this cosmic-sounding calendar moment. I distinctly remember lots of naked people and a man sharing out muesli from a giant communal cauldron. So it was touching to be there again, 30 years later, with my own 6-year-old girl.

When we got back I had to do four laundries in a row, and chisel the dried mud off all our boots, Elsa's buggy, the backpacks and the tent. I was in a bad mood that day. The rain hasn't stopped since, though, and have you seen on the news? Parts of the country are totally flooded. Maybe it'll make people think about climate change and the planet. Or maybe not.

What about you, May? I hope you're OK. Are you busy? Write soon – I hope I get to hear from you before we leave. We're going on Sunday to Colombia for three weeks, but I'm taking my mobile phone so I'm still contactable.

Big hugs and love to you

Bee XXX

20.07.07

Calling London. Are you there?

Hi, my lovely friend

Are you back? I long to hear from you and keep checking my emails but you must be still in Colombia. It will be good to be able to talk to you properly by email.

By the way, I sent Kate from CARA my documents and she said that she would try to find me a PhD acceptance at a university. She has also written to my supervisor and a couple of friends, asking for recommendations, and has asked me if she can request a recommendation from you. I said of course, when you are back from Colombia. Who knows, it may just help.

Anyway, I have to go now. Send me pictures of you and the LOVELY nieces of mine in Colombia, and say hello to Justin.

Love you always

May XXXXX

PS A man is taking a walk in Central Park in New York. Suddenly he sees a little girl being attacked by a pit bull terrier. He runs over and starts fighting with the dog. He succeeds in killing the dog and saving the girl's life. A policeman who was watching the scene walks over and says, 'You are a hero – tomorrow you can read it in the newspapers: Brave New Yorker saves life of little girl!' The man says, 'But I'm not a New Yorker.' 'Oh, then it will say in the newspapers: Brave American saves life of little girl,' the policeman answers. 'But I'm not an American,' says the man. 'Oh, what are you then?' The man says, 'I'm from Iraq!'

The next day the newspapers say: 'Islamic extremist kills innocent American dog.'

27.07.07

Back among the raindrops

MAY!

Well, we got back from Colombia two days ago. It was epic. I savoured every moment – every sight, sound and smell reminded me why I fell in love with the place. Apart from my personal nostalgia and catching up with important friends, it was also a perfect family trip. Eating weird fruits, snorkelling among coral reefs, horse riding. Eva's godfather Emilio has a huge coffee farm where we spent a dazzled week. Words can hardly describe it; the air is full of flowers and brightly coloured birds. We went to a wedding in Medellín. My friend Maria Clara who's Catholic married a Jewish man; it was a beautiful mixture of both ceremonies. And of course a lot of lounging around in hammocks with rum-based cocktails.

Her Majesty Elsa became royalty over in Colombia; everyone went just crazy over her curly blonde hair and blue eyes, but the problem is that now she waves at every person she sees in the street, expecting the same level of attention. Today I put all three girls in the bath and sprinkled them with fresh pink rose petals from the garden. I call it a goddess bath. Elsa tried to eat the petals.

Well, I can't wait to hear all your news, May, and great news about CARA. You must tell me more. What did Kate say? What have you been doing, and how is Ali?

Lots of love and hugs to you

Bee XXX

11.08.07

CARA

Dear dear Bumbo Bee, my lovely friend

I could be dreaming but I'm keeping my fingers crossed. Kate arranges fellowships, which are placements at universities. She tells me if all goes well I could do my PhD at the University of Bedfordshire. I would be coming on a student visa, and Ali could come too. I don't know how long it would take to organize, though. She cannot promise anything but I am sure she will do her best. CARA have been helping academics since the 1930s so I trust their judgement.

CARA says the university fees are covered but mentions a figure of £30,000 for living costs for the three years of my PhD. As students we are allowed to do some part-time work too. Do you think it can happen?

I'm so happy to hear about my lovely Elsa. It is absolutely fascinating. This baby means such a lot to me; I love her so much, and you of course and the girls. Must go now.

Love and kisses for them all

May xx

14.08.07

Latest news

My dear May

This news from CARA is the best thing yet and it's hard not to get all my hopes up again. I'm trying to think of ways we can raise the rest of the money and I wonder if an interview with you, a news item or an article would help with this. I don't know.

What's it like out there? Have you settled in, or made any friends? Do you feel in any way a bit more at home in Damascus? Write soon. I love to hear the latest. Am feeling quite out of touch with you . . .

B x

04.09.07

Missing

Hello, my bonnie wee sister

We live in an area that is overpopulated with Iraqis. Syrians are a minority here. It is inhabited by the Iraqi ex-middle class. Most of them are Sunni and many are a bit prejudiced, but only in thought and not in action. The flat I live in is situated in the middle of a marketplace and is very noisy. The furniture is shabby and worn out. It is very small but it has the basics, such as a washing machine and an iron. The plates we eat off are plastic and broken. We've bought two or three cups (for our tea!) and some new plastic plates and things like that. The heater is old but part of it works and that's the important thing.

Life is monotonous, as you can imagine. To be honest, Bee, I am safe but not very happy. I miss my life. I even miss the streets, pavements and the destroyed city. (It is my home.) I miss my bed, my books, my china. Oh Bee, I even miss the bombs. I feel so lonely, and so out of touch, but I guess this is what war is all about.

The internet café here is always overcrowded with people, mostly Iraqis trying to get in touch with their families, and it is heartbreaking to see the separated families reconnecting through the internet. By the way, Bee, I can't write as often as I used to because I hate standing in long queues just to get hold of a computer, and while I'm waiting it hurts to watch how miserable the once comfortable Iraqis have become.

Tell me, how are the lovely girls? News of them keeps me going.

May XXXXX

16.09.07

Your nieces

My dear May

I'm so sorry you're missing home. I thought so. Oh, it's all so sad. I don't know what to say. So here is some news of your nieces. I hope it helps. Elsa is impossibly lovely now, May. People just love her when they see her, and I think she really is the happiest baby I've ever met. Her world is a place where everyone loves her and everything tastes nice – can you imagine such a life? Eva is happy at school and bursting with energy. But Zola is very tired at the moment;

sometimes after school she runs upstairs and hides in her room saying she wants 'some peace and quiet', and if I knock and go quietly in she will have created a miniature world out of all her dolls and bears, all very intricate. Perhaps she misses being the baby of the family. I think I should get more exclusive time with Zola so she doesn't feel left out.

OK, May. I'll write again soon.

HUGS BXXX

18.10.07

Back after a mad week

Hi, May

All the emails I've written, sitting here at the end of the wooden table facing towards the small apple tree in the garden. One day you will join me in this kitchen and I'll make us tea. You like it black with sugar, don't you? I like milk no sugar.

Anyway, May. We need to have a chat about the plans. I am a bit worried about the financial backing that will be needed to support your fellowship at the University of Bedfordshire. Justin and I can write the letter of recommendation and could borrow enough money to show the necessary bank statements. But I am going to be blunt, May: we simply cannot afford just to give you and Ali £30,000. You will need to pay rent and food. Ali can't speak English. Would he be prepared to do unskilled work? The minimum wage here is £5.52 an hour. Are you prepared to take on any extra work as well as your PhD? The fact is, I know neither of you have done anything like this before, because of your backgrounds. You probably won't be very good at it. But you must think very hard about this. You can't expect to get everything for free, May. You will be getting the PhD for free but you will also have a lot of hard work to do to support yourself and Ali.

Sorry to put it like this, but I feel I need to. Do you understand? I hate talking about money (I'm very English in that regard).

Loads of love and hugs to you, May

Bee XXX

21.10.07

Good intentions

Lovely Bee

I've imagined us sitting drinking tea after so long a wait. I've also imagined the girls playing around us and calling me Aunty May. By the way, my tea is black as you correctly guessed, but without sugar. I only take sugar when I mix it with milk – crazy, ha?

Now let's become serious, Bee. You are quite right, but I really do not expect to get things for free. Ali, for example, is still young and says that he is prepared to work 18 hours a day to keep us both, but I worry if he can do this after what he has been through? Maybe he would break down, and become more of a burden than help??

These are not good intentions, dearest Sis, but facts. Am I prepared to work very very hard *and* study for a PhD? Easier said than done (taking into consideration my age and the amount of suffering I've been through). I know that at least one of us will have to work, even with the presence of the fund, because of the high cost of living in the UK. But at least we will be secure to some extent and will not die of cold and hunger. Tell me if you understand my point.

I have realized from your emails that it is very expensive to live in the UK. I need to know how much it would cost to live there modestly. Bee, I have never, ever expected you to take responsibility for us, because it is out of the question. You have helped us more than enough already.

Must go now. See you in another email.

May XXXX

Intentions aren't enough

May, you have already been told how much it costs to live modestly in the UK : that was the figure CARA gave of £30,000 for both of you for three years. So the university estimates £10,000 a year. There is student accommodation, which is quite cheap but not free, and basically this is the figure we are looking at.

Justin and I would have to borrow the entire amount in order to show that kind of money in our bank account. Naturally Justin is worried that if you two became unable to pay your rent for whatever reason, then the university would send debt collectors straight round to us, because we guaranteed your visa. I want to explain it properly, as it's a worry for us, but I'm not saying it's an insurmountable obstacle. There must be a way to do this, I just know it.

But I'm not sure I completely understand you: you have answered my questions (and I know they weren't nice or polite questions) with more questions of your own, such as whether Ali can work 'after what he has been through'. And can you be expected to work and do a PhD given your age and the suffering? Well, May, the fact is you will not have a choice. There are people who have been through even worse than you, and they still have to work and support themselves. That is the stark reality.

You mention 'the presence of the fund' but, May, there IS NO FUND. Your university fees are being waived but there is NO MONEY on top of that. Don't you understand? So what is the alternative? Perhaps Ali might be allowed to stay in Damascus and find some work there, and you could try to visit him every month? That may be a possibility, and it could be less frightening in some ways, but there is the personal risk for your own safety.

Once again a pretty unpleasant email and again I'm sorry about this. May, you know I love you and only want things to work out happily, but I just have to make all of this as clear as I can to you, and I wouldn't be a good friend if I didn't say things because they're uncomfortable to say.

Bee XXX

23.10.07

Honesty

Dear Bee

You are my best friend and I am really grateful for your honesty with me because it shows that you are really worried about my well being. I think maybe I did not understand how the supporting fund works.

Love

MAY XXXXXX

23.10.07

RE: Honesty

Hi, dearest. Sorry I got cross. It's been a crap week for me and the children being ill and everyone (well, nearly) at the BBC getting the sack. They're cutting costs by making people redundant and it makes the atmosphere horrible. Anyway, CARA are quite clear: they say that the university will cover your fees, but: 'We still need to get together sufficient funds to support you and your husband in the UK over that period.'

The funds Kate is talking about is that £30,000 that we do not have. We still don't know where to get it from, but without it you will not get the visa. That's what is worrying me so much. WE WILL THINK OF SOMETHING.

I'm at work today and tomorrow I'm taking the girls up to York on the train to see my mum until Saturday. Will be back in touch next week when I get back.

Take care meanwhile.

Hugs

Bee XXX

03.11.07

A bit of explanation

Dear Bee

I have been thinking about what you said, and I can see how you might wonder how I have suffered. I want you to try and understand that as Iraqis (leaving out private and personal pain) many years have worn us down. Ever since my family returned to Iraq in the 1970s nothing has been easy or smooth; we've been in and out of problems for so long that I think we have forgotten how to live in a normal manner.

Twenty-two million of us (or maybe more) need rehabilitation. I used to joke about it back in the 90s. I remember telling a psychiatrist friend, 'Doctor, we need 22 million beds all the way from Kurdistan in the north to Kuwait in the south.'

You have to understand our background. The people awoke one September morning in 1980 to find we were at war with Iran. All that can be said about the eight-year-long war is that it was an emotional nightmare for most Iraqis. With men at the front, women shouldered all the burdens and responsibilities. And this was nothing compared to the fear and anxiety engulfing families with at least one male in the military services.

Burdened with all kinds of worries, each young soldier would leave with the memory of a special woman spilling water on his trail (a traditional way for wishing the speedy return of a loved one). I was no different from other women. I had a husband at the front and the nine o'clock news was something I wouldn't miss for the world. I remember waiting to find out where fierce battles had taken place. If the battles were not in Basra, where my husband was, I would try to figure out who of all the people I knew was serving near the battlefield.

When the ceasefire was finally announced in August 1988 people thought that it was time to pick up the jigsaw pieces of their lives. Therefore when the leadership announced that the people could celebrate in their own way, people spontaneously went out into the streets, dancing and splashing water at one another in extreme joy. At this time Saddam was still genuinely loved by many. No one ever thought that history would repeat itself so soon, but we woke up on 2 August 1990 to discover that the country was at war again, with Kuwait. And now we live in a war zone yet again.

I know you think I was just being ungrateful and lazy, but the whole truth is that I feel on the verge of collapse. You said that many people have gone through worse times; well, you are right, but each person reacts in a different way. You do not know much about my previous life and how psychologically worn out I have been. Ali's entry into my life smoothed out some of the creases but not all of them. There are permanent scars, and these scars have made me the woman I am now. Of course, when I come to England Ali and I will face different challenges, and they will be difficult. But I am telling the truth when I say that we are both tired now, and I worry about our strength.

My love to you as always

May

Fairy tales

God, May. I am sorry. All those years of war must have sent you
and all Iraqis crazy. Do you mind me asking: why were you visiting
a psychiatrist back then? Did it help? I love the tradition of pouring
water on to the trail of someone who is leaving, so they will return
safely. It's like something from an old fairy tale. I know you have
been through so much, and I hate to think your spirit might be
squashed. I just want you to know that it isn't always a fairy tale
here in England. But I hope we can find a way for you both to leave
soon.

Love always

Bee xxxx

7.11.07

Return to Baghdad

Dear Bee

This must be a short email, but I had to tell you our plans and
thoughts. My dearest friend, we are completely fed up here in
Damascus. I haven't been able to extend my visa for another three
months and so, my dear, the only choice we have left is to go back
home to Baghdad. My leave at the college has also expired, so I
must return quickly to take up my teaching job again.

My love to you, as always

May

A warm hello from Baghdad

Bumbo Bee, my dearest

At last I'm back home. Though it is unsafe and the scene is full of destruction everywhere, I still think I will feel more me than when I was in Syria. Bee, you are right in sensing my spirit is all squashed. You see, it felt so dreary and hopeless just sitting in Damascus. Doing nothing all the time is something awful. I tried searching for a teaching job, but there was no hope – and even if there was, the salary would be equivalent to £50 a month in your money. I remember I had high hopes at the beginning, but they just evaporated.

Oh Bee, I don't think I can ever describe fully what it was like. The Syrians started to get irritated after Iraqis began to compete with them in everything from jobs to public transport and rents. And the presence of the Iraqis raised prices in a very sick way. For example, if a flat was worth only $3,000, Iraqis would pay $20,000. Even taxi fares were tripled. The Syrians started moaning, then this turned to open anger. Anyway, I wasn't part of all that, thank God, but that idle life made me so depressed and I am so glad to have left.

You asked why I saw a psychiatrist. Well, first of all the man I mentioned was a friend but I did consult him at one point. The reason for going to see him was that during that time I was trying to get a divorce. My late husband had convinced me that it was not his drinking that made me unhappy, but rather it was something wrong with me, and so I had to get a professional opinion before filing for a divorce (taboo here). He told me that there was nothing wrong with me, but as the years went by I felt very depressed and went to another doctor who gave me a mild dose of antidepressants to take at night. I do tend to get more depressed when things don't work out, but these episodes soon pass despite the bad circumstances.

Did I tell you that most Iraqis depend on the food provided by the ration card, which is issued by the government? It has the basic monthly food requirements – rice, sugar, flour, cooking oil, salt, tea, soap and a small quantity of detergent. Educated Iraqis joke about wanting Valium to be added to the ration-card items. This, I think, will give you a clear picture of how Iraqis feel; many are eaten up by fear, anxiety or depression.

Anyway, my lovely, I am finally home. Although my destiny is unknown, at least I have a job to go to, and friends and colleagues to speak to. Which, in my opinion, is much better than staring at four walls in a shabby flat in a foreign country.

Coming back has been a relief, albeit a mixed one. People in our neighbourhood, shop-keepers and others warmly welcomed us; my mother cooked a hearty meal for us and brought us cheese, bread, marmalade, sugar, detergents and coffee. Tomorrow I will be going to the university. I phoned my head of department and she was both happy and relieved that I was back. I also talked to a couple of friends on my mobile and we laughed about our situation and made jokes about our government and things like that. For Ali, however, it is not the same. He is not safe here.

Must go now, my love. I still have a lot of work to do.

Love you for ever, my wee sister

May XXXXXX

15.11.07

Hugs from chilly London

Hello there, dearest! It's a relief to be back in touch.

How nice that everyone made a fuss of you on your return. I'm sure you'll feel much more like yourself now that you're back with people who know you. How are your students? They must be glad to have you back. I love hearing about all that.

I'm having a lovely day at work, wearing a new black wool dress. Oh, I look great, hee hee! I can tell you there is nothing like striding to work in a foxy dress to dispel the blues. It's such a relief to get into the office and think about the rest of the world and have a look at the newspapers etc.

But I had a bad start. Justin is away filming and I'm still terrible at doing the mornings on my own. I can't seem to do enough. I end up doing laundry at midnight to keep up with it all. Everyone's ill apart from Eva, but then she got angry about having to go to school on her own. Off she went, my heartbreakingly lovely, skinny girl – all weighed down with her school bag plus swimming bag plus violin in a tattered case.

And I've had a big fat row with Justin. Can you believe he's started nagging me to have another baby? Yet he keeps working at weekends and leaving me on my own with them all. I mean, I love babies but another one would just push me over the edge. Already it's mad trying to do things like public transport with three girls, but with four it'd be in a different league; I wouldn't even be able to go to people's houses. So I said he should stop bloody working all the time if he wants more babies so much.

I have a joke for you (well, it's Eva's actually). Why do goats wear bells? Because their horns don't work.

OK, I'm off again.

Catch you later

B XX

HI, MY SWEET

Dear, dear Bee

It is so nice to write to you in the privacy of my home. A cigarette, and a cup of tea to go with it.

I really couldn't write much in Syria because I was always distracted by other people. Everyone looked at everyone else; and the voices of people talking via the messenger to their relatives, and sometimes crying and sobbing, always made me nervous. Thank God it's over.

I went to work last Sunday and, like you, dressed up for it. I wore a black suit and a white shirt with a feminine tie to go with it. They welcomed me very nicely. We joked and laughed and all of them said I looked much better! I will not be teaching third-year English literature this year because I came back too late, so it will only be human rights. Our university regards this as a subsidiary subject so I don't need to work very hard, and at the same time the salary remains the same.

As for the Baby 4 project, Bee, I don't think it is such a bad idea, if you can get Justin to promise to help. I think he seeks an heir because all men do. They say it has become easy to determine the sex of the baby if you go to a specialist clinic, so why take the chance? Just do it right from the start. (I think if your no. 4 is also a girl, he will soon be asking for no. 5.) So if you do it this way, I think you will be a happier mother. People all over the world aim to have both sons and daughters. And they prefer boys to girls for a number of reasons, most of which have to do with their own welfare after they become old and weak. A baby boy is exactly what you need – he will make you both very happy and contented.

Must go now, dear. The electricity will go off in 15 minutes. See you in another email.

Love you for ever and a day

May XXXX

16.11.07

Your human rights classes

MAY!

You know, you really sound like your old self again. Your emails from Damascus had become sort of paler and paler, but now you are back in glorious technicolour again, with a cup of tea and a ciggy in your hand.

Just a thought. When you talk about teaching human rights to your students, I can't quite picture it. What do you say to them? How do they relate to your lessons when they are growing up in a war zone?

Bee XX

18.11.07

RE: Your human rights classes

Dear Bee

Teaching young Iraqi females the principles of democracy and human rights has never been an easy task! So I try limiting the topic to basics.

I will never forget the first lecture I gave. It was the first year after the invasion. I went into the classroom to find that they had turned their backs to the blackboard, facing the window, and when I asked for the reason they said, 'We are living in a state of democracy.' I smiled and told them about a little incident with my nephew, who was about 6 when the former regime collapsed and people began to talk about democracy. My nephew wore his underpants back to front and when his mother asked him why he had done that, he simply said, 'It is democracy and we can do what we want.' Then I explained that democracy does not mean wearing underpants back to front or turning our backs to the right thing. They laughed and changed their chairs to face the blackboard.

In class I usually begin by reading an article, then stopping for a moment to check their reaction. But what I usually see is blank expressionless faces staring back at me. I then read again and translate into Arabic, fearing that the language difficulties may pose an obstacle, but the faces of the young women with their covered hair remain expressionless. At first I used to return home irritated, thinking I was a failure, but then it struck me. I realized that it was impossible for these oppressed young females to comprehend that there are freedoms granted to humanity in general. It was like describing colours to the colour-blind, I thought to myself.

I decided to simplify matters a bit further. So I explained that human rights in their simplest form mean the right to do what you want and say what you think, without harming others. Maybe I can start from this point with a little provocation, I said to myself. I mentioned that family is like a miniature society, being the smallest unit, so it can easily be compared to a country with the father as head of state, the mother as prime minister or cabinet and the children as the people.

There was a stir and some light shone in their eyes, but they remained silent. It is not easy to get these 18- and 19-year-olds to talk, since they have been trained to say yes and never argue or ask questions. Asking questions here is considered rude and insolent by parents, teachers and society and might get a person into serious trouble. But I feel it my duty to change this old Iraqi discipline.

Imagining the father as head of state stirred some reaction, when I asked whether the right to argue your case with the head of the family was granted at home. To my surprise the reaction was strong; many of them said that they had no say over the simplest decisions related to their personal lives. Some said that they couldn't choose what to wear, or how to dress, or what field to choose for study. Three students said they had been forced to study English by their family while a fourth said that her husband had forced her to study English while she preferred law.

Some of the strongest reactions were stirred when we reached Article 16, tackling marriage and the freedom to choose one's spouse. Many young women said that either they or another female member of their families had been forced to marry people whom they didn't want, or actually had been. One student said that her cousin, who was an uneducated outlaw and is currently serving a prison sentence, was named as her bridegroom. I asked her how on earth such a marriage could succeed. The answer came, sad but simple, 'These are our tribal rules.' I wasn't convinced and probed a little further into the matter, asking where her father was. The reply was that he was dead, and the uncle had since taken charge of the family thus naming his outlaw of a son as the young lady's future husband.

The right to work was another controversial subject. These young women know for a fact that it is not the rights granted by law that organize their lives, but rather traditions set by their great-great-grandfathers or even the generations preceding them. The right to work is in many cases not a matter for the women to decide. Yes, it is granted by law, but it is in the hands of the husband, the father or the brother. I remember a relative of mine broke her engagement to one of her cousins (our traditions are less strict, by the way) because he insisted that she stay home after graduation. She married a distant cousin who was less suitable but did not mind her getting a job. Years of embargo and invasion finally kept her at home raising her three children.

As for the free question I gave them on 'How I would improve society if I were to assume an important post in government', well, most answers talked about stabilizing security, improving the financial situation and improving education, but what struck me most was that a couple of papers advocated sending young inexperienced teachers abroad for training courses to master the language they are teaching in!

Have to go now, lovely.

Hugs

May XXX

19.11.07

Tempestuous weekend

MAY May-Maybe Baby!

May, I was most surprised that you advised me to have another baby, but I've been thinking about it. Maybe you and Justin are right in the sense of taking a long view rather than thinking of the short-term chaos. But I just can't help thinking I would be in a bad mood for about three years if it happened. Like today: Justin was doing his new TV presenting thing this morning so I had all three girls on my own. Elsa has a constant stream of snot coming out of her nose and running down over her mouth and chin, no matter how much I clean it. I remember before I had kids seeing children with snotty noses and thinking, 'How disgusting: what bad parents to let their children go about like that!' But now I know it's nothing less than a Sisyphean task.

But now Elsa is having her nap and the girls are watching TV, so I can tell you my news. Well, I've had a funny couple of days. When I last wrote, I was in a huge strop with Justin about his absence due to work, and the fact that he wants another baby. Well, it all came out on Friday; I just had a total attack of hysteria. I was screaming at him at the top of my voice about everything that had annoyed me over the last few weeks. The worst thing for me is him not seeing the kids often enough. They ask for him constantly and it's hard to know what to say, as I don't always know when he'll be back. And there was the tedious old stuff of things going wrong at home when I was at work, like the recycling not being put out and so on. ('And another thing!!! . . .')

Then right in the middle of it he said, 'Bee, things are much better than you think. We are so lucky; you are lucky in every way.' And in the middle of my fury I thought, 'God, he's right!' And I nearly lost my track. But why let a small obstacle like the truth put me off? And so I finished my rant, and then we made friends. We went for lunch in a pub nearby and I was exhausted and had a sore throat from crying, but strangely I felt much better. I don't even have PMT so don't know where it all came from. Poor Justin, I really am a madwoman at times, especially if it all builds up and I haven't seen him much.

Then on Saturday we galloped around with the girls all day and in the evening went to a gig. It was a salsa musician called Larry Harlow – he's a giant from the 1970s New York Latin scene, which is the music I love and collect (I used to DJ too on obscure student radio stations!). He had a 15-piece band with amazing brass. The crowd was good, lots of Latinos. A friend of mine from Colombia came who is a brilliant dancer, and we danced like crazy.

Oh May, after reading about your students I'm quite shocked. I'm torn between praising you for your creative efforts, and disbelief that they can't understand you. I really don't want to be rude about your society, forgive me, but it sounds like my idea of hell. Why even bother sending them to university, if that is their miserable fate? I have always been brought up to ask questions. I know it's controversial and I apologize for making generalizations, but I just don't think Islam is much good for women. Seems to be great for men. But what's in it for you, May? Really?

Oh your students, May, what will they do without you? You are like a benevolent public service. I bet they're too shy to tell you, but I would love to know how they feel after being in your class. It must be almost like going into a forbidden world. I wish you could bring them with you. Or, at least, the one who's been promised to the guy in jail.

Will send this now but hope you are well . . .

More soon.

All my love

Bee XXX

21.11.07

Questions

May! Now that he is back in Baghdad, how is Ali coping?

Listen, I know the last few months have been a nightmare of uncertainty, but what do you two as a couple really wish for? I can't tell you too much, but we are still all working away at the plan to get you here through CARA. I know I really hassled you about the money circumstances, and I'm so sorry for putting pressure on you, but I was worried that you didn't have a grasp of things. But if we can get the funding, this will be much less of a worry.

But how do you feel about all this? Does Ali want to come to the UK? If it all happened, would you both be ready to come over? Probably the last thing you want to think about after all the stress, but I really want to know what you both think about it. On the radio this morning was a debate about how it's become much safer in Baghdad. Apparently attacks are down by 50 per cent and lots more people are returning from Syria to Baghdad. Is it true? But does this mean that if the coalition forces withdraw then there will be a return to violence?

Better go.

Hope you're well . . .

B X

RE: Questions

Dearest Bumbo Bee

You asked about women and Islam. Let me start by recalling an old saying: 'Traditions start like cobwebs then turn into thick chains.' We all abide by them to a certain extent, depending on how we look at it.

Bee, Islam (contrary to all that is said and circulated) is greater for women than men; that is, if people really follow its principles. Women, first of all, have their independent financial status, keep their maiden names after marriage and are a separate and sovereign entity. On top of all that, women are not responsible for their living expenses, unless they wholeheartedly desire to be so. The money they gain from work or inheritance is for their own use and leisure. Costs of living, housing, clothing, food etc. are the man's responsibility, whether father, brother or husband. In the absence of these men, then it would be the responsibility of the nearest male kin.

Women are not banned from work, and they have their own say. If you want my view, I think Islam puts the pressure on men more than women, but what we see today are traditions that have been exploited and manipulated by many people and by the clergy to serve their ends, ignoring the real religion.

Forced marriages, for example, are prohibited by law and religion, but they are seen as a tradition and are mistaken for religion. Most women are neither banned from seeking knowledge nor from education. But the key point is that a helpless woman cannot possibly raise healthy men.

Let me put a finger on a sore spot. The two most important decisions in an individual's life — education and marriage — are the targets of the greatest interference. Many of my friends chose the seemingly easy way; they followed Mum and Dad's instructions, and in some cases these were literal orders. They joined colleges and majored in fields they loathed and eventually graduated with a hatred for everything to do with their speciality. Many married people whom they did not love, but who were highly recommended by their families, and ended up miserable and stuck in the golden cage of matrimony. They pleased others and tortured themselves. Many of them are now grandmothers in their late forties, wailing over their long-lost youth.

What bothers me is how anyone can become creative in a situation they detest or, at least, feel true to themselves.

As for coming to the UK, and the security conditions in Iraq, it is true that many, many people have returned. But the real reason for their return was not a safer Iraq, but because Syria did not renew their visas. Many of those who returned also had jobs they did not want to lose, or they had used up all the money they had brought with them and had to return to get some more. In turn, Syria would not allow them to re-enter, and so they have had to stay. The situation is not 50 per cent better, but it is a wee bit better. Even now on the news, they found five bodies buried in the garden of a house with their identities all erased. Fights break out every now and then between the government forces, made up of the Shi'ite militias, and the Sunnis, who are called the 'armed groups'. As for the Iranian gangs, well, their assassinations of university professors and the highly educated continues.

As for us, well I know I won't be rich, Bee, and we both plan to work to make ourselves a better life. We want to start from scratch and build ourselves a new life. It is useless to wait for things to get better. I've waited for 35 years with nothing to show for it at all. It is always getting worse. Ali hasn't been out of the house since he got back. Our 'safer' area is now controlled by the army, and we do not trust them, because every now and then they carry out arbitrary arrests of Sunnis.

So, Bee, England is a dream place for us. At least we will live without fear and we can work freely, and go out freely with no one to fear but God. We are both law-abiding citizens, and I think you have sensed that in us, so we will be much happier. You know, Ali wants to improve himself and acquire further education in addition to work. He is full of hope and he tells me that he wants to be like me: 'a fighter in life'.

Must go now. Electricity will be cut off. Will write again.

Love you always

May XX

23.11.07

Freezing

Hi, May

This is a bit like back to the old days, isn't it? We've had all the ups and downs, and now here we are again, writing between London and Baghdad.

I like hearing about Ali. He's an unknown quantity for me, and sometimes I worry about his traditional values. But then you tell me things like what he said about wanting to be a fighter like you, and then I like him. Anyway. While we're on the subject of the male species, May, it's all very well you and Justin wanting me to have a baby boy (has he been secretly in touch with you to use your influence?) BUT have you ever spent time watching boys? They just run around hitting things, all day long. The idea of changing a nappy with a penis in it horrifies me. Girls are almost always advanced with talking, reading, toilet training and so on, you just have to wonder when/how precisely it is that men suddenly take over the world. Naturally if I had a boy I'd change my views on this 100 per cent, but even so I resist the notion that I should want a boy just because most other people want them.

(Two caveats: teenage girls are frightening and that's probably when it's best to have a son. Also, this morning I took Elsa on the 168 bus and she behaved appallingly, thrashed about, head-butted me and screamed her head off. She might as well have been a boy, haha.)

It's still freezing cold here; I can't keep warm and I keep making cups of tea and then finding they've gone cold really quickly. YUK!

Better go and collect the girls. Am taking them to ballet later.

Love you, May

Bee XXXX

26.11.06

DIRTY WATER

Dearest Bee

I'm writing to you and the weather is just beginning to get cold. I know it is freezing in London but it is also cold here.

Today I got the worst disappointment. I was so excited when my friend phoned and said that she had managed to get me 60 litres of kerosene for the heating. I got in the car and went to collect it, but something was nagging me all the way back. I didn't know what it was till later. When I got home Ali was so happy that at last we were going to have some heat in the house. Suddenly I thought to test the kerosene before filling up the heater tank.

And so we brought a piece of paper, put it in the kerosene and tried to light it. To our surprise it didn't start. The whole quantity turned out to be dirty water. Imagine buying 60 litres of DIRTY WATER for $45!! My friend had also been cheated and we both cursed those black-market cheats.

Write as often as you can. Do not wait for answers, just write and warm my days, my beloved wee sister. Love you always.

Must go now.

May XXXX

29.11.07

Ahh-CHOO

Aaarghgrhr, May! It's the Christmas Fair on Saturday and I've got a streaming cold and even Justin's ill now. He's never normally ill.

Have to go now and do the never-ending, never-ending bloody eternal laundry. (Do you know, sometimes I dream about laundry? I hate it so. You can't imagine how many dirty clothes a family of five makes, and Justin is the worst of all – he just chucks his socks and stuff all over the place and only wears things once, even though I go mad with him.)

Just ate a very large tray of baklava and drank it with a coffee. Tried it no sugar, like you, and liked it. And that's about all. Not very interesting, but wanted you to know I thought of you as I ate the baklava and drank the coffee, and sent you a nice thought.

Hugs always

B XXX

(PS I can write more next week – after the Fair, life will be normal again.)

Iraqi Hell

Dear Bee

A man dies and goes to Hell. There he finds that there is a different Hell for each country. He goes to the German Hell and asks, 'What do they do here?' He is told, 'First they put you on an electric chair for an hour, then you lie on a bed of nails for an hour, and then the German devil comes in and beats you for the rest of the day.'

The man doesn't like the sound of that, and so he moves on. He checks out the Russian Hell as well as the American Hell, and many more. He finds that they are all more or less the same as the German Hell.

Then he comes to the Iraqi Hell and finds a long queue of people waiting to get in. Amazed, he asks, 'What do they do here?' and is told, 'First they put you on an electric chair for an hour, then you lie on a bed of nails for an hour, and then the Iraqi Devil comes in and beats you for the rest of the day.' 'But that is exactly the same as all the other Hells – why are people waiting to get in here?'

'Because maintenance is so bad that the electric chair doesn't work. Someone has stolen all the nails from the bed, and the Devil is a government employee so he comes in, signs the register, then goes off to the canteen!'

May xxx

30.11.07

VERY IMPORTANT!!!!

MAY

This is extremely important, and I want you to read it with an open mind because I think it could change everything. Up until now I haven't told you what I've been up to, as I couldn't bear to get your hopes up once again, but now I think I have to tell you, and you will understand why. I've been trying to find ways of raising the £30,000 we need for your student visa application. I and some friends applied for six places on the London Marathon so that we could raise the money that way, but we didn't get the places. So I have been looking for other ways.

A long time ago Professor John at CARA suggested writing a book, but at the time I never considered it further. But now we need that money to get you and Ali out. Well, Kate has a friend, Adrian, who is a literary agent and publisher. He is a lifelong friend of Kate's, and has helped CARA in the past. So I went and met him, and told him our story. He loved it. Then (this is the bit where I think you're going to kill me, but please just hear me out) he asked me to send him all our emails, every single one, and I did. He thinks they could be published. I know what you're thinking: they're private emails. And you're right, we never meant them to be read by anyone else. But what if they can realize this new possibility?

An advance on a book could cover your cost of living which should be sufficient for a UK visa. Then you and Ali could come to the UK. Then, and ONLY THEN, would a book be published: **after you both were safely here**.

I feel extremely nervous telling you this.

What do you think?

Love always

Bee XX

WOMEN CAN CONQUER THE WORLD!!!

Women make the world go round, the world go round, the world go round . . . Heheeeee. I am not just excited, I'm going mad! At last we have great news. I hope we don't get disappointed this time. Oh Bumbo Bee, you can really buzz quietly – or, how do you say? Discreetly. I never suspected something so big. Well done, my lovely. Hope to hug you for real this time and hug the girls and kiss you all.

When I come (I hope) start thinking of that wee baby boy and I will help you with him and his wee 'P . . . s'. Hehee.

Love you for ever and a day

May XX

30.11.07

We'll just have to see what happens

Dear May

You're brave, as always, to want to give it a try. I thought you might go mad with me. Of course it's not certain, but we have to try every possibility, don't we?

I'll keep you posted. Sorry it's only a few lines but I have to go over to school now for setting up tomorrow's Christmas Fair. ARGH!!

B XX

03.12.07

All mixed up

Dearest Bee

Can't describe how I feel. You are so kind to keep trying, but there have been so many setbacks and false dreams that something inside tells me not to set my hopes on anything, while at the same time pulling me towards the opposite view and telling me soon I will reach the light and the sunshine and finish climbing out of this long dark tunnel.

Things are bad here again. It is freezing cold and we do not have a drop of fuel. The violence has returned and there is absolutely no hope that the country will settle down, not in a hundred years.

How can a country settle down and be stable when all the big fat greedy politicians pursue their own welfare and forget about the people? I've been watching sessions of our parliament on TV and all they seem able to discuss is their salaries, their security and immunity – these are the only things that they worry about and are able to take decisive measures to improve.

As for the rest of the country's problems, well, the population (who are poverty-stricken, hungry and freezing) can go to hell for all the politicians care. From all the sessions I've watched they have never discussed the people once, and if they ever attempted to do so they would probably postpone the session and fail to take any serious action.

Ali has gone into a silent phase. This phase is broken now and then by a question: 'Do you think we can make it?', 'Will we be ever able to live our own lives again?' and things like that. By the way, he has been sick since we returned and he has lost quite a lot of weight. I think it is mostly psychological, and a result of the freezing-cold house.

Must go now.

Love

May

Sparkly Germany

Hi, dearest May! We're back.

Sorry to have been silent, but we went to visit my German family in Freiburg. Up in the Black Forest mountains, the snow was deep and brilliant and we sledged on our tummies right down close to the snow, which sprays up in your face. My dad was nice and tolerated my demands not to smoke near the kids, which I know he hated. My granny didn't look very well – she was all skinny. I haven't seen her since August 2006 so it was a shock. She is still quite tough, but she complains constantly and I struggle to keep up in my not-very-good German. She exclaimed, 'When you're 85, yes, well, THEN you'll think of me, won't you!' And I said, 'But I already think of you, Oma.' So she said, 'Well, just you wait till you're 85 – see what you think then.'

So that was a bit glum, but otherwise she was delighted to see the girls. Of course, she thought that golden Elsa was amazing. Elsa is a bit of a performer at the moment; she shouts 'Bye-bye' if someone leaves the room and then blows them a kiss. She knows it sends all the adults into a fit of joy. Zola got dressed up in lots of 1950s children's clothes and strange old-fashioned gear. Eva galloped around; Oma's house is bizarrely enormous and has about 12 sofas arranged all in one huge room. All three girls stuffed themselves with Lebkuchen (German chocolate gingerbread that's traditional at Christmas) and had chocolate-coated faces for most of the holiday.

We got back yesterday and I'm still finishing the laundry.

I wish you were here, May. I wish it with all my heart that you and Ali could just be here and be able to relax and not be afraid. Is there any chance Ali could go to Damascus again for some time? Just so he doesn't go mad. What is your money situation? Write soon; I miss your letters.

Bee XXX

19.12.07

Funny how life goes on

Dearest Bee

Today is the first day of the al-Adha feast. I don't feel very bright because the day reminds me of many things in the past. I woke up this morning feeling rotten, but that's the way life goes, and it has to go on whether I like it or not.

I keep thinking about what your granny said. You see, getting to a certain age is something we cannot sense until we get there. When I was 16 I thought people at the age of 30 were very old and about to die. I remember when I had my tonsils removed at the Glasgow Royal Infirmary, at the age of 15, the matron came and asked if I had dentures and I burst out laughing and replied that I wasn't old enough to have false teeth. The woman looked at me hatefully and went away (I think she had dentures) and even today I still feel ashamed for being so impolite.

You know, something just happened right now. As Ali was working outside in the back yard trying hopelessly to fix the generator, the US helicopters detected him and they began to fly above him. It is so funny and sad at the same time. I mean, it is they who are intruding on our privacy in our house and in our country. Do you see the irony of the situation? How would you feel if someone came into your house, destroyed the furniture and kicked you out? Wouldn't you hate them with all your heart?

As for my work, well, I have a long holiday now because the opposing sects have named different dates for the feast, and so there will be no education until *all* the opposing parties have enjoyed their feasts. It is really weird what is happening here, because this feast depends entirely on the rituals that are carried out in Mecca. The feast begins when the pilgrims go up a certain mountain called Arafa. They ascend the mountain and come down again. There should be no problem, because this is the decisive ritual which determines that the feast will take place on the next day.

OK, love. Must go now. Give my hugs to the three little princesses, a big hug and a kiss to you, and my regards to Justin.

Love you for ever and a day

May XXX

20.12.07

Outburst

May, I feel wretched: I know you are miserable and there is nothing I can do. I've been thinking about you a lot. I know I always say that, and it's true, but I think about you in different ways. And at the moment I feel that somehow you need me to think about you and send you my love. I know it sounds stupid, but I can just tell that you're not OK. And neither is Ali.

I feel like we've lost momentum, we're just stagnating. At least in the past, May, when we've been through crises of various kinds, it has always been dynamic in one way or another, and it seemed to be moving somewhere. But this is strange and it makes it hard for me to write to you, as I feel my words are more useless than ever.

Anyway, I've just been out for a drink with a friend who is in a troubled marriage. Often our conversation turns to men: what bastards. And then I experience a secret feeling of joy and relief about Justin, and how lucky I am. But tonight I didn't get that feeling. I didn't tell you this, but Justin and I had the most horrible fight in Germany. It was on the first day out there and we were all waiting at the bus stop in the cold and I was grumbling, but not in a significant way. It was me and him, my dad and my brother and the girls. Justin suddenly called me a bitch in front of my father, saying to him, 'Has she always been like this?' I felt like I'd been slapped. I have always had a fraught relationship with my father, and I am painfully proud whenever I see him. I certainly don't want him patting me on the back with a worried look because my husband's just been horrible to me.

I was mortified, May, and I'm still angry with him. I'll admit that we are both pretty tempestuous. I'm easily as volatile as he is, and probably more annoying, BUT at least I keep it private, instead of involving other people. I just wasn't brought up with public displays of emotion like that: with my mum and brother we are all quite respectful of each other in our own way. Justin's from a bigger, louder family so maybe he thinks that's OK. I can't make sense of it. I was so very, very hurt.

Well, for the rest of the German holiday (which was otherwise as lovely as I told you) I was in a boiling fury, and couldn't stand the way Justin ate or talked or even breathed. Hmm, I guess it will blow over. We're going to Dorset on Saturday and will be there for the whole festive period, during which time both our respective families will visit (separately), so let's see how that goes.

May, I am so very frustrated about not having anything good to cheer you up with. I feel like I have used up a small and inadequate bag of tricks, and now everything is still the bloody same as before. Exactly a year ago we were sending each other those gifts, via Andy – remember? What a year. All I can say is that I think you are lovely and I miss you. And I hope you have a huge cup of black tea and a cigarette, and your day starts well.

All my love

Bee XXX

PS Elsa met 'Father Christmas' yesterday at a baby Christmas party, but she didn't like him, and she cried. She's also started dancing and singing, and can sing the whole tune of 'Twinkle Twinkle, Little Star'. She sang it at the top of her voice today on the Northern Line of the London Underground, and a whole row of hatchet-faced Londoners actually smiled at her.

2008

02.01.08

Occasions only come once a year

Dearest friend, HAPPY NEW YEAR!

I got your text message last night just as I was beginning to wonder what had happened to you. I imagined all sorts of things, good and bad. As I settled for bed your message came through, and I really was relieved just to hear from you and fell into a deep slumber immediately. I woke up a bit late and hurried to work. We've had an on-and-off holiday during the past two weeks, but the first-year students are very different this year: they've been attending classes even in their holidays. This is a very good sign and I sure hope that it continues, but I very much doubt that it will.

Our area is full of armed forces. Their behaviour is unpredictable, and their reactions are largely dependent on the security situation in the district. One day they are nice and friendly, and the next day they are very nasty, but in general they are OK with women. Men usually avoid them and go out as little as possible because there always is the threat of arbitrary arrests, especially for Sunnis like Ali.

Ali is still home; he doesn't go out and his temper is getting worse. I try so hard to console and pamper him but the depression sometimes engulfs him. He breaks down, sobbing so hard that I stand helpless and stricken with anxiety.

I did not write to you in the past few days because I did not want to spoil your Christmas and the fun. The problem, dear Sis, is that

I've been told that my name is on the list of those to be assassinated, as are the names of many of my colleagues. Some of them have left Baghdad, others have been killed, and the rest of us wait hopelessly for something to turn up. I have asked Kate and now I am asking you: if anything happens to me please, please don't stop your efforts to get Ali out of the country.

How was your New Year holiday? Did you enjoy it? As for us, we spend whole afternoons watching TV. The street generator goes off at midnight and, like Cinderella, we have to retire as the clock strikes 12, otherwise we will freeze to death. We sit by candlelight or kerosene lamps, returning to the Middle Ages.

We watched the festivities all around the world, among them Britain and the US, but we never celebrated anything, not even the al-Adha Eid. My mother bought a lamb, had it butchered and distributed the meat to the needy, and of course members of the family got their share. My share was the kidneys and liver, and I cooked them for Ali (I don't like this part of the meat). My brother and sister went for lunch on the first day of the Eid to my mother's; this is traditional. I fried fish, but with no batter, and I made different kinds of salads, such as Russian salad and hummus.

There were a lot of things I wanted to tell you about but they just seem to have evaporated. I will tell you when I remember. But to be honest, we were both a bit nostalgic for our past, and you know these occasions need friendly surroundings and gatherings. Anyway it is all over now, and we don't have to deal with it till next year – and who knows what will have happened by then?

OK, love, must go now. I really miss you.

Love you always

May XXX

Tell me more

May, that is awful. Who did you hear it from? Is it safe for you to go to work? Surely your boss will let you have time off if you can show her the list. I am worried sick. It makes me wonder whether it's better for you to know about the list, or not to know about it and just carry on, because either way there's nothing you can do.

For myself I feel quite happy, but I do feel uncertain about this year. Last year was full of empty promises one way and another – not terrible, just disappointing. So perhaps this year will somehow deliver, or maybe it will offer up its own new agenda.

For the moment I'm just focusing on the microcosm of my family. Especially Elsa, who is in such an interesting phase. She will start nursery school in June, when she's 2. I know that that is a big step away from me and I want to enjoy this last little chapter with her. She's become bossy and assertive (can't think where she gets it from!) and loves copying sounds and gestures, so you can have quite a long conversation with her, made up entirely of weird noises, shrugs and expressions.

Zola is really accident-prone at the moment and has endless bumps and bruises. But she gets huge pride from her injuries and talks about them endlessly, adding a theatrical moan or a little shudder now and then. I have to go now; we have no au pair at the moment so I'm doing everything (sounds spoilt, I know) until our new one arrives. It takes me for ever to do all the laundry and cooking and tidying up and get them all to bed bla bla bla. Made some fabulous hummus yesterday, though – still eating it today.

Oh, I still haven't told you about Christmas etc. I will get round to it, I promise, but meanwhile PLEASE take care, dearest, and write when you can.

A million hugs

B XX

04.01.08

Life goes on

Dearest Bumbo Bee

How nice to hear from you and to know that there still are loving people around the world, and that life is functioning normally and children are growing up nicely. I've told you all our recent news. Life is just dreary and monotonous.

I heard about the assassination list from an acquaintance, who claims to have seen boxes with lists of all the university teachers. I was discreetly told that my name is on that awful list. The instructions are to kill university teachers 'mercilessly'. It applies not just to political activists, but also to university teachers who don't belong to a religious sect or party, or who are termed technocrats.

The 'seculars' pose a threat to the religious extremists from both sides. Believing that my name was on the list was hard to comprehend really. I spent every day of the al-Adha feast worrying and thinking of ways to escape. We are keeping a low profile as much as possible. The religious parties have imposed their ideals on the Iraqi streets as part of the new democracy. I've heard of horrible things happening to others, so I've decided to stick to the street rules. That's why I drive to college with my hair and arms covered. In the car park the transformation takes place as I pull off my head cover and remove my long-sleeved jacket. I enter college looking my usual self.

We have just heard about the assassination of an acquaintance and former colleague, Mohammed Al-Mayah. He had been the dean of the Mamoon University College and was previously assistant dean at our college. How is all this going to end? I am really scared and feel trapped. I've even given Ali instructions regarding what I want him to do after I'm dead. It didn't feel real, telling him about bequests to certain people, and asking him to bury me in a place where there are trees, if possible.

Anyway, life has to go on and I just hate to stay at home feeling frightened and going mad like Ali. I am scared a bit, but I don't want to give in to this because it will ruin me, as it has one of my friends. She has stopped driving because of the threats she and her family received. We used to go out for lunches and shopping, but now she totally refuses to leave the house. I don't want to become one of the 'living dead' so I still drive to work, and go shopping for food and groceries.

Our internet connection is getting worse every day; I think it is because they are overloading it, and also because the Americans are in the area and they make it more difficult with their transmissions. Anyway, let's move on to a better topic. I have bought two metres of black cloth, and lining to go with it. I think I will take it to a tailor (next salary) and get him to make me a pair of trousers or a skirt (which one do you think is better?) and a top to match.

Ali just went outside to the garage and saw our neighbour at the gate. Part of their family is leaving the house. There is a rumour that there will be arrests, and if there are more than two men in a family they will take half the number. You see, I can never shift to a more lively subject. I keep returning to the same (bl . . . .) topic, and that is security.

Ali is passing through a phase of self-hatred. He blames himself and tells me that it was all his fault for tying my fate to his. He says I would have been free to leave the country, and it would have been easier to get the funds, and many other depressing thoughts. I object to what he says and tell him that to me he is worth life itself, and I would never desert him for any reason whatsoever.

Will he start cursing the hour we met and cursing the marriage that got him into such a prison? He has never said a word about it, and he still loves me and pampers me like a child, but who knows what will happen if things continue the way they are? Well, I hope I'm dead before he turns against me and decides to leave or start a life somewhere else. Today he was talking about being jobless and he said that he is prepared to do any kind of work. Then he said, 'But all the doors shut in my face.' I felt terrible but calmed him down with the hope of leaving for England, saying it may be sooner than we know, and adding any other optimistic statements that I could think of at the time.

The zodiac signs for this year promise Librans a decisive year. It says they will either walk away or stay. It also promises legal proceedings.

Time to go, love. Will write again soon.

HUGS UNLIMITED

May XX

05.01.08

Latest

Dearest May

Don't worry if your writing keeps returning to the horrible themes of what surrounds you; it's important to let it out. It's really no wonder it preys on your thoughts so pervasively. Ali sounds in a terrible state and it's very worrying, but his reactions are positive too: he wants to work, he wants to move on and develop. He is unable to, but that's not his fault.

I promised to tell you about Christmas/New Year. To be honest, my expectations were a bit low. We were in Dorset for 10 days and had loads of people coming, so I thought it would be exhausting. But it was brilliant. First my mum and Dave, and my brother and his girlfriend, and my mum's two dogs Bella and Meg came to stay.

On Christmas Day Justin cooked a fabulous meal. He was utterly charming to my family. (Remember how upset I was about that scene in front of my father in Germany? He promised never again.) Anyway, after they all left Justin's family came: his parents Penelope and Charles, his 3 sisters and their husbands, and 10 kids. Imagine! After they had all left we spent one day on our own, and then two sets of friends came down for New Year's Eve. We did some long walks by the sea.

One morning we woke to hear Eva's voice piping up outside from the garden: 'No, it's fine. My mum says I'm allowed to!' I peeped suspiciously out of the window. There she was with her friend Tommy (he's 7) and they were climbing over the back wall into the meadow. They ran far away through fields of sheep until we could hardly see them. I thought it was beautiful. They can't do that in London; someone is always watching them and stopping them. After that, they did it every morning, coming back with bare feet and pyjamas soaked with dew.

OH, I have to go! Justin took them all swimming this morning but they're just arriving back so it's all about to go mad any moment now.

Love

B XX

09.01.08

LIFE

Dearest Bumbo Bee

I've had no connection for the past few days and the service is still very bad. A lot of awful things are happening these days. One of them was that Ali's elder brother was assassinated, and with your knowledge of Ali's psychological state you can imagine how it has affected him.

At first he said that he would go to see his family, and asked me what I thought. I told him that it was OK with me, as long as I had nothing to do with them. Then he changed his mind and said that he had heard something from a friend, or it may have been a relative. (I don't really know, because all the people in Ali's province are related to each other. They marry their cousins and their cousins' cousins, and so on. This is part of their tribal traditions.)

Anyway, we were just starting to get over this when we heard a news item announcing the assassination of Ali's secondary school teacher, who had later studied for a PhD and become a university teacher. Ali broke down again, and it took me a long time to calm him down.

The latest blow came this morning. We woke up around 10.30, and just as I was making tea and preparing breakfast a bomb exploded outside. The smoke covered the garden. It turned out that a member of the municipal council for our district had stopped by the shops near our house. Someone had planted a bomb in his car, and as soon he got into his car they blew it up and the poor man was torn to pieces. I think I will soon lose my mind; things are truly terrible. They have exceeded the limits of my comprehension.

Why did the bloody Americans invade us? Dictatorship with security and safety is much better for civilians than the blood-thirsty democracy they have brought us. Five awful years with no sign of improvement. It is just making us lose all interest in life. There are many times when I've felt that the right way to end all this is by taking my own life, instead of waiting for someone else to take it when I am not prepared. I know this sounds horrible but at times I just can't help thinking this way.

By the way, I have found another job to get some extra income, but my work depends completely on the internet and emails. The connection is very unreliable, and I don't know if they will tolerate this or not! I translate items for a news agency and send articles via email. They tell me which article they want, then I look it up on their website, translate it and email it to them. I went to the interview and passed the test, but since then the connection has been so bad that I haven't been able to get a single piece of work done.

We are supposed to have another holiday tomorrow, but they haven't announced anything on TV yet. It is the beginning of the Hageira year (the Moslem calendar) so I don't know if I'm supposed to be going to work or not.

Bee, can you really comprehend what life is like for us? Do you really have a clear picture of how it is? Sometimes I think that I shouldn't tell you these things because it is impossible for you to comprehend. I sometimes can't comprehend, so how can you?

I must go now; I am exhausted. I will write again as soon as I can. Don't stop writing.

Love you for ever

May XX

11.01.08

Comprehension isn't the main thing

Hi, dearest

I am glad (if glad is the right word) that you tell me the dreadful things that happen, but you're right to wonder if I can comprehend it all. In a factual way, of course I can: journalists regularly document other people's abject misery and the plight of humanity all over the world. The difference is when it's someone you care about, and so every time there is a bomb or atrocity you wonder how they feel about it. Were they close? Did they hear it? Are they afraid? So really, the part I cannot comprehend at all is how you carry on: how you keep going, teaching your students, supporting Ali, writing emails and just trying to be normal.

But the most important thing is that we connect in spite of all that madness. We have so much to share; compassion is stronger than comprehension. And also it's important for you to be able to describe the horrors, because even if I can't fully imagine it I think it's somehow good for your mind to get it out. May, I won't give up. Please remember I always love you and am wishing all the time for a way out of this.

I can't write any more. It's pouring with rain outside, and Elsa and I are trapped indoors going a bit crazy. She keeps popping up and climbing on to me and bringing me books and things, so I know she's getting very bored. We will just have to go out and face the downpour.

Take care, dearest.

B XX

15.01.08

GUESS WHAT!!!!!!!!!????????

MAAAAY!

Adrian, the agent friend of Kate's, called me today about the you-know-what. A publisher has read our manuscript, liked it and wants to meet me next Monday!!!!!!!!!!!!!!!!!!!!!!!!!!!!!!! (There aren't enough exclam-ation marks for how I feel.)

The phone call came at about 4 p.m. I was on my own in the house and I didn't recognize the number on my phone. After the call I was totally hysterical; I didn't know what to do so I ran about trying to find a piece of music with an appropriate sense of triumph. I picked Janis Joplin ('Get It While You Can') and put it on at top volume, sang and shrieked as loud as I could and spun about kicking my legs up in the air, dancing like Kate Bush and whirling all over the kitchen, and then I burst into tears.

May, I know we've both tried hard to be cautious and not get too excited but this is truly the BEST news I've had for ages. It's not certain yet, but it's a great start. Now, for God's sake just make sure nothing happens to you or Ali; just stay safe. Please don't take any risks at all – if anything bad happened to you now that we are so close I couldn't bear it.

HURRAAAAAAAAAAAAAAAAAAAAAAAY!!!!!!!!

A MASSIVE HUG OF JOY, MADNESS, AND SHEER RANDOM LUCK!!!

B XXXXXXXXXXXXXXXXXXXXXXXXXXXXXXXX
XXXXXXXXXXXXXX

16.01.08

HIP HIP HURRAY

Dearest Bee

Read your email. It's so good . . . I'm so happy. I sure hope it will work out this time. Oh Bee, what you've done is a great humanitarian deed. I thank you. I really love all this, and as a Libran I adore publicity. I really can't wait for Monday and hope it will come soon.

You know, I've been thinking a lot and I've reached the conclusion that even if I don't live to see this, I would still be happy for the world to find out how people can have a genuine affection for one another even though they live worlds apart. Funny how the most precious people in my life came into it through fate and long-distance communication. Remember my meeting with Ali? And of course you know how you and I became so close.

By the way, I forgot to tell you a funny thing about the extremists in our district. They have banned putting cucumbers near tomatoes. They say there is a sexual implication in these vegetables and it is wrong and sinful. They have also ordered the shepherds who roam around with their herds to make the goats wear nappies, because it is sinful to exhibit an animal's genitals. Imagine, Bee, the 21st century with all its scientific discoveries still has idiots like these.

Anyway, I will tell you about today. I finished my first lecture at 11.45 and was then called to attend a departmental meeting. The meeting was hilarious. No one took it seriously and, no matter how the poor head of department tried, no one really paid much attention. She told us we must attend college four times a week, and I retorted that they must provide electricity, security, water, fuel and salary increases before they demand work. The funny thing is that we are not being asked to give lectures, but to sit and wait in case any students have any questions.

Anyway, everyone started to make fun of the issue, and then I said today was supposed to be payday and they were not paying us because tomorrow is a holiday and they are scared in case a large sum remains at the accounts department without adequate security. I don't understand how these people think they can delay paying us our salaries, little as they are. It is our right to be paid promptly.

We spent the rest of the time talking at length about the water shortages and the dirty toilets, and each person who spoke suggested something funnier than the last. One suggested buying buckets to be kept in the toilets with clean water for washing, and another talked about buying better-quality soap, instead of the soap with no lather that is available on the ration card. So these are the concerns of university staff in the new Iraq.

On my way back home the army stopped me and searched the car. I asked the soldier if he had planted a bomb on me. He was annoyed and asked why the Iraqi people did not trust the army. I told him there had been reports of such incidents, and when I got home Ali searched the car. There was nothing, thank God.

Would you believe that we don't have a single penny in the house, and all our money has gone on fuel? We've been getting our groceries from the store on credit.

Love, as always, with hugs and wishes of luck for our project

May XXXX

21.01.08

Today was the day

MAY!!!

I'll start from the very beginning.

I woke up quite early, just after 7 a.m. I noticed how it's started getting light earlier, and I had a nice daydream about making a box of stuff for you and Ali when you move into your student accommodation. I lay there thinking what supplies you'd need, such as washing-up liquid, cooking oil, that sort of thing, and then I got all excited about putting in some Yorkshire tea. We have always talked about cups of tea, and Yorkshire tea is – with customary Yorkshire modesty – the best in the world. Its boast is that one tea bag is strong enough for two cups, and the box depicts such Yorkshire delights as Brimham Rocks and men playing cricket. I have converted several friends to the cause. I can't wait to get you on to it too.

Yes, yes, you're thinking – but get to the point! WHAT ABOUT THE MEETING WITH THE PUBLISHER??!! HAHAHA. Well, I'm building in some suspense, May, to make it more exciting. So, I wore high-heeled boots and borrowed a black trench coat with a cinched-in belt from my most glamorous friend, Amy, and off I went. I met Adrian in a grand reception area and we were taken up into a white office space full of shiny elegant people. I told them our whole story, took out my photos of you, and we talked about everything. Basically we've been talking about you all day! Now we have to wait and see if they want to make an offer. Adrian said he won't have an answer for a while . . .

Right, I have to go now. I'm tired – it's been a mad one.

Love you always!

Bee XX

PS Don't say thanks, it's both our work.

22.01.08

Too good to be true

Dear Bumbo Bee

You've done a great job; I hope it all ends well. I can no longer put my whole heart into one thing and sit and wait. You have a saying in English: 'It is too good to be true.' So I'll just wait without involving my emotions.

Today I had a good laugh. As I was washing the dishes I heard Ali talking to someone via the messenger. He said, 'Hello, Mali . . . how are you? . . . am so happy to meet you . . .' Then he said, 'Mali, are you OK?' It turned out that he was talking to an English-speaking woman, and he was repeating what he had learned when we were supposed to come to the UK in the summer. I laughed more when there was a sort of Arabic–English pun. The woman told him that she was fine. The word 'faayen' as used in Ali's province means bad or degrading and it is used when someone's luck is running out, and I heard him reply, 'Faayen, yes, faayen. My luck is quite faayen,' and I just couldn't hold my laughter in.

You remember I told you about the new job? My editor is going mad because the internet keeps failing and he told me that I have to do something about it. I can't do a thing of course. He told me that my translation was excellent, and this made me happy because it's been ages since I worked in the media. Anyway, I will be happy for as long as it lasts.

I start work after I come home from the university, from 2 p.m. to 6 p.m., so I am working a whole day. I do get very tired, though, and Ali isn't very helpful. As soon as I got up from my seat this afternoon he smiled at me and said, 'You are tired.' And immediately afterwards he asked what was I going to make for dinner. I got mad but didn't say a word. I made tea and brought out some milk, cream, cheese and jam and sat down to eat. He said he wanted me to fry meat and eggs for him and I snapped, 'Fry them yourself.' He got up and went and did just that.

I feel sorry for him but I think he has been spoilt, and he needs to be more modern. In his province the women do all the housework and the men bring in the money. They live like caliphs and are waited on by the women. I have tried to make him understand that it is not because they are men, but because they bring in the household income. He looked at me and said, 'You know, I hadn't looked at it that way.' So at least he realizes the reason, but he still forgets all the time (quite handy).

Time to go now, lovely Bee.

Lots of love and big hugs

May XXX

24.01.08

Advantages of a boring country

Dearest

I don't blame you for saying it's too good to be true. You know I am an incurable optimist. So let's just wait and see. Great that Ali's learning English. Best of luck with your 'modernizing' process, haha! Were there servants in his old life, or just the women in his family?

I'm back at work today. What a relief – I've been missing it. I came in early and read all the international stuff, as it's a bit nerve-wracking when you haven't been in for ages and don't know what to say about Gaza or whatever. It's good to see everyone. And after the days and weeks of rain it's suddenly sunny and bright outside, so I went for a walk during my lunch break. I walked over Waterloo Bridge on one side, with brilliant sunshine reflecting off the Thames and looking across to the London Eye; I could see Westminster and Big Ben. When I got to the other side I crossed over and came back, enjoying the view of the City and St Paul's Cathedral. It's the best bridge in London. I always walk over it in my breaks from work. It makes me feel just like I'm in a film. I'll suddenly realize I'm walking along like a superstar, then want to burst out laughing.

I'm so pleased for you about the second job with the news agency. Today's my first day in since before Christmas and I think I go a bit weird if I don't work. But we were starting a new au pair, so I needed the time off. She's called Tina. She's Swedish and was telling me today that she thinks Sweden has no extremes: no one is very rich or very poor, or leans to one extreme or the other, everyone is 'neutral'. She thinks it's boring. I said at least it's not a small country acting like a big one and waging wars. (Don't you wish Iraq was a bit more boring?) But having said that, I'm extremely proud of British culture, and I suppose that never came from being neutral or boring. Reminds me of the cuckoo clock speech by Orson Welles in *The Third Man*, remember?

I've just got lunch (cheese baguette with cheese and onion crisps squeezed in) and brought it back to my desk. I'm getting World Service's Burmese Service to translate and read a love poem that hides a coded insult to the country's military leader. The poet, Saw Wai, has now been imprisoned as a result. (If you read the first word of each line it spells out: General Than Shwe is crazy with power.) A military leader, afraid of poetry. As if beating up unarmed nuns wasn't enough to make him ashamed of himself.

Take care . . .

Bee XXX

25.01.08

Hello

Dearest Bee

How nice that you're back to work. It really makes a person feel more glowing and lively. I was working yesterday when your mail arrived. This, you see, is one of the good aspects of working online. You're kept informed of new emails and their senders. After I'd finished I read yours immediately, and started imagining the streets of London. I discovered that I didn't really remember all that much. I do remember Piccadilly Circus, Trafalgar Square and the pigeons, the Royal Albert Hall, Oxford Street, the zoo, Madame Tussaud's, Wandsworth Common and Shepherd's Bush. But that's about all.

As for my students, well, they seem better this year. You know that I'm only teaching democracy and human rights this year, because I returned after the beginning of the semester. You should see how silly I look when I talk about the subject. I keep reminding the students that this is how it should be, but then I get scared in case there are government agents among them, so I reconsider by saying one day it will be like this. Sometimes the students ask questions that are a bit tricky to answer, and I have to twist a bit to get out of trouble. But in general it is fun to teach about contradictions.

For example, there is an article that says everyone must have good pay and suitable working conditions, and I smile at them and say, 'See, just like we have: very cold classrooms in the winter and very hot in the summer,' and I laugh, and they all laugh too. I can't of course talk about arrests, exile or everyday dangers, because they might create a problem, so I just skirt round them in a very cautious way. But I talk freely about marriage, working conditions and education etc.

Ali, on the other hand, makes my life a happier one. When he sees that I am tired or worried he becomes an angel, and this is what counts. It doesn't matter if he is a lazy bum on ordinary days, because I can cope. You asked if his family had servants. No, they didn't. It is the females of the family who do the work. They did have slaves when his grandfather was alive (he was the sheik of a tribe), but not now.

Now that I come to think of it, we had servants for a very long time, but not any more. I had a home help until I married Ali, but things have now changed and the situation has deteriorated so much that I have to do all the work. And because I hate housework and Ali isn't a tidy person, my house isn't as tidy or as clean as it used to be. But to tell you the truth, I don't care, because we no longer entertain or have visitors.

I must go now.

Love

May XXX

31.01.08

JACKPOT

BEE, that was the best text message of them all. Penguin have said yes! Tell me all about it. I think we can say we made it. I can't express how I feel, can't really describe it. But, in short, I'M HAPPY. I can't really believe it. I've always wished in my deepest thoughts to do something rarely done by women in my country. And I've always wished that my life would come to an end in the

UK. I don't know why I thought this way, but that is how I've always felt.

Before the fall of the former regime I used to say to my friends, 'All I want is to find true love, and if I have ten years left of my life I would gladly give five of them in exchange for living in the UK.' And then I would laugh and add, 'With an open chequebook of course.'

When you first told me about the book I started to think of our early emails and how you did the phone interview. Then Elsa's birth and the rest. Then I started to wonder: what have I written, how much private information did I talk about, what will the reaction of our friends and family be? And similar crazy ideas.

Ali seems quite happy about the book and he is looking forward to the great event of leaving here. He has started thinking about bolts and locks and such like. He doesn't like the idea of exposing our lives to the public, but he knows that this is our only chance. I don't really understand why he feels this, after all we've been through.

Do you remember Ali was thinking of contacting his family after his brother was killed? His family don't want him back unless he divorces me and declares his repentance in front of all the family, including very distant relatives. My family and I, on the other hand, have always been distant and even if Ali left me I have decided never to go back to them. We already lack mutual understanding, and I think at my age it is stupid to look back, because the future is much shorter.

Time to go as the electricity will soon be off.

Love you, wee sister

May XXXX

01.02.08

RE:JACKPOT

Oh May, when I got the call yesterday I felt lifted up by a hundred balloons! I was round at my friend Terka's house and we'd been talking about it loads. I was saying I couldn't bear the waiting any longer and was feeling down. (She works in publishing, and helped me out with the original pitch.) Suddenly my phone rang and as I scrabbled around in my bag I was saying, 'Oh, please be Adrian, please be Adrian . . .' and it was! He said, 'Good news! Penguin have made the offer,' and I started to twirl about and shriek and dance. (Terka's little boy Max had just woken up and looked unimpressed by the cavorting woman in his kitchen.)

I hope you and Ali have been celebrating. I haven't told my mum yet, but we're going up to Yorkshire next week (our anniversary; J. and I are going to stay in a hotel and leave the girls with my mum) so I'll tell her then.

OK, May, over and out for now. I hope you're feeling as uplifted and delirious as I am . . .

Hugs

B XXX

01.02.08

The shore can be seen

Dizzy is inadequate to describe how I feel . . . Delirious? No . . . Dreamy? No . . . I think I am going crazy. We keep talking about future plans, past sorrows and how we are going to leave them behind. I think the journey is nearing the end. The shore, though distant, can be seen, in my mind. Do you think that I will one day put my feet up (metaphorically) and sleep the whole night without being awakened by the sound of explosions and bullets?

Will I bid farewell to the sight of blood, chaos and damage? Farewell to those ignorant and uneducated traditionalists who wander around trying to get their revenge from anyone who is even slightly well-off or educated?

Will I be able to take a shower whenever I want, and dry my hair when I choose without having to put the generator on and then turn it off to save on fuel?

Will I be able to go out for a walk and breathe fresh air?

All I want from life is to be able to live and talk freely without any fear. I don't really know what I'm saying. The words keep tumbling out. I have no control over them. I am so happy that it is making me scared. Nothing so good has ever happened to me since my return to Iraq. I've told you it has always been my dream to leave for a better world. A place where I can have peace of mind before anything else.

There are other things I would like to tell you about the Old Man, but they are taboo. Sometimes I think it is like this wizard in Harry Potter who is described as 'He who must not be named'. Yes, we have always been scared. But to tell the truth, we are still scared in one way or another. I will write about it later.

Time to go now, lovely Bee.

May XXX

11.02.08

Our anniversary

Hi, May

I've just come back from the perfect romantic break. It wasn't our wedding anniversary but the anniversary of us actually meeting for the first time, eight years ago. Swinton Park is a rambling country mansion with wooden floors, soaring gold-patterned ceilings and oil paintings glowering down. You enter via a long sweeping drive, and the grounds go on for miles with deer and woodland. But instead of being stuffy and posh inside everyone is friendly and Yorkshire-y. The food was amazing and we were greedy. Justin said if I got pregnant there we could call the baby Swinton Rowlatt. I said no, both to getting pregnant, and to having a baby that sounds like the villain in a Hardy novel.

There was a moment when we had tea in one of the splendid rooms. I looked into my teacup and saw the reflection of the chandelier in my tea. With any small movement the image splintered, shaken into random sparkly lights and bits of rainbows, then gradually resolved itself back into the chandelier again. This happened over and over again. I was hypnotized by my own teacup.

By Saturday afternoon I'd got used to pretending that I actually lived there, but we had to leave and go back to my mum's. We stayed a night and left yesterday after a bit of a row with my mum. I'd got all bottled up about feeling that she always has to take me down a peg or two, and as though I have to downplay the good things that happen to me in case she thinks I don't deserve them. I don't know what brought it all on, but I got very emotional and shrieky. She just didn't know what I was on about. It wasn't good. Well, it was awful actually. But I hope it's OK now. As my family is so small I get very upset about family arguments. Still digesting it in my mind.

Hope you're well – and how's Ali?

Write soon

Bee XX

PS I'm sitting here writing with a big bit of toast with pâté on and slices of raw onion that are stronger than I thought and v smelly, HAHA! You're lucky you're so far away.

11.02.08

Flames of love

Dearest Bee

So glad you enjoyed the mini holiday. I think it is kind of refreshing to a marriage and rekindles the flames of love.

We've been having the mid-term holidays and will be back on Sunday. I haven't been out of the house at all. Not even to the garage. I've been hearing all kinds of explosions and gunfire. They are quite close but I don't really know where. A couple of nights ago there were searches and arrests in the area but, thank God, no one knocked on our door. They probably know who they are after and know that we are just ordinary people.

Ali has bought a game of snakes and ladders and we play all the time to combat the boredom. I usually win, and you should see his face and how he starts to stamp his feet and call me a cheat. I laugh so much at him. It is really not so much the game that I enjoy as Ali's reaction. We make all kinds of bets. Some of them are unrepeatable and we laugh and laugh at one another.

I made chicken with tomato sauce and rice for lunch and a huge bowl of salad to go with it. Work was dreary and I don't have much energy today. I don't know why. I slept for 10 hours last night so I should feel very energized, but that's how I am: always contrary.

Is there any news about the book? What happens now that Penguin have said yes? Do we now have everything we need for me to start thinking about visas? This is the best news we've had and I want to start planning, but I don't want us to go through the pain of planning only for our hopes to be dashed. Please let me know what I should do next.

I can't stay long now because I have to go and take a shower. We haven't had electricity for the past four days, and so no hot water for a complete wash. I leave the rest to your imagination . . .

Love you, dearest

May XXXX

19.02.08

By the fireside

Hello, lovely May

You'll be back at work now, and probably exhausted, but I just love hearing your news. Is everything OK?

First things first. Adrian tells me all the details of the deal have been settled, but then the contracts have to be drawn up and signed so that there is money available to cover your living costs when you and Ali get to England. The money from the book makes up a big chunk of the money that we need to raise, but Justin and I are thinking about ways to raise the rest – as soon as we hit that £30,000 mark, CARA can confirm all the details and you can start applying for your visas. It's feeling a lot closer.

It's freezing here. I've dragged the heavy sofa across the room so it's right in front of the fire, which is banked up and glowing. Now I'm cold on one side of my face but hot on the other. There's a programme on TV about lizards by the wonderful David Attenborough. (When I was little we didn't have a TV and the only thing my mum let us watch was his nature programme *Life on Earth*. We'd go round to a friend's house.) It's been freezing all day; really beautiful and clear too, but so cold, and I can't stop eating.

We had a small gang of the girls' friends over today after school. They dressed up in some weird clothes Justin got from work. There was a charity sale of celebrity clothing from reality shows at the BBC. He bought some for fun, and came back laden with tacky items that look like prostitute's clothes: a sequinned red dress, silver high heels, a gold sequinned miniskirt, and finally the real shocker – a pair of knee-high shiny bright red extremely high-heeled boots. They're like transvestite boots.

Naturally the girls fell upon this inappropriate bounty; they think it's some kind of exquisite princess clothing. Even Elsa tried to totter about in the red boots. So this is what the girls and their friends most enjoyed, and luckily the parents didn't come back in time to find their children freakishly dressed up in my house. Elsa has been a bit ill (high temperature and not eating) but when the girls were all playing she really cheered up and tried to join in with them.

May, do you ever get sick of me rambling on about the kids? I don't talk this much to anyone else about them, and you don't even have kids yourself. Well, I'm quite sleepy now; I quite want to go to bed but the fire is so nice, I always feel it's a shame to leave it still glowing. I'll wait up for Justin, I guess. He's doing a speech some-where and will be back late.

I hope you're well, May.

Write soon

B XXX

PS OK . . . I'm going to tell you a SECRET: I've decided to get pregnant. I've hinted at it with Justin and reached the final decision in my own mind. I feel a lot of dread about it; I truly hate being pregnant and look on it like a jail sentence. But I adore babies. When I see them I get tears in my eyes. It means the world to Justin (he's obsessed with having another one, as I've told you) and I think if I'm going to do it I should hurry up, as I'm 37 this year. But am I crazy? I think people will think it madness to have four kids. Three is just about OK, but with four I will be a freak show. Oh dear, oh dear, now I'm talking myself out of it . . .

27.02.08

My mum

May, I'm not feeling great. My mum called and she's got a small lump in her breast (it's called a ductal carcinoma in situ). I can't get it out of my mind. She is going into hospital on Monday to have a lumpectomy and will go home on Tuesday. She has a deep terror of hospitals and anaesthetics so that makes it even worse for her, but she said the doctors were very nice. I asked Dave if I should go up and visit but he thought I might just add to the hassle. After the lumpectomy I guess they should know how serious it might or might not be. It makes me feel awful and I'm very gloomy at the moment.

Have to head out to the shops now with Elsa and buy loads of food. It's my book group tonight and we're having it here for the first time, so I have to cook for everyone. I'm nervous because Justin always does the cooking, so I hope it goes OK (plus the book is *Housekeeping* by Marilynne Robinson, a maudlin monotonous book with sentences so long and tedious you can't keep your eyes on the right word).

Hope you're enjoying your work.

Love

B XX

28.02.08

Yesterday's email

Dear Bee

Sorry to hear about your mum. At the same time, thank God she found out about it early enough. It is much better to check the growth at an early stage. Tell me about any developments; I feel really worried about her.

The funniest thing happened today when I was cleaning upstairs with the mop. I accidentally hit a wooden block the size of a fist. It fell right on Ali's bald head and I just couldn't stop laughing. He was cursing and calling me names and I just giggled and giggled. After that there was a small lump on his head.

As for your little secret, dear, I don't think you should be scared. Go on with it BUT go to a clinic to make sure it is a boy, if this is possible. You will be much happier if you have the two sexes. As for age, well, this is nothing; you are still very young. We have women of 50 here having babies – sometimes both mother and daughter get pregnant – so age is really nothing, especially as it is not your first pregnancy. I love the idea and I think you are a good mother, so why not? Go ahead and do it. But what made you change your mind?

Tomorrow is Friday, my day off. The house is clean and there are no dirty clothes, so I think I'll just rest and mark some papers, that's all. I don't really mind but my joints and bones hurt and my body is not as flexible as it used to be. Well, I hope this will end soon when I start exercising again. The thought of being able to walk around freely in England keeps me going and, yes, you are right, it feels so close now but I know that it will take time. I cannot thank you and Justin enough for everything you are doing for us.

OK, love, must go now. Kisses to you all.

Love you always

May XXXXX

03.03.08

My weekend

Hi there, May

Yesterday was Mother's Day. Eva and Zola made me breakfast in bed (it was toast). Zola put honey on it but forgot the butter, then added the butter on top. Eva put heaps of Marmite. They'd made very sweet cards and brought some daffodils to put next to my bed too. We all squeezed in and ate toast in bed; there were crumbs everywhere and Elsa thought it was very funny. Then we went to Whipsnade Zoo, where we saw a baby rhino playing with its mum and skipping about. Imagine a rhino skipping! We ate a picnic even though it was freezing.

It's so cold I have to keep moving, so end up doing silly things like clearing out cupboards, 'aerating' the lawn and so on. Last night I went to our local Neighbourhood Watch meeting. We meet once a year to discuss security – burglaries, that sort of thing. All the neighbours are furious about some gates to an alleyway behind our houses being taken down. We're campaigning to get them put back. I'm only telling you this as it must seem quite comical, given how it is in your neighbourhood.

Justin's filming in Scotland. My mum is in hospital and I haven't heard from her yet but she should get sent home later today or tomorrow.

Bbrrrr, I'm off to make more tea. I'm going to make a big shepherd's pie tonight. Sometimes I think my life revolves almost entirely around food. But that's a good thing.

Write soon

Bee XXX

PS Thanks for asking about my mum. Still feeling a bit strange, May. To be honest, since she told me about this operation I've been really distracted; it's in the back of my mind constantly. We've chatted on the phone a couple of times and she sounded her normal self. The worst bit is that the last time I was up in Yorkshire we had that huge row. That's so typical, isn't it? Now I wish I'd kept my mouth shut. But then feelings have to come out, don't they?

04.03.08

Holidays all year long

Lovely Bee, love

Couldn't write for various reasons, but the most awful thing happened yesterday. As you know, we've had the mid-term holidays. These were followed by the fortieth commemoration of the Imam Al-Hussein's death (he was killed in a battle between Moslems and from this incident the Sunni–Shia conflict originated) during which college was also closed for a week, as was everything else. To top all this we have had President Ahmadinejad of Iran on a two-day visit and so there has been no school or college.

Yesterday my hairdresser called; I haven't had a haircut for as long as three months and it looked awful. She said she was in her shop, so I asked if the road was OK and she said yes. I took my mum with me because her hair was looking frightful. On the way back I stopped to buy a takeaway lunch for Ali and me. As I got close to our neighbourhood a bomb exploded; it was so near that it shook the car. The soldiers were everywhere and they started shooting in the air and shouting at us in a very rude manner to all get out, turn our cars round and drive back to where we'd come from.

I did, and decided to take another route. As I got close to our area again, I saw that there was a roadblock. The soldiers came and told us to return to wherever we'd come from. In the end, we didn't get home for over four and a half hours. I arrived home exhausted and almost in tears, and my mother was just a nervous wreck.

I didn't work on my translation article and went to bed early.

I have to go now – starting work. Say hello to your mum from me if you get in touch with her.

Love you lots

May XXXX

PS I am now researching a topic I'm thinking of working on for the PhD. I want to work on 'fallen women' in nineteenth-century English literature. I need to know how journalism tackled this during that period. Can you help?

05.03.08

Dangerous hairdo and PhD thoughts

May, thanks for writing. Please don't risk your life again for a hairdo! I'm sure your hair didn't look that bad. I can only hope you got your highlights done too, seeing as you went to that much trouble.

Yesterday it was awful — on the radio I heard the most gruesome reports from Baghdad about people being assassinated INSIDE hospitals, actually in the treatment rooms, by Shia militia groups. The reporter said, 'If this was in a movie, it would look too far-fetched.' So don't let Ali go into hospital for any reason.

My mum came out of hospital yesterday. The lumpectomy went OK and she has to go back in next week, on Thursday, to talk to them about the results of the tests. I'm going to catch a train up for the day and go along with her. I thought I was OK about it all, but yesterday afternoon I was out running on the Heath. I was listening to a song called 'Hey Mama' by Kanye West and I just started to cry; I had tears pouring down my face as I ran along. It's a song I listened to a lot when Elsa was born. The thought that if my mum died soon then Elsa would not remember her came into my head, but I tried to banish it. Of course she's not going to die. She is a tough one, as I've told you, so there's no point in me being all tearful about it.

Let's change the subject. I'm delighted at your idea for your PhD. You've chosen one of the best and juiciest eras of literature. The person who springs to mind is Christina Rossetti. She actually worked with so-called 'fallen women' at her sister's nunnery, and her poetry combines strange religious fervour with quite overtly sexual imagery ('Goblin Market'). At our wedding my friend Alice read a Rossetti poem, 'A Birthday'. Does it have to be the nineteenth century? Mary Wollstonecraft is the century before, but is of course the original feminist in literature. Her life story is unbelievable, daring and tragic.

How exciting. It's a good distraction for you too. What a luxury to sit and think about great literature and amazing women. I've just glued a load of marshmallows on to small cakes; that's my contribution to humanity for today. (It's Eva's class tea today, and cakes with icing and sweets stuck on fetch a much better price.)

Take care

Bee X

PS This is the one from my wedding.

A BIRTHDAY by Christina Rossetti

My heart is like a singing bird
Whose nest is in a water'd shoot;
My heart is like an apple-tree
Whose boughs are bent with thick-set fruit;
My heart is like a rainbow shell
That paddles in a halcyon sea;
My heart is gladder than all these,
Because my love is come to me.

Raise me a daïs of silk and down;
Hang it with vair and purple dyes;
Carve it in doves and pomegranates,
And peacocks with a hundred eyes;
Work it in gold and silver grapes,
In leaves and silver fleurs-de-lys;
Because the birthday of my life
Is come, my love is come to me.

06.03.08

Ice cream in a hot desert

Hearing from you is like an ice cream in a hot desert. We are so depressed and bored. Stuck within the four walls of our small house, not being able to go anywhere because there really is nowhere to go. Talking to Ali and emailing you are just about the only conversation I get!

How are things? Is your mum OK? Did you go to see her? How is she? Although deep inside me I don't think it is very bad or anything, feeling your worry has got me worried.

As for the situation here, well, we die several times every single day. Doing my hair was an ordeal but I did have highlights – it is very blonde and I like it. Since I wear a head cover when driving, I don't attract much attention but at work and at home I take it off and my hair shines. Working on fallen women has probably got something to do with it (hehee).

I have just finished work and am absolutely exhausted. The electricity has been playing hide and seek and I've had to start the computer several times and recover material. Oh, it's been awful. But it is good for my brain because I keep cursing and swearing, which makes me feel alive. Otherwise I would think I don't exist.

To tell you the truth, I like this work more than teaching (although I do get brain congestion at the end of the day). It gives me instant satisfaction and a sense of accomplishment. Teaching is nice but it has a by-product – marking papers, which I really hate.

Media work has also changed. Now there is a certain amount of competition between the various media establishments. Before the invasion we had only a handful of newspapers, and perhaps three or four magazines, but they were the mouthpiece of the government and there was little difference between one and the other. The invasion changed things and there was an explosion of journalism – I think around 50 newspapers and magazines in my estimation, although some people say there were far more than that. But many newspapers have since disappeared. We now have about 20 (I am not good with numbers). Each of these is a mouth-piece for one party or another even though their titles suggest that they are independent. Very few of the people I know read newspapers because of the numerous untruths and the bias contained in them, but these must have their readers or they would have shut down like the others. The news agency I work for is an Iraqi one, but it really is independent and luckily does not take sides with any of the conflicting parties we have.

OK, love, must go now to dig for info.

Love you always

May XXXXX

06.03.08

Swearwords and very bad mood

MAY! Hi, Blondie! Bet you look lovely. You must teach me your best Arabic swearwords; I'd love to learn them. (I learned some very satisfying swearwords when I lived in Colombia, although they are all v misogynistic and about people's mothers.)

Well, your email cheered up my day. I'm in such a bad mood at the moment. I want to cry. I feel like I'm in a limbo (even been listening to 'Sitting Here In Limbo' by Jimmy Cliff) and I hate it. Not knowing about my mum, not knowing when you will get here, not knowing yet about That Secret Thing I told you. And, most of all, I'm bored and I miss my work. I missed out on a month of shifts as my old email went wrong (that's why I've changed addresses). I feel agitated and sort of mentally itchy.

And I hate March; spring isn't here yet but everyone is waiting for it. I don't even like March as a name for a month. (I am terrible at handling boredom. If I'm on a long car journey, about two hours in I usually start trying to aggravate Justin and pick an argument with him. He just laughs and says, 'Bored already?')

Bye for now and big hugs

Bee XX

08.03.08

Shock grey discovery

May, I really don't know why I was looking behind my ear the other day, but I found a big clump of GREY hairs, loads of them hiding there impertinently. Shocker! I thought, 'Right, your days are numbered,' and booked a long appointment at a posh salon up in Hampstead. So I am going this afternoon for a cut and colour, and I just can't wait: the very prospect of sitting still for hours and reading glossy magazines while people bring me tea is just too good to be true.

B xx

09.03.08

Grey hairs

Dearest Bee

About grey hairs, I know how it feels. They appeared on my fringe and sides when I was 27, and I didn't bother too much until one of my colleagues, who was a dear friend, told me to do something about them. I felt so embarrassed! I went home feeling bad and wanted to buy hair colourant but at the time of the blockade – or what the allies call 'economic sanctions' – a tube of hair colourant was more than my month's salary. As an Iraqi, I tried a substitute and used some shampoo and hydrogen peroxide, plus some yellow coloured spices from the kitchen, and dyed my hair myself. It turned out to be a disaster, of course, so I ran to my mother and she gave me money to buy hair colourant and cover the mess.

Haha

May xx

10.03.08

Greys? What greys!

Hello, my dear May. I love the mini-drama of your hair under the embargo, and your mum coming to the rescue. Was it just things like hair dye that were hard to buy back then? I had no idea we foreigners were messing up Iraqis' lives and hairdos for so long before the invasion. My greys are now all GONE, oh joy! I'm officially young again. My hair is blonder too and quite a lot shorter.

Love

Bee xx

11.03.08

Embargo talk

Dear Bee

Just got some time for myself now. I still think about my family life, even though it is in the long-distant past. I've always kept myself as busy as possible in order to get my mind off things, and this is usually quite successful.

You asked about the embargo, and how we lived at the time. The problem with the developed world is that people don't really understand what it is like to live under a dictatorship. The embargo was not really imposed on Saddam but on us – 'the ordinary people'. His life was not in the least affected. On the contrary, he built many, many palaces and his wealth increased, as did that of his relatives and close aides.

The highest salary an employee received was somewhere between 3,000 and 4,000 Iraqi dinars, which is no more than $2 a month. Thus not only luxuries were out of reach, but also necessities. People had three or four jobs, trying to make ends meet, and it was incredibly hard. I remember working in the media, studying at college and also doing private teaching. All this hard work earned me peanuts at the end of the month.

This economic hardship left Iraqis tired, and they lost interest in everything. Bribery and all sorts of corruption spread through society like wildfire. You could never get any job done, no matter how legal it was, without paying bribes. Of course things are worse now, but it all began with the embargo.

The ruling class lived in a separate world. They enjoyed all the luxuries life can offer, and in turn this paved the way for a lot of moral decay. You'd be surprised to know how the people surrounding them behaved, and the lifestyle they enjoyed.

Hatred and bitterness prevailed during the 13 years of the embargo. I think this was the precursor to the invasion of Iraq. The people were too exhausted to care or to defend the country, and most of the people wished for the end of the regime. But it never occurred to any of us that the situation would become what it has.

It is hard to explain what life was like during that time, but perhaps if I give you some examples you can imagine it.

- People stopped visiting, entertaining and exchanging gifts.
- No chocolates or sweets – the price of sugar was scary – no such things as ice cream or baklava, and if one did get them on the black market the price was astronomical. (But there

was always enough sugar to celebrate the president's birthday, and to bake thousands of cakes all over the country.)

- Children fainted in kindergartens because they didn't have breakfast. I remember people talking about a child who had fainted, and when he was revived he told his teacher that it was not his turn for breakfast that day.
- Army generals, especially those who were retired, sold their furniture. One in our neighbourhood tried to sell a new pair of shoes to buy medicine.
- Doctors and surgeons drove taxis after working hours to earn some extra money.
- Engineers went to Friday junk markets to sell the tools and things they treasured.
- Some men travelled abroad (mostly to Libya and Yemen) to find jobs, leaving women and children behind and weakening family ties, which Iraqis used to cherish.

In our case my mother did her best to cover for the shortages we suffered, but still sometimes we would feel embarrassed to ask and ask. I remember going for 10 days in a row having only some dates and a cup of milk (a luxury) for lunch. The Iraqis endured all this and waited for the nightmare to pass, but it seems like it's been replaced by something even worse.

Love to Justin and my little nieces

May xx

11.03.08

A small sadness

Hi there, May. I'm feeling really sad this morning as my period came. It was a couple of days late (I'm never late) and I had become convinced that I was pregnant. I'd even begun to feel some of the feelings you get. But I guess I must have just made it all up.

Amazing how after being so opposed to the idea, I am now actually upset not to be pregnant. It's put me off a bit; I don't know what to think now.

Oh, I asked Kate at CARA about your PhD offer. She said that your offer is already there; you have the offer from the university and therefore you have the invitation to come to the UK. She suggested that you might want to do some research on your thesis proposal. She thinks it's good for you to be in contact with your tutor, and to be thinking about the ideas, if you have time. It is a question now of securing the remaining funding so that you can take up the place.

OK, I really have to go. The girls are about to eat dinner, and Elsa and Zola have that bad cough and everyone is getting a bit fraught. I've just been typing away furiously in the middle of them all plaguing me and asking for things, but I can't ignore them any longer.

Love

B XX

12.03.08

Sons, mothers and militias

Hi, Bee

Things are all so disheartening. My colleague told me a story about a family: a mother, her son and daughter. The son was a former officer. She said that the militias came and asked where he was. She told them that he was not in the country. They came the next morning, shot the two women and blew up the house. She was telling me how part of the kitchen wall was demolished and how the cooker could still be seen with the morning kettle on it. I couldn't help myself, I cried. Oh Bee, why are people so cruel to each other?

Around 11 o'clock I had an exam with postgraduate students of chemistry. It is part of the curriculum requirements to study English in order to be able to undertake the research necessary for their degree. I had reluctantly agreed to repeat the exam for those who had failed, and I wasn't happy about it. They were bad and their English was awful, both oral and written, but I was sort of embarrassed to refuse. The girls came up to me, crying and saying that they would be expelled if they didn't pass. One of them is married and pregnant. I just don't know why they want higher degrees if they are not up to it. It is a trend now that students come to college to study, then fail, and then go crying and pleading to the teachers, making the situation in the country and the lack of security an excuse for their poor grades. They gain the pity of the teachers and then pass. This has been happening over the past five or six years. It embarrasses me to be the odd one out and so sometimes I give in and award them 50, which is the lowest pass mark. I hate myself when I do it.

I must stop now – I will continue tomorrow, when I will hopefully feel stronger.

Thursday. Not much better. On the way to work cars were being stopped and searched. When I arrived at the checkpoint a young officer said good morning and waved me through. When I thanked him he said, 'Not at all, Aunt.' This is a phrase to show respect for one's elders!

Ali has been quite a nuisance recently. He doesn't understand (or maybe he pretends not to) my need for the computer. I need it more now for work, and to search for PhD sources.

We ended up having a row over it and he started yelling that he didn't want to go to a country where he couldn't speak the language. He threatened to stay in Syria or Jordan. I got so angry and told him he can go to hell if he wants to; I will not be deterred, no matter what happens. After a while he apologized, and then he showed me an accessory he had bought for the car. Even though a big part of the row was over expenditure and the money we spend on fuel and repairs etc. Ah well, I think this is how it has to be.

Waiting for your email

May XX

14.03.08

What a wonderful relief

Morning, love!

After so much worry about my mum, yesterday was just amazing. It was me and my mum, and Dave. My mum was getting more and more apprehensive as we got closer to her appointment. She's been putting on a brave face for the last few weeks and now it had really got to her and she was just so scared.

We got to the hospital and had to wait in a room painted a cheerful yellow with nice friendly flowers and pictures, presumably so we didn't think about death. My mum went white and asked me to tell her stories about Elsa, so I began to gabble away about cute and funny things that Elsa has done recently and showed her photos of the girls on my phone. Then we were called into a room with bright strip lighting. We couldn't think of anything to say so we just sat there. After a while three people came in, one of whom was her surgeon. They had big smiles and I felt like I was staring into bright lights. But then the surgeon said, 'It's fine, you've nothing to worry about.' My mum and I burst into tears. He explained a bit more and then he left.

A lovely nurse sat with us and explained a lot more, using pictures showing the inside of a breast. The lumpectomy had been completely successful, and even though the carcinoma was a high grade one (which means it could have become invasive if left alone), it was still non-invasive, which meant it hadn't spread to anywhere else in the body. So all that happens now is that they will check my mum again in six months, and then she'll just be scanned each year.

We all walked to a café, sat down and then realized we were all too shaken up to eat or drink anything, so we left again and walked to the Museum Gardens in the centre of York. Slowly the euphoria came. We looked at daffodils and spring flowers and felt amazing. My mum said it would take longer to sink in, as she was so exhausted from the worrying. But I just felt like we'd had a dreadful jail sentence lifted, as though someone had shown a huge act of mercy to us and let us off. I kept taking massive deep breaths, as if I hadn't breathed properly before. I thanked God and bought some champagne, which we drank from plastic cups. I've never really understood the fear of cancer before, but I can tell you it's awful – and it wasn't even me who was at risk. But you just feel so vulnerable and afraid, and the hospital ward seems like a place where you can be condemned to death, almost at random.

Got back to London to find my home full of illness and mess. This morning Eva's got the temperature and cough and she had to stay off school and miss her assembly. Justin has a temperature of 102 degrees; he is mad with boredom and in a foul mood, and I have to admit I'm not very patient. If I'm honest, I find illness quite touching and sweet in the girls but in a great big hairy man it is just plain irritating.

Oh, I'm so happy about my mum! And, you know, it has also made us appreciate each other more as I think we've had a spell of being distant, and now we're not. I feel so lucky to have her. Also, she has a big party coming up (she is 60 and my brother is 40 so they're having a joint event) and now we can just get on with it without horrible thoughts and people trying to be all sympathetic.

PHEW! Massive, MASSIVE sigh of relief.

Hope you have a lovely day .... B X

Controlling cancer is a bliss

THANK GOD

Dearest

I was so worried sitting here waiting for news about your mum. I hate cancer; I know how you must all have felt. We have a history of cancer in my father's family. My father died from it when he was only 39. I think about him often. Our family was shattered by his death. My mother changed after that and I ceased to be Dad's favourite girl. I was just like the other two, and being the eldest I had to bear some emotional responsibilities that I felt were unfair because my friends didn't have to suffer them. My mother became 'the angry type'. She was never satisfied with anything. She had money, a degree and a good career, but her anger with life just surged through her. Pain was reflected in all she did.

Anyway, good news here too, but of a different kind. We had electricity all day today. Imagine, I didn't know what to do with it. I put chicken in the microwave for tonight 'just in case'. For lunch I made dolma. I never used to cook fancy dishes in my previous life, but Ali is different – he loves food and it is a great pleasure to watch him devour all the dishes I make. I don't want him to feel that he is missing out on things that used to be part of his home life.

Talking of your mum's illness made me remember something I wanted to tell you. Did you know that Iraqis don't usually go to doctors for illnesses requiring antibiotics? Instead, they diagnose and prescribe medicines for themselves. They will say, 'Ah, it is flu or just a cold,' and ask the pharmacist for antibiotics. I am one of those Iraqis, by the way. Unfortunately I am allergic to certain antibiotics, but I still use the kinds that contain sulphur, and I prescribe cough syrup for myself, and so on. I know that these things are mostly given under prescription in the UK, but they are like Maltesers here.

By the way, *The Old Man and the Sea* is on TV and Ali is watching it. I keep telling him to keep in mind that: 'A man can be destroyed but not defeated.'

OK, love, try to be a wee bit patient with your big hairy boy. All men are really babies on the inside. Fine on my part to say this, but I do get edgy and angry seeing anybody sick. Even when I fall ill I don't want much attention, I just want to be left in peace (hehee).

Big big hugs to you all

May XXXX

25.03.08

Post-Easter chocolate come-down

Hi, May

Had a lovely long Easter weekend break, but now Justin's away again and this morning wasn't good. I'm feeling all achy and tired, I burned the porridge, tried to hang out the laundry before we set off for school, then the girls' hair was all tangled and they screeched when I brushed it (apart from Elsa, who rushes up and demands the same as her sisters, even if it hurts). On the way to school it was so windy my eyes were streaming and it looked like I was crying. Zola's teacher said I looked tired – well, hardly a surprise as I don't even get time to brush my teeth let alone put make-up or proper clothes on. And I really hate my hair at the moment. I have to put all sorts of gungey stuff on it just to stop myself from looking like the nun out of *The Sound of Music*.

Well, that's all the latest from this end. I'm going to make tea now and read the papers for a quick break before Elsa gets up. I'm at work tomorrow (yippEEE!) but please write to me soon. I really want to hear from you.

Lots of love and Easter hugs

B XXX

26.03.08

I hate this

Bee

Are you there?

I am so depressed. I feel like killing myself to get rid of the load I have weighing on my mind. First of all, Ali's stupid monkey of a friend formatted the computer without my permission and has LOST so much of my work. I haven't even had a chance to say all the nasty things I wanted to because Ali became so angry and started blaming me for being careless and not backing it up. But how was I supposed to know that he would format the computer? I usually explode when things like that happen, but with Ali I'm scared he might get violent. I've had enough of that in my previous marriage. So you see, it is all bottled up inside.

The second thing is that I received a letter addressed to me with the word 'Confidential' stamped on it. I found that it had been opened. Although nothing of great importance was in it – it was a research paper sent to me for assessment – the point is: HOW DARE THEY OPEN A CONFIDENTIAL LETTER?

The third thing is that the local generator has been out of order for the past four days, and of course the house generator is not designed to run for long hours. I just hate the darkness, especially when the weather is turning hot. Just imagine, it is 39 degrees centigrade.

And one last thing. We were awakened at 6.45 a.m. on Saturday by heavy bangs on the door (not the outside gate) and the army burst

into the house for a search. They searched the whole neighbourhood and we were so scared and upset.

Am I overreacting, Bee?

Sorry to pour it all out like this, but I must tell you.

Hugs, love and XXXX

May

29.03.08

1,2,3 . . . 144 chocolate cakes

Hi, lovely – really quick one. Sorry, but it's been mad. I don't
blame you for being furious – what a terrible time! Especially the
thing about the computer. I don't know how you managed to keep
from going mad with Ali, but well done.

Yesterday after work I baked 144 chocolate cakes for a party for my
my mum and brother tonight. Finished cooking at 10 p.m. in a really
bad mood as Justin kept trying to eat them. I feel so tired. Trying to
pack today before we drive up north, so I'd better rush. We're back
on Weds but might be able to write to you from my mum's.

Lots and lots of love

Take care

B XXX

29.03.08

Cakes for sale

Dearest

I could never bake a cake, and certainly not 144. How did you
manage it? Bee, I think you are talented. Why don't you start a

bakery business? I think it will be profitable. Or maybe we can work together: I'll make some Middle Eastern foods and appetizers, and you can make European pastries and cakes. But we'll have to ban Ali and Justin from entering our shop because there'll be nothing left to sell!

Will go now. Write when you can.

May XXX

01.04.08

The joys of living?

Dear Bee

I know you're at your mum's but I still need to write to you. Here tension is worsening; there is fighting all over the country and I fear that it may spread. The schools, universities and shops are closed: life has almost stopped. If the fuel we have runs out then we can no longer function. There are some efforts being made to contain the crisis, but I read today that some Sadrists say they are being oppressed, just as they were in the old days. (These are mostly illiterate followers of a young 'cleric', who are accused of extensive looting and also killing a vast number of Sunnis, and even burning them alive. They suffered oppression before, but now they are doing even worse things.)

I just don't know what the Americans have gained by ruining the country. They could have just toppled the president and left the people to resume their lives. Do you know that over 80 per cent of the population is out of work? One of the richest countries in the world suffers from poverty and all kinds of shortages.

I was flicking through the TV channels we have and one showed a lawyer defending the members of the previous regime. He was complaining about the Iranian influence on the court and how the judge and guards hated the defendants, because the judge had asked them to remove their head covers, which represented 'an insult for old men of tribal background'. I switched to another channel and it showed children who had been blinded by bombs that contained dangerous chemicals. Tears were streaming down my face as I flicked to another channel showing something about Mother's Day, but it kept mentioning the suffering of Iraqi mothers and how many have had their sons killed in all the violent events that have rocked the country.

We've had enough. You know, I miss everything – from the smallest pebble on the street, to sitting with friends in a club or a restaurant, just smoking and drinking coffee or tea. My brain feels different. I hate myself, my house, Ali and everything around me.

I haven't been out of the house for eight days, but will risk going to work tomorrow just to see people. I sometimes wish I could spend a night or two away from home, talk to people who are on the same wavelength as me, but there is no one left to talk to. Most of my friends have emigrated to someplace or another. And anyway, they are from my old life and I don't think even if they were here that I could communicate with them. Ali doesn't like meeting people, particularly those from my previous life, and he hasn't got any friends of his own. Even if he did have, their wives would either be young or from a world completely different from mine.

I can't stand this life much longer and, I confess, if our little project does not go through within this month I don't know what I'll do to myself, but I will do something to ease all the tension inside me once and for all.

I MISS LIVING, I really do.

Oh, I can't go on any longer. I will end my email with love and hugs to you all.

May XXX

Be strong!

Oh May, I'm sorry. I just don't know how you pull through. But you do, May, you always get through. Normally I'd say you shouldn't go out as it's dangerous and I want you to be safe, but I think for your mental health you really must get out. Going to work would be the best thing you could do. Is it at all possible at the moment? Can you get to the hairdresser's?

I've heard about the curfew in Baghdad. What about having a coffee with colleagues inside the university; is that safe? I know they're trivial suggestions but it's all I can think of. Please cheer up, May, I feel awful with you being so sad and trapped.

Well, as usual I can't really give any proper advice or help so I'll just tell you about my stuff and what's been going on. I feel like it's just me yapping on but at the very least it might distract you for a moment.

We drove up on Saturday and I was still in a mood with Justin for eating an extra cake. We had all eaten one, leaving 139. That night Justin wanted another, but I said no. But when I went to bed he ate it anyway as he thought I was being stingy. In the morning I was furious and accused him of being like Elsa: seeing something, demanding it, not capable of understanding it might belong to someone else. We had a big row and I was grumpy on the journey up, which was rainy and tedious.

We got to York and began to help my mum set up the village hall for the party. Everyone was in really high spirits, and I managed to keep the cakes and the photo display secret. (Had blown-up photos of my mum aged 20 and my brother as a baby.) We went back and got ready, and I did my mum's make-up. She never normally wears make-up, so I did it quite subtly and she looked gorgeous. It was a lovely intimate moment, prancing around, listening to Aretha Franklin and sorting out our outfits.

The evening went brilliantly: the band was great, there was lots of food and drink and friends, and everyone was dancing. The girls wore a combination of Indian wedding outfits and cowboy hats. Elsa shot on to the dance floor, grabbed two helium balloons and then ran in circles jerking them behind her. She did this ceaselessly, and when people tried to pat her or dance with her she just swerved past them and carried on like a demented bumble bee.

I grabbed some people to hide away and help me light the candles on the 100 cakes which we'd put on a catering trolley. When we wheeled them out everyone sang 'Happy Birthday'. By the end my feet were killing me as I was wearing my orange sandals with a six-inch heel, so the clean-up was a pain, but everyone was so happy and it couldn't have gone better.

Well, May, I know I'm just talking about cakes and you're possibly still feeling quite suicidal. All I can do is send you a massive hug and hope with all my heart that you're better than you were when you wrote that. Please try to think about the beautiful things in the world. You have lots to live for, May, and lots of people who love you.

Always

Bee XXX

04.04.2008

A mixed bag of spring and blues

May, how are you? Thanks for sending a text; I was so worried. Hope you're still feeling better and have managed to get outside.

Well, I got very upset and cried today, May, as I think my period's come again, and I'd just started thinking I might be pregnant. I know, I know this happened last month too. I'm so contrary: of course, if I found out I was pregnant I would complain and moan and be frightened and resentful and so on, but once again finding that I'm not is also secretly a disappointment. I guess I'm from the generation of women who think we can control everything in our lives, and then it's a shock when we can't.

But we went to the Spring Show for the local gardening society. It was brilliant. Totally lifted my spirits – it was so English. There was nice tea in proper teacups with saucers, lots of friendly old ladies and cakes, plus all the flower and veg displays. The girls entered the two children's categories. Eva made an Easter bonnet with yellow chicks all over it, while Zola's was an edible nest of chocolate and cornflakes, squished up with eggs and chicks in, all on a bed of straw. They both won first prize (there was no competition to speak of but that didn't matter to them, hehee).

Oh, Justin has had some great news at work: he's going off filming in Alaska and chasing polar bears LATER THIS MONTH and although I'm really happy for him and leapt for joy, my second thought was the dawning realization that I'll be on my own with the kids for two weekends in a row. Argh! Weekdays are OK, but the weekend is just a wretched time to be a single mum. But still, quite amazing news so I have to look at the long-term picture.

This email is a right patchwork, isn't it? I'm all over the place. Will we still email this much when you live in Bedfordshire? It's 10.30 p.m. now, so if I start getting ready for bed then this'll be an early night.

'Good night, sweet May, and flights of angels sing thee to thy rest.'

B XXX

05.04.2008

Just hold on

Dear Bee, it will happen. I am sure of it.

My mum just came to the door. She and my brother's family had been invited to lunch by some old friends who have rented one of my mother's houses. She hadn't been out since I told you about our visit to the hairdresser's more than a month ago, and she was happily telling me about their outing. I think that seeing friends is worth the risk, don't you?

OK, lovely, when will Justin leave? Tell me so that I can send you more emails and stories about our life to keep you busy for a while.

Love you, wee sister

Hugs

MAY xx

06.04.08

My wicked children

We went to some friends' house for a big Sunday lunch – they have young twins. Our girls played beautifully with their twins and they all put on a little show together with music and dancing. But when we got back much later on Justin discovered that Zola had a lump under her jumper, which turned out to be a little plastic necklace she had taken from their house. She first tried to hide it from him, then claimed to have 'found it on the pavement', then finally admitted to taking it but begged J. not to tell me.

Did I tell you about the time when Eva nicked a sweet from the chemist's on South End Green? I marched her down there with her money tin and made her tell them what she'd done, apologize, and then pay for the sweet out of her own money. Later on I lectured both girls severely, saying that stealing is wrong, but most of all, and worse than anything, I didn't want to be lied to. I delivered this in a weighty manner, hoping they'd never forget it. But Zo thought about it for a moment and came right back with: Actually, Mummy, I prefer lying. Because if someone lies to me, I don't care, but if they steal from me then I don't have that thing any more.'

OK, dearest. I'm off now.

Bee XXX

14.04.08

Hello, big sister

I felt bad for not writing last week. But do you know what? I'd been reading through a load of our recent emails and it just made me depressed. I know we have everything to celebrate, and it's only a matter of time, but it seems that every time I am saying the same thing: oh, it'll all be happening any moment soon, blah blah, constantly cheerful and upbeat. I just couldn't bear it again; I've run out of patience and it all makes me feel sick. I suppose I feel bad being here while you're still stuck over there, going mad.

I don't normally experience guilt, but basically I just felt sick of always trying to cheer you up. I seem to say the same things again and again and I couldn't face it this time. Sorry.

My words about not stealing went unheeded: Eva and Zola were caught by Justin stealing chocolates in London's Borough Market on Friday. Eva had a pocket stuffed with really expensive chocolates, worth about £5. He made her give them back. I went mad and told them I'd hand them both over to the police if it happened again, but this weekend Zola came back from a friend's with some small doll's things in her pocket. She could've brought them by accident, I suppose, but I was furious and don't know what to do. Anyway, they're both up at my mum's now until Friday, so it's only little Elsa and her flying fists of fury this week.

Am in work today – I love it. I talked to our Pashtun Service about a florid Indian soap opera that might be banned in Afghanistan despite huge audiences, and am chasing Burma and Kenya too. It's a great news week, so much going on in the world.

Better go – more chasing to do. You know I think of you always.

Bee XXX

14.04.08

Hello, wee sister

Hope you're well. We are still locked in our houses out of fear. I keep myself busy with lots of human rights papers to mark, questions to set, and also I have just completed a paper on 'Social Satire in Jane Austen's *Persuasion*'. And I hope to start one soon on 'Sin in the Victorian Age'.

By the way, I've had an idea about the chocolate incident with Eva and Zola stealing things: maybe the girls' behaviour is jealousy of Elsa and they are trying to attract your attention. I know that you do your best to treat them all equally but the girls are just babies as well and do not comprehend that Elsa needs more attention than they do. Well, I don't know but that is what I think!

Love to the naughty ones.

Love

May xxx

15.04.08

Elsa's poo!

Hi, love. Thank God you're OK. I was at the gym and there was rolling news about a car bomb in Baghdad, so I texted you straight away. Just imagine, it is only these technological advances that have kept us together all these years.

Guess what — we had a big moment in Elsa's life last night when I got home from work. I took her nappy off and she played around, sitting on the potty while I sang some songs and showed her books, then suddenly she picked up the potty, ran to the other side of the room and placed it carefully on a rug, then did a big poo in it! I realize that poo isn't the noblest of topics but I have to tell you about it as it's a big deal for her and was her first ever try. She stared at it, looking all worried and doubtful. I began to cheer and clap her and praise her. I took a photo with my phone to send to Justin (apparently he showed it all round the office, oh lucky colleagues!). She began to be delighted and clap her hands, then we flushed it down the toilet, saying, 'Bye-bye!' She stood there waving and shouting bye-bye to her own poo long after it had gone.

As for your thoughts on Eva and Zola being jealous of Elsa and stealing in an attempt to get more attention, it's possible. I do appreciate your comments, as you're able to see it from afar whereas I'm up close and can lose perspective. I worry about them not getting enough individual attention; it's one of the hardest things to sort out. Eva was just 15 months old when Zola arrived and I guess she doesn't remember anything else. But Zola remembers being the baby of the family, and she used to love it. She never much wanted to do 'big girl' things like use the potty or learn to walk. She was just happy being a baby.

I spoke to them yesterday and they sounded so happy. My mum had taken them pony riding and they were about to eat pancakes.

Have to go now. Write soon!

Hugs

Bee XXX

15.04.08

I thought Elsa's poo was all I'd get!

Hi, Bee

Do you know what happened when I tried to open my email? It was so funny that I have to tell you. I had only 45 minutes left of the local generator's electricity and I just felt there was an email from you, so I thought I would use the time. I got to Yahoo and did everything. The new Yahoo shows your inbox and the titles of the new emails. I tried to open it and got 'Bee Rowlatt' then 'Elsa's poo!' and the time. I pressed the one that showed the email but the page expired, so I tried again and again – about 10 times. Every time Elsa's poo just stuck there. At last I burst out laughing, saying to myself, 'That is all I will get tonight: Elsa's poo.'

The page finally opened and . . . ah, how sweet of you to let me share in Elsa's growing-up process. I know the subject isn't a noble one, as you say, but it is reality and part of nature. I remember one of my very close friends (we've lost contact now) had a baby boy back in the 1980s and she used to call and describe his poo in detail and I used to listen, though not with much interest. It was part of our friendship to share events, even the 'smelly ones'.

You know, I was watching *Sense and Sensibility* when I got the feeling that there was an email from you. I'm glad I got up and opened it and found your email there. At least I have hope, while others here don't. So I guess I am luckier than many.

May XXX

16.04.08

Thoughts on government

MAY! That's got to be the maddest thing that happened in all the madness of Baghdad yesterday: a distinguished Iraqi academic and chief editor clicking away for 10 minutes on an email entitled 'Elsa's poo!'.

It's been really cold outside again and so I made some cakes today, filled the house with baking smells and ate a load. Tonight we're going out for a curry. Honestly, May, I really eat like a heifer (sadly don't have two stomachs) and if I didn't do so much exercise I'd be a right blob. I know you can't do any exercise in your current circumstances, but when you're here maybe you should. It works as well as, if not better than, antidepressants apparently.

As I was walking back from the gym I started thinking about you saying how we in the West don't understand what it's like for people who live under a dictatorship. You are right. I can't understand it, and I don't want to make you angry, but isn't there any way Iraqis could have got rid of the dictatorship themselves? Would Saddam have been there for ever? I know that after the Gulf War there was an uprising of the Kurds that was crushed, but didn't anyone else try to join in? Don't all dictatorships crumble in the end? Aren't people at large responsible for taking their fate into their own hands? Can Islamic countries be democratic?

Anyway, if you get time (and electricity, of course) do please answer me about democracy.

Loads of love and hugs to you, big Sis!

Bee XXX

Democracy and a lost country

Dear Bee

I am afraid I don't agree. To start with, S.H. did not assume power and become a dictator right from the start, he climbed a couple of steps before that. He was vice-president for some time and had succeeded in earning people's genuine love. They adored him so much that they were ready to sacrifice anything for him. His nationalization of oil was a brave patriotic step and I think it was what ignited western animosity towards the man.

If I remember correctly, it was sometime in 1971 or '72 when there was a fuel crisis all over Europe, and also in Britain. We were in the UK at the time and the TV showed Europeans walking or riding bicycles to work. This was a disaster for the West, but for the people here it was a source of national pride. He also did quite a lot of things internally, such as combating illiteracy, initiating building projects and giving people a good standard of living and land on which to build homes. He also had a direct line that anyone could phone to ask for his assistance on all sorts of difficult matters. I phoned and even met him a couple of times. I will tell you all about it when I feel I can.

When he assumed full power, most people did not even bother to question how and why. There were others among the senior party members who did not approve, and he got rid of them at once. There were several attempts to overthrow him but he moved quickly to crush all attempts. I have a book, written by his half-brother, entitled *The President's Assassination Attempts*. It was later withdrawn from the market. His policy was not just to punish the people who had collaborated against him, but also their families too, although they were punished less severely.

Gradually people understood and feared, and this fear created hypocrisy; they started saying and repeating things they did not mean or believe, like parrots. So the dictatorship arrived in small doses, not all at once.

I think your voting system does really work as it should, and that is why you cherish your right to vote because it will make a difference. In Iraq voting tends to encounter a lot of difficulties. Falsifying votes and intimidation are not uncommon. I did not vote, because I didn't know a thing about the constitution and I didn't believe in any political party.

Islam is a different issue. Religion has never been in favour of dictatorship, and the Holy Quran states that matters should be solved through 'shura' (consultation and deliberation). After this has been done, a leader is chosen who must then be followed in order to maintain unity between people and parties. According to this mechanism it would be quite impossible to choose a bad person through shura.

Islam also states that no coercive measures may be exercised to force anybody to do anything. There is, however, punishment for anyone who breaks the norms or indulges in bad conduct, such as adultery, theft or usury etc. What we have today is not Islam but a misinterpretation of it, mostly for political or financial gain. Most moderate people recognize that, but they cannot really change the prevailing circumstances or they will become scapegoats.

When I was writing my thesis I had to read the Bible, and when I did I became convinced that there are no major differences between the two religions. Reading Chaucer, on the other hand, and some criticism of certain works in *The Canterbury Tales*, shows how religion can influence people's lives, and how anyone with perverted ideals can easily exploit the simple uneducated people. This is a universal problem and may happen anywhere. At the time of Chaucer, Moslems were ruled by the Caliphs, who were just and governed according to the real laws of Islam. Life in general was very good, whereas Britain was still in a primitive state with the

Church imposing its tyrannical rule and deviating from the true course of religion. Now it is the other way round.

Do you think I've talked more than enough (hehee)?

Big hugs to you all

May XXX

PS I drove to the hairdresser's today. All was quiet and nothing disturbed the peace. It turned out later that half of Baghdad was closed, because Condi was on a surprise visit. My hair had reached a depressing point. I haven't worn it long since the Gulf War when electricity was destroyed by the allies. So I told her to cut it in my pre-Ali hairstyle (like James Watt's hair), then I got highlights and returned home safe and feeling much better.

21.04.08

WHAT!?!!!

WHAT? May, do you mean to say that you actually met Saddam – are you kidding? I can't believe you never told me this! You are SUCH a dark horse, May, it makes me wonder what on earth you'll come out with next . . . You must tell me about it; I'm dying to know. Why haven't you ever told me before?

As for James Watt's hairdo, do you mean the Scottish inventor? I can't quite see it, but at the very least it sounds like you've had a wonderfully normal day. I think hairdressers are underrated in the nation's hearts, they should be treasured for cheering people up and simply listening to them. Well, apart from a guy on Haverstock Hill who once dyed my hair purple instead of blonde, and made me cry. But apart from him they should be encouraged for the greater good.

Oh, I had a great day at work today. I'm getting the president of the UK Beekeepers' Association to come in and talk about bees in danger. My colleagues laughed as obviously my name indicates a certain bias, and maybe it's because of my name, but I've always loved bees. And currently UK bee keepers are just getting over mass attacks of the varroa parasite that kills bees, and now are in a panic about Colony Collapse Disorder. I don't know if in your circumstances you have the emotional energy to feel sorry for bees, May, but up to 80 per cent of bee colonies have been wiped out in parts of the US. It's mass unexplained death. And did you know that bees are responsible for pollinating around a third of all the food we eat?

So although it wasn't on the same scale as Condi's trip to Bahrain trying to get Iraq's neighbours to be more supportive (we did this too, of course), I got tremendously motivated and made it the mission of my day to get bees on the programme.

Oh no, it's 10 o'clock already. See how the evening rushes away. That bit between 8 p.m. and 10 seems to go in about 45 minutes somehow.

Love you . . .

Bee XX

23.04.08

James Watt

Hi, love

Yes, it is the Scottish inventor who had short straight hair, ear length. But I don't think he had highlights (hehee).

A nice thing, or rather hilarious thing, happened at college this morning. The fourth-year students decided to continue their graduation celebrations and they came in wearing fancy dress. Some wore pyjamas and nightdresses, others wore bridal gowns and some wore national costume and hired a local band playing awful music. They climbed on the desks and chairs and went through the department singing and dancing. I stood watching them and couldn't move. Two conflicting feelings came over me: the first was that this was not really decent behaviour, and the second was to let them enjoy life while they can. The second feeling won. I thought to myself that they probably chose to do it in my room because they see me as a mother figure and feel they can trust me. They moved away and I tried to undo the damage they'd done to the furniture.

Bye, love. Write soon.

May XXXX

27.04.08

Moment of peace

Hello, May

I was dreading Justin leaving for Alaska, but now he's gone it's not too bad. The saddest part was Eva – she was so upset, she cried every time she thought about him leaving. Zola shrewdly asked him if he likes his job more than his children, then to ratchet up the emotional blackmail Eva drew a series of pictures showing herself weeping while he walked out of the door with his bag. So it's been quite dramatic, but he set off yesterday with all his special winter gear, waterproofs and woolly socks etc.

I had my book group on Thursday and it was miles away in South London. I'd forgotten to RSVP to the woman who was hosting it, so she was surprised to see me. To add to this, after a second helping of rhubarb crumble with custard I leaned back in the chair with a sigh, and it made the most enormous CRRACK noise. I leapt up in horror. We couldn't find any cracks, everyone laughed and she was very kind about it, but I felt such an idiot. But I do love book group. The other women are so bright, and their diverse reactions to the books are an eye-opener. It makes me realize how swiftly I judge things. Sometimes I'll just hate a book because the length of the sentences annoys me. (Anxiously scan this email to see if the sentences are too long. No . . . looks OK, phew!)

I loved your fourth-year students going mad and partying on the tables, especially when you think what their lives must have been like these last few years. I'm glad you let them do it. It's precious to be silly sometimes.

Love

Bee XXX

06.05.08

Return of the explorer

Hi, May

It's all back to normal here again, hurray! J is back, the sun is out, coffee together in the mornings, everyone happy. By Sunday afternoon we were really counting the hours to his return, and I was running out of things to do. We went to the park and got ice creams, came home, and as we were sitting in the garden Justin arrived with all sorts of strange Alaskan food and polar bear socks for the girls. Yesterday was a bank holiday so we all had a quiet day together.

Last week on the way into school I took the girls into the polling booths to vote in the London mayoral and assembly elections. I let them draw the crosses on the first and second choices, then post the papers into the ballot box. So they have taken part in the democratic process, even if Justin failed miserably to do so. (I nagged him for days to sort out his vote before he left for Alaska, and he didn't do it, so now any undesirable outcome will be all his fault.)

You know, when Justin was away Eva decided to write a letter to the Queen. Not to be outdone, Zola wrote to the Prime Minister.

I helped them write, but the questions were their own. Eva asked, 'Do you like gardening and what is your favourite flower?' And Zo asked Gordon Brown, 'Why are there more cars? I'm worried about pollution.' (She spelled it 'plooshun'.)

It's been really hot and sunny here this week and today I filled two paddling pools in the garden. So you can tell the weather's changed: the next-door neighbours have lit a barbecue and it smells delicious. It's making me really hungry. I'm off now, going to find something to eat.

Are you OK, May?

Drop me a line if you can.

Bee XX

08.05.08

Disappointment, distant hope

Dearest Bee

I know you are a bit worried about me. I am OK really. But I am beginning to lose hope and patience. Could the book plan be a mere dream?

I haven't been feeling comfortable at college over the past two weeks. It seems that they've all noticed that I haven't been myself. One of my colleagues (your age) brought me biscuits, another brought me a book, a third has called me for three days in a row asking how I am, and a fourth has visited me.

All the usual things – power, Ali, my boss – are wearing me down, but on top of these nerve-wrecking things there is the problem of the ration card. It has become a form of ID and is requested as identification wherever you go. I haven't used mine since the invasion, and Ali has left his with his family (and it is in another province anyway, and therefore not accepted here) but now I need mine as ID. When the military operations and the terrorists were in our area I was too scared to go and get one, and then we left for Syria and they registered me as displaced, or something of the kind. When I returned and tried to get one, it was awful – I hired a man to get one for me but he took the money and didn't do it. I just don't know what to do now.

I worry about the book and the funding for my stay in the UK. Where will the money come from? What makes the whole thing so slow? I have my plans, and my supervisor said my thesis proposal was promising. I've also received an email asking for my address to send me a formal letter of acceptance, but where is all this heading?

I didn't want to burden you with all this.

Love, hugs and kisses to you and all the family

May

08.05.08

We couldn't wait

Hi, May. I feel you can't go on waiting any longer to find out what will happen, and neither can I.

So we're changing the plan.

As you know, Penguin are giving an advance, but it's not enough. We've been trying to get the rest elsewhere, but it's too slow. So I talked to Justin and he thinks we should borrow the remaining money right now, because it is this delay in getting the funds up front that is stopping everything else from happening.

Once the money is in place with CARA, your visa applications can go ahead as planned. And so I've asked my mum, and Justin's mum, to help. Between the two of them, and me and Justin, we are borrowing the money. My mum said it will take her three weeks to get hers. I was nervous, of course – I hate asking for money (who doesn't?) – but both mums were brilliant and are pleased to help.

Guess what, I also swam in the pond today for the first time this year! Went up with Talia in the very hot sun at midday; she'd just come off a shift in the local hospital and was full of tales of her mad patients. We lay around and read the papers in the meadow and had the most wonderful afternoon there. It was like getting a secret holiday in the middle of the day. The dark blue sky was almost shimmery in the heat, the water was smooth with ducks and geese nesting around the edges. Occasional petals blew across the water. It was fresh but not freezing so we swam around for quite a while.

Write soon.

Bee XXX

09.05.08

What a day!

Dear Bee

Your news is wonderful. I see rainbows and my heart flutters. I am scared and keep trying to calm myself. We have begun to talk about the things we will do before we leave, the things we need to take with us, how to lock the house up and who to give the keys to etc. Of course, no one knows a thing (except one of my friends, and he doesn't know where or how). I just told him that I might be quitting because I want to do a PhD abroad. He smiled at the time, as if he thought I was dreaming.

I do hope things work out this time. I reread your email just now and feel that I can never ever repay the good things you've done for me. I sure hope that you will find me worth the effort when we meet face to face and see each other regularly, as friends and family do in normal circumstances. I am also grateful to Justin and to the kind mums you both have.

I must tell you about this morning. I woke at 9.30 and checked in with my boss online at 10.00. He is just back from a four-day leave. After saying our usual morning greetings etc. I told him that I wanted to make some tea before I started, and he asked me to just translate one item before I did, so I said OK. I thought the item would be so vital that it couldn't wait for 15 minutes. Guess what he assigned me? A call made by a very unglamorous MP demanding the government provide water tanks for a hospital. The item is humanitarian, I know, but since no one but the government and the US forces can do a thing to help, what was the point of translating it before my morning mug of tea??

Anyway, I did it. Then, when it was time to finish, he told me to stay for an extra two hours because the other translator had gone to the dentist. So I finished at 4 p.m. and the electricity went off immediately. It is 7.45 now and I'm going to mark some exam papers and read a little bit for tomorrow. I am happy, sad and anxious all at the same time. I do hope everything works out well.

Ali sends his love.

May XXX

12.05.08

Sweaty office and no custard creams

May. I'm so glad to move into a new chapter. I don't know how long it'll take to get the paperwork all in place. My main fear is about what it will be like for you and Ali, in Jordan or Beirut, waiting for the response from the embassy. I think that will be a horrible wait, but nonetheless there's absolutely no reason it should go wrong: everything is legitimate and correct; we will have all the paperwork and finances in place.

I'm at work. Sun burning through the windows, hot stuffy office air, and loads of natural disasters around the world. Burma cyclone, China earthquake. The death toll just keeps rising.

I ran down to the BBC canteen to get biscuits and tea. There were no custard creams in the biscuit tray so I stood there at the front of the queue, digging around searching for them, with a load of annoyed people huffing and puffing behind me. But you have to have the right biscuits. In the end I opted for jammy dodgers and chocolate bourbons.

Bee XX

12.05.08

Back again for more

Hello again! I'm back from work now. Just spent an hour watering the garden; my back's killing me. The heat has suddenly made the jasmine plants burst into flower – two tall bushes covered in clustering small flowers – the smell nearly knocks you over as you walk past. I've been checking on all my new small plants and making sure they're doing OK. It struck me that it's rather insane to spend a day at work looking at the death toll from an earthquake rising by thousands upon thousands without any particular emotion, then get home and go berserk if I find that someone has trodden carelessly on a seedling.

Then from downstairs I heard Elsa wailing so I went up and looked in on her; she had a dirty nappy and was pointing at it. I changed her, and put her back to bed all clean and happy. How wonderful it is to be able to help someone; just make them go from crying to smiling in one simple action. It's unusual in everyday life, but it's one of the most satisfying small details about being a parent.

You know, May, I'm sorry to be nosy but I once asked you about whether you'd wanted kids, and you said no because you didn't want to bring them into this mad world. But then another time you did say that you once wanted them with your first husband. So did it just never happen? (Ignore me if I'm being too nosy.)

Bye for now, Big Sister!

B XX

13.05.08

My secret

Dear wee Sis

I've always wanted to tell you about this point in my life, but it is painful to talk about and I seem to want to brush it aside. But since you've asked, I'll tell you. Here is the whole story.

At the age of 7 I got very sick and doctors failed to diagnose the reason. When I was finally taken to a surgeon they discovered that an ovarian cyst had burst, requiring the removal of one ovary. I was in intensive care for five days. After that I was taken to the UK every six months, where doctors on Harley Street checked whether I would menstruate or not. At the age of 9 I finally did, and they said I was as normal as any other female. Even so, I heard some remarks from the older and uneducated female members of my father's family about me not being able to produce children and changing their minds about taking me as a wife for one of their sons. This suited me fine at the time, although I did feel a little heartbroken.

When I got married at 17, I never thought twice about being abnormal as all the medical reports from the Harley Street doctors confirmed that everything was OK. But as the years went by (1980s by now), people began to ask questions, as children are regarded as a necessary factor in marriage here. I began to think about the subject, since I felt lonely at heart and thought maybe a child would make my husband quit drinking.

I had some medical checks and then one of the gynaecologists asked for a sperm count from my husband. The results were disastrous. He was given medicines and hormones. My tests said that I was normal, but he never accepted the fact. He kept telling me it was my fault and reminding me of my operation. By that time the war had started and he was at the front, spending his seven-day leave getting drunk and aggressive. Every time I used to request him to take his medicine he would accuse me of using my mum's medical connections to forge his lab results.

I solved the feelings of loneliness by getting a dog. Then, in the 1990s, I made another attempt after we remarried. I had divorced my husband, but three years later we remarried, after he had stopped drinking and had turned religious. My medical examinations again proved normal. The doctor advised us to try something called artificial insemination, or something like that, and we did. I was 37. The doctor said we should have several attempts until it succeeded, but it was costly and we couldn't afford it. My mother offered to pay, but I refused. If others were paying for me to get pregnant, how was I supposed to bring the child up? I hated myself for the mere thought.

I told Ali all the details of my childlessness before we got married. He was very optimistic about it and was sure that I would become pregnant. I had doubts because I was 45. I again went to a doctor and she gave me injections to activate the ovary. I missed my period, but the test was negative. I broke down and cried all the pain of the past 30 years. Ali was very kind and said it did not matter. I stopped trying, but thought about it a lot now that I had Ali in my life. Every month was a heartbreaking event.

The last time was in Syria, last summer. The doctor this time announced that my missed period was a symptom of the menopause. I had my last breakdown and cried so hard, and then deleted the matter completely from my mind.

I think I was never meant to be a mother, and I have accepted it. But sometimes I feel hurt, and as if I am not a complete woman. In

Iraq they think a childless marriage is lacking, and they always blame the woman (and try to get the man to marry another). Unmarried women here think a childless man an easy prey to catch – as you know, a man is allowed here to have more than one wife, so a childless woman always feels threatened.

So that is my secret.

May x

14.05.08

May XXXXXXX

Oh May, what a deep long sadness. That is heartbreaking.

Your life is full of extreme events that you have managed to overcome, but this one I found the hardest to read about, and the hardest to know how to reply to. I knew it would upset me, and it has. Tears are stinging my eyes. You deserve to have as much love in your life as possible. There are still many possible outcomes, you know. I think you can't have conceived in Damascus because of the huge stress, fear and uncertainty. But whatever happens, you are special to me and my family; my girls love their Aunty May and can't wait to meet you. I hope very much that you will have a role in their lives.

With your kindness, wisdom and funny sweetness any person is lucky to have you close by, be it your family or students or anyone who loves you.

It makes me realize how lucky I was to have the babies without any worries or hassle; it's even more of a blessing than I knew. I feel foolish for having moaned on about my period coming these last few months. I didn't stop to think that it might have upset you.

I just think you're wonderful, May, and I will always love you.

Your Bee XXX

Thinking of you

Dearest friend

Got your lovely and very kind email. The tears ran down my cheeks. I was so moved by your words. Yes, you are right – when I look back I realize that my life was and still is full of extreme events. But I don't really regret or mind anything I've been through, simply because any experience in life has its benefits. If I hadn't suffered with my late husband, for example, I probably wouldn't have appreciated the second opportunity I was given. If I hadn't suffered economic hardship, I wouldn't have felt for the needy when my economic status improved. You know, I think God has always been merciful to me and has always helped me through. So let's just look on the positive side of life, though it's very difficult to see from where I am right now.

Before I start talking about something else, I just want to say that you mustn't ever think that the subject of you getting pregnant upsets me or anything. No, I swear to God that I never ever compare my situation to anyone else's. And second, I do feel that I am part of your family and we should confide in each other. So don't worry; talk about whatever you want, my bonny wee sister.

Let me tell you about yesterday. I woke up around 8.30 and sat thinking with my third cup of tea about the good people who are helping me, through you. I so much appreciate their faith in me. Then my mind turned to Ali, and I was just thinking that I should wake him when a big explosion shook the house and the windows rattled. Ali woke of course, and came running to me. I hugged him and said, 'I was thinking of a way to wake you up, and my wish came true at once!' There was a time when we were woken by birdsong. Now it is bombs.

It turned out that it was a car bomb that had killed 3 people and injured 26. The area turned into a battleground with ambulance sirens, helicopters and the army etc. This was the second incident in our street this week. The first was in a shop, which was completely destroyed.

Will have to go now, my lovely. Hope you are in the best of shape.

May XXX

19.05.08

Deep Monday breath

May, lovely May

I was struck by you and Ali having both been brought up with birdsong to wake you in the morning, but now surrounded by car bombs and sirens. Memories are so delicate and should be 'taken out' often, particularly when they hold meaning for you both. My day started very well: no special sounds, but do you know what Justin did? This is so sweet. He had to set off late last night to go and film down in Cornwall somewhere today. I grumbled that I wouldn't get my morning cup of coffee in bed. So he made me a flask last night before he left, and put it by our bed. I woke up all excited, put on the radio and poured out my coffee, feeling like royalty and thoroughly pleased with the world. It was still quite early, so I then crept in on the girls and got into Zola's bed and cuddled her. Eva heard me and she came down her ladder and joined us. We were all dreamy for a short while, then the girls began to squabble so I got out and went to get Elsa.

Hope the bombings on your street stop. Have to dash now; I have a meeting about the book. Tell you about it later. A deep breath and off I go.

Buzzing Bee XXX

21.05.08

Celebrations can wait

Hello, dearest May

So. We signed the Penguin contract, including an extra clause that we cannot publish it unless you're *out* of Iraq. Then I handed over the cheques to Kate at CARA. It was exhilarating at the time, and as I signed I felt a rush of 'How did it all come to this? How on earth did we get here?!' But afterwards we had a long chat about the next step, and it stopped me in my tracks. It made me reflect on what we still have to get done.

Really, I think that's why I'm not feeling my usual self. I've sent you so many triumphant bursting emails in the past, haven't I? But the next part is stressful and I'm so worried about you and Ali. Kate has said that she will send you detailed instructions about everything that you need to do. Don't get me wrong — there's no reason you should have any problems. This will not be like the last time. It's a proper fellowship scheme and we have all the right paperwork and the money. Kate has just been to Amman, so she knows what's happening and which way is best to proceed.

So I'm going to save my emotions and the real celebrations for when you are actually here. That's when I will celebrate. But after the meeting I met my friend Amy, who was working nearby in Soho. We stopped at a Greek place, had baklava and made a little toast to you.

Yesterday I threw myself into the PA Summer Fair with a vengeance, and by mid-morning had secured a hotel break, a family trip to Legoland, and various nice local meals, as prizes or for auction. I was so delighted with myself and then plodded up and down the nearby streets doing more begging from shops, restaurants, hairdressers and so on. It's exciting when it works.

Today I was taken to the famous Chelsea Flower Show by my friend Tsam, and it was like being in a cartoon world. There is too much to see and smell – a massive wall of sweet peas with over-powering perfume, a tunnel of climbing roses in changing colours as you walk through. By midday our eyes were somehow exhausted and we lay down for a picnic. Next year I might take you and Ali; it's a very English thing. The people are so passionate about their plants – you get specialists who do nothing but one plant, maybe dozens of different strawberries all heaped up, and they talk about it like it's the only thing in the world. There's something about flowers, the sheer voluptuous unnecessary beauty of them, that can make you feel differently about the world.

A hundred hugs . . . B XX

21.05.08

Things are finally moving

Dearest Buzzing Bumbo Bee

I am delighted with the developments. I guess things are finally moving. As for you, well words are never enough, and the same goes for dear Kate. So now I think it is down to me to organize visas for Ali and myself and think about England!

A lot of things have been going on but the most important is that I have asked for a letter from the college saying that I am still a teacher there, which is necessary for obtaining the visas to Amman. Anyway, I applied yesterday. It will take about a week for the letter to get through college, then another week at the university, then another at the ministry of higher education, then I don't know how long it will take at the foreign ministry, and then finally I can take the letter to both the Jordanian and Syrian embassies, which will also take some time. If they are convinced, I will get a visa to enter their countries (it should work OK).

Must go now, love. I am glad the meeting went well, even if there was no sign of your usually happy and hope-inspiring reaction.

Love

May XXX

22.05.08

Light of day

. . . light of day, light at the end of the tunnel. We've never been this close before, May. I'm half elated, half sick with terror. Basically I can't seem to sit still. I feel like a tin of Coke that's been dropped on the floor but not opened. (May, if it goes on like this I will be a gibbering nervous wreck by the time you get here. You might take one look and jump on the next plane back to Iraq, haha!)

Some calmer thoughts overtook me yesterday when I was at the flower show. I wanted to describe to you how it gave me a feeling of goodness and rightness in the world. It's quite probably the diametrical opposite of what is happening now outside your door. It was like a true expression of civilized humanity (I don't just mean lots of posh people swanning around in hats, although there were), love for something that is ultimately superfluous to our survival. I mean, who needs a flowery garden? It may sweeten life every day but, like music, no one would die if it were taken away. (But we would certainly be lessened.) I don't know what on earth has brought on these thoughts; the pollen must have gone to my head.

I had a similar reaction when the bombers attacked London back in July 2005. The day began as usual, in fact I was swimming in the pond, of all sacred places, when I found that Justin had called me to say all trains on the London Underground were cancelled and something bad was going on. Then all the phone lines went dead;

it was very scary. All morning I watched the breaking news getting steadily worse. I collected Eva and Zola from nursery, cried and squeezed them tight, brought them home and made a huge batch of lemon cakes. As though cakes could restore goodness and make everything OK.

Swam in the pond this morning and it was freezing again. The temperature has dropped to a shivery 14 degrees. But I saw my first ducklings of the year, tweeting around so fluffily. Soon, May, you're going to visit the pond with me; you just have to see what I mean about it being special and heavenly. You don't have to swim if you don't want to! My limbs were aching with the cold, my skin felt sanded with sandpaper and it was hard to do my shoes up afterwards, but a flask of tea and some Viscount biscuits brought me back to life fairly swiftly.

I'm now in packing mode, running up and down with laundry, bags everywhere, lists upon lists, to get us ready for our long-awaited Dorset trip. We're leaving today after school and staying until a week Saturday. J has tried to sort out the internet connection so I hope I'll be able to write to you from there. I am so happy we're going away. Justin's really tired and hasn't been himself since Alaska, and it feels like a long time since we had some nice relaxing family time. I plan to eat loads of food and be barefoot as much as possible.

All my love

Bee XXXX

24.05.08

A lot of distractions

Dearest Bee

This is the third attempt within half an hour. The electricity keeps going off and coming back on. I couldn't write over the past two days and catch you before you went to Dorset because there was so much to do and a lot of repairs. The car, the generator and the computer. They took all my salary. Yesterday I spent all day from 9 until 4 cleaning the house from the impact of the successive dust storms we've had over the past month.

The computer keeps crashing and I am just fed up. I've never had such problems before Ali, because I never visit strange websites. But he does. I don't like it and keep warning him not to do it, but he just brushes it away. There are other things annoying me, and I think I have to sort them out with him before we move on to the next step. Otherwise, life will be unbearable for both of us. I just hope he keeps his word if we agree on some changes in our life together.

I have to go now, lovely wee Sis. Hope you get my email while in Dorset and I wish you a very nice stay.

Hugs

May XXXX

25.05.08

I was the bad guy

Dearest Bee

You seem to be in outer space (Dorset). I hope you are having a great time. I just wanted to tell you that yesterday's computer crash wasn't Ali's fault, but the news agency's. They kept denying it and telling me the sites I needed could be accessed from my computer. Poor Ali was a total wreck after I finished lecturing him about indecent sites and computer viruses, then he blew his top and said, 'Won't you stop! I don't go into such sites; I did when I was first introduced to this technological miracle, then I stopped. So SHUT UP!'

I shut up but kept grumbling, and then my colleague called and said he was also having problems. I felt so ashamed of myself and had to apologize (a thing I hate doing).

We talked about my fears and about how he must change some of his habits when we get to the UK, such as getting slim, studying and working even if the job is menial. He gave me his word, so I went to bed feeling happy and quite reassured.

I'll go now, as I have just finished work.

Love you always

May XXX

27.05.08

Apology to Hemingway

Dearest Bee

I just got your text message. Lovely Elsa will be 2 tomorrow! Her birthday marks the age of our friendship. We've been through some difficult times together, haven't we?

I was thinking about Hemingway. My feelings for the novella's main theme have changed. 'A man can be destroyed but not defeated' is the theme of *The Old Man and the Sea*. My pre-invasion reading of the novella used to boost my morale. I thought of all the encouraging statements that could incite the desire to resist the oppressive life that Iraqis lived during the 1990s and early 2000s. But in my post-invasion reading, Hemingway's words are no longer effective. I feel silly trying to teach things I do not feel. It seems futile trying to inject these young women with passion and resilience, while everything around them is a wasteland. What future awaits them, or me for that matter?

The whole society has been faked. People fake their names, qualifications, backgrounds – and even religious beliefs are subject to counterfeiting. I feel an apology is due to Hemingway because I am no longer capable of teaching his theme of honourable struggle and engagement with life. The successive blows dealt to humanity in Iraq have taught man to accept defeat to the point of gladly destroying himself. It is rather funny how the same words can ignite two such opposite feelings and reactions in one person at different times.

Will have to go now, lovely Bee. I know you are still in Dorset and can't read this immediately, but you are so very near even when you are away.

Love

May XX

28.05.08

A soggy greeting from Dorset

Dearest May

I've missed you such a lot since getting down here and not being able to write. Right now I'm on Justin's laptop, sitting in a café in Swanage and looking out at the pouring rain. It's my only chance to drop you a line! His computer is an Apple and v annoying so sorry for all the typos.

You seem to have found an optimistic core in Hemingway that you feel is disproved by life in today's Iraq. But May, you mustn't let Iraq be the prism through which you see humanity forever more. Do you think you'll ever let go of the fear? I have to say Ernest Hemingway has never been my cup of tea. I don't much enjoy those macho American writers, Norman Mailer, Cormack McCarthy etc. But Hemingway did once say a very good thing about writing: it should be done as though you are sending a telegram i.e. limited, as though paying for every word. That will mean nothing to the generation who don't know what a telegram was, who can burble infinite words around the world for free (= our relationship, haha.) However, it's a style tip I admire even if I don't always follow it.

Elsa's birthday has been a bit of a washout, with persistent grey rain from the moment we woke up. However, we made a fuss of her and she enjoyed opening the presents: we got her a small pink scooter that she's just starting to learn to balance on, J's parents got her a posh teddy bear and we also got her a very pretty dress. She'll have another little birthday party when we're back in London so I'll do the cake and candles etc. then.

Have to go now, sorry. Am thinking of you lots.

Bee XXX

31.05.08

Depressing TV

Dearest friend

I just had to write to you and tell you. At this very minute Ali and I are in tears because of what we saw on TV. You just can't imagine what is happening to Iraqis abroad. Just five minutes ago they showed a former Iraqi officer of high rank. This man is now very sick and needs an operation. He is appealing for people to help cover the expenses of his operation in Syria. His daughters are with his relatives in Baghdad because he can't feed them. The room he lives in with his wife is practically empty. There is nothing in it, Bee, nothing but a thin mattress. There is no carpet, no television, no fridge, nothing. They haven't been able to talk to their daughters over the phone because they haven't enough money, so the TV network gave them credit and the wife called the girls and as soon as one of the little girls picked up the phone the mother burst into heavy sobs and couldn't continue and gave the phone to the father, who in turn burst into tears.

You ask about fear. I've been scared even of my own shadow since 1975 when we moved back to Iraq. I have always tried to be extra nice to everyone, just in case they had connections or might unjustly accuse me of one thing or another. Sometimes I start imagining all kinds of things, and scaring myself to the point of a breakdown. I ask myself – we haven't done anything wrong, so why the fear? I don't know if it will ever leave us.

Oh, I am deeply moved and exhausted by the sights I see on TV. Can't the peoples of the world extend a hand to help end our people's misery? Can't people just go back home and live in peace? Unending misery seems to be everywhere. I was at the market area the other day. It has changed so much. It used to be a posh market that sold only high-quality and expensive imported things. The streets used to be clean and the cars parked at the sides were mostly German and Swedish. Now most of the old shops are either closed or have been sold off. The stalls on the pavements sell cheap glittery things and the sellers are clearly very poor, and quite probably work for richer dealers.

As I walked through the stalls an old man standing by his stall begged me to buy a girl's cream sleeveless dress with a short-sleeved top to go with it. He looked at me so pleadingly and when he said, 'I haven't sold a thing since early morning and maybe my luck will change if you buy from me,' I took it, even though I had nobody to give it to.

As I drove out of the car park with the things in the carrier bags a man in his early forties ran after me asking me to stop (I know it is dangerous nowadays, but I just couldn't help it). He told me that his wife was undergoing an operation to remove a cancerous tumour and he needed help. I gave him some money and he broke into tears saying that he had five girls to look after. I asked him how old his daughters were – he said the eldest was 17 and when I asked about the youngest he said 6, so I pulled the cream dress out and gave it to him. He was so happy and in my heart I felt that all this was planned by God to help this man. I am glad I could help him even a little bit, but I wish I could have done more.

Well, I just wanted to tell you that the problem is not just that of May and Ali, it is the problem of millions of people who just want some space to breathe.

Must go now, love.

MAY XXX

02.06.08

Catch-up

Hello, I'm back. Sad to read your latest emails. Who knows how far and wide the effects of the war will go on? How do you get a civil society back, once it's been blown apart? The feelings of injustice can carry on for generations. It is bleak.

I got your text saying Kate's been in touch about the documentation, so that's good. Can I send any money via Western Union? No doubt it'll cost you to do anything once you're over the border, and I understand you have to pay a considerable sum to the embassy just to make the visa application in the first place. So let me know if there's anything you need.

The holiday was just right, and I'm still basking in the afterglow. It takes a day or two to get into the rhythm of doing things together as a family and getting the pace right, but then it was quite relaxing. Each morning the girls crept downstairs secretly and made their own breakfasts. We did some long walks to beaches and Elsa always insisted on taking off all her clothes and her nappy, then running into the sea (just like her dad – but without the nappy!). My friend Terka came down with her family for a few days, and we went on steam trains and ate crab by the sea. Basically we did everything that you should do on an English holiday, apart from get rained on (the only rain was Elsa's birthday when I wrote you that email from Swanage). The girls scraped their knees, fell in bushes, fell in mud, fell in rock pools and got covered in sand almost every day.

On Sunday we did a little party for Elsa. It wasn't like a usual kids' party with loads of toddlers milling around, as she hasn't really got any friends her own age. It was more like an Elsa Appreciation Society, just a few friends and neighbours all making a fuss of her. We opened champagne that I'd been given when she was born and have been saving ever since (Elsa had a little taste). I'd made a chocolate and cherry cake covered in jam, we sang to her and she blew out her candles very graciously. Eva squeaked out a rendition of 'Happy Birthday to You' on the violin. All very charming.

Feels good to write to you again; I missed you when we were away and kept describing things to you in my head.

Hope you're feeling well.

Love always

Bee XX

02.06.08

Two frights in a row

Dearest

Hope all is well. So nice to know that you're back and I can write and you will see my email the same day, or the next day at the latest.

Today and yesterday were shocking. I received two frights that really upset me. Yesterday morning I was getting ready for work, putting make-up on with probably my sixth cigarette burning away in the ashtray on the dressing table. I heard Ali shouting at me to cover myself, because the army were in the house. So I put on a robe, buttoned it up and came downstairs to find the house full of soldiers. There was a raid and search campaign in our area. Some went upstairs and opened the cupboards, looking at our clothes, while another opened the storeroom door. They searched drawers, looked into the kitchen pots and even our unmade bed. Then one of them asked if we had weapons and I said, 'Yes, kitchen knives.' He looked at me, then apologized for the inconvenience, gathered the others and left.

They woke my mother and asked her if she had any weapons. Coincidentally she also said, 'Yes,' and then held her walking stick up for the soldiers to see, telling them that this stick could break bones if needed. They laughed. Can you just imagine? An old woman without her dentures talking about beating the soldiers with a stick! I think a sense of humour is a blessing in these circumstances because it relieves the tension.

The second shock was today, and this really gave me the fright of my life. As I was working at the computer my friend called; we talked about college, the possibility of a pay increase and the department's problems. While I was chattering away Ali called for help and collapsed on the ground. He hadn't fainted; his eyes were open but he wasn't breathing. I ran to the kitchen, brought some sugar and pushed it into his mouth but he remained motionless. I slapped his face hard but he was just like a stone, except with his eyes open. Oh God, I thought he might be paralysed.

I put a long-sleeved shirt on and went outside to call for my mother. She left her pharmacy and came running. She pressed his chest so hard, and he came back to us. Life returned to him just as I was trying to find someone to get him a doctor (as you know, hospitals are out of the question). I gave him orange juice and he recovered fast. My mother says it is psychological, but whatever the reason I was really scared.

The final exams start next Sunday. I have been asked to set three different versions, and a committee will choose the one for the final exam. Even the teachers will not know which one is to be used (this measure is new – I think they are trying to combat corruption).

OK, lovely, I will go now because I am so sleepy. Good night and thank you for your offer of help. I will of course seek your help if I am broke. But for the time being I am OK and managing well.

Hugs

May XXX

03.06.08

RE: Two frights in a row

May! I'm worried about Ali. That attack sounds scary. I've been thinking how hard it will be for him here; it will take a while for you both to feel relaxed but it'll be so much easier for you than for him. But there are loads of Arabic speakers here in the UK and I'm sure he'll make friends after a while. I just wonder about adapting to a whole new culture and all that this entails. I bet you will notice big differences since you were last here, and not just higher prices for ice creams and fish and chips! What are you most looking forward to?

I can't stop thinking about the next stage and how it will all go. But then sometimes I get annoyed with myself for thinking about the future too much. As if life always seems to be focused just around the corner, or perhaps in the middle of next year. It must mean losing something from the present moment. There has to be an ideal ratio of time spent thinking about the past, present and future.

Talking of nostalgia, it's Justin's birthday on the weekend and I've just decided what to get him: I'm going to get the girls' portraits done (photos), wearing these amazing ancient old dresses we found at Justin's dad's. Apparently they were his grandmother's and are hand-made exquisite lacy children's dresses – fragile like cobwebs, should probably be in a museum. It gave me the idea to have their photos done and so we're going this afternoon. I just hope the girls cooperate. They may be able to look like Victorian beauties but their behaviour might not live up to the same standards.

OK, lovely May, have a good one.

Love

Bee XX

05.06.08

Dreams of freedom

Dear Bumbo Bee

I hope you are all well. Ali is fine. I don't really know what it was, but it's gone now. Real Iraqi summer began with the advent of June. It is over 40 degrees centigrade and movement outside the house is an ordeal. The air conditioner in my car doesn't work and can't be fixed. A friend of Ali's broke it by fidgeting with the air vents in the car. The frame slipped inside the duct and fell under the button which changes from heating to cooling, and we are now stuck with hot air. So driving is a very tiring business.

But today was not so tiring because I didn't go to university, and the news items to translate were rather short and easy so I did my share and retired 45 minutes early. We had tea, cream, jam and biscuits and I think I ate more than I really should have, but they tasted lovely and I just couldn't stop until the teapot was empty. I kept pouring tea (no sugar) and eating away at the cream and jam etc.

As for the changes I will find in the UK, I know for certain that they will not be in the things I miss. I miss freedom of movement, expression, freedom to to wear whatever I like, sit on a bench in a park, visit a museum, a cinema probably. But what about smoking? Where can one smoke? Can we smoke in a café or in the park? It worries me to think about having to limit my beloved cigarettes.

I dream of renting a bicycle on a quiet Sunday morning and cycling for as long as I can. Do you know that women never cycle here? It is out of the question and even considered obscene. I used to cycle with my friend Susan McLeod back in the 1970s. We would go from Glasgow to a loch outside the city, passing breweries on the way, and then sit for a while before cycling back. I remember a sign saying 'An Apple A Day Keeps The Doctor Away'. I feel nostalgic for these little freedoms and the blessing of non-interference.

Love you always

May

05.06.08

Filthy cigs

Oh dear, May, you're in for a shock: it's hard to light up anywhere in the UK now. It's been banned from pubs, clubs, workplaces and anywhere serving food. People mostly cluster outside on the streets to do it, even in the rain. I'm sorry to say that I've become one of those censorious types; I scowl at people flicking their ash anywhere near Elsa (in her buggy she's just at cigarette height). It started when I was pregnant and could smell smoke at 50 paces, and I've never liked it since. As a teenager, I sometimes nicked them off people if I was drunk. I never bought my own, and boasted about not being addicted. Looking back, I can see that wasn't especially endearing of me. Justin was a massive smoker for around 20 years (he was renamed Justin Roll-up), but gave up before we met. I promise I'll try to be tolerant of your smoking, though. After all, if anyone deserves to light up, it must be you.

I couldn't believe it when you talked about riding a bike to the loch: May, I think we have done the same bike ride! I did it with my friend Amy; we lived near Maryhill in Glasgow and one evening we rode along the canal to Loch Lomond. We did it on impulse and it wasn't quite as scenic as it could have been. There are bits where you lose the path altogether and have to cycle under dark tunnels with crunchy broken glass, and the canal was full of shopping trolleys and plastic bags. But when you reach Loch Lomond it's peaceful and pure. We had a pint and a bag of chips, then caught the train back home as our bums couldn't take any more. When you're here, shall we do that bike ride again?

It's been a stressy and busy day. Justin's away (can't even remember where, plus we had a big row about his work making us change our holidays repeatedly) and I woke up really tired and only just got everyone ready in the morning. It's like a miracle when they're all fed, with shoes on and bags ready. Elsa is included in this, as she's now officially starting nursery. I'm heartbroken, May! We got there and I sat down to 'observe'. My baby just ran off with the other kids, and did everything they did. The nursery staff sent me out, just to see if she missed me, and she didn't even notice. I'm proud of her, but oh, it hurt to see her running away to a new phase of her life. Normally we are so close up that I touch and smell her all the time. But this was like looking the wrong way through binoculars; she looked so small and remote.

Do you know what I did, May? I bought some ovulation tests to try to get the timing right. You have to wee on them like a pregnancy test, and it tells you if there's a hormone surge indicating ovulation. It makes it seem a bit mechanical, if I'm honest. I'm feeling ambivalent about that whole plan at the moment. Partly I feel the loss of Baby Elsa becoming Child Elsa, but then I think of Justin being away at weekends and during our holidays, and what it's like getting three of them ready for school. When it was just the two of them, Eva and Zola used to take it in turns to cry. But now there's three, sometimes they all go at it at once and I feel like I'm going mad.

Love you loads

Bee XXX

06.06.08

Countdown and teddy bear

Dearest Bee

Things are moving. Kate is such a great person. She is very efficient and I think she is absolutely fantastic.

It seems that the countdown has started, but we still don't know how to get out of the country. The only easy route is through Syria, but that's no good because we can't get a UK visa from there. I am waiting for the letters to arrive so I can photocopy them and attach the Jordanian visa application, though it is not guaranteed that they will let us in. There is also another option, and that is to go to Syria and then try to get a visa for Lebanon or Jordan through their embassies there, but I don't have a clue whether it will be successful. So I am just keeping my fingers crossed.

I haven't told a soul at university about my plans. Final exams start on Sunday and we have to go in every day. They say that if we don't attend every single day, we will only get half our normal salary. I will of course be going (I hope). On Sunday I'm supposed to receive the letter of support from the college to the Syrian and Jordanian embassies to say that I am still a member of staff.

I am so happy for Elsa. She is moving towards childhood. It is so nice. She will soon have her own circle of friends, and before we know it she will be a young woman dating and dancing and going to college etc. I saw a big pink teddy and I want to buy it for her, but I still don't know if I'll be able to take it when we leave. Maybe I can send it by FedEx, which I heard about recently from Kate (I never knew we had such a service here). If the letters arrive safely then I will be sending Teddy with them.

Oh, I forgot to tell you we almost got burned down last night. I usually boil the drinking water, using an electric kettle. With the power shortage I decided to boil our water on the gas cooker. The first amount boiled perfectly, and I stood there admiring the kettle and thinking what a great housewife I am for having kept it so shiny. I filled it the second time and put it on the cooker, but then forgot all about it and went to bed. I was woken at 2 a.m. by Ali screaming that I had almost burned the house down. I tried cleaning it today but the stainless steel was black.

By the way, I'd love to cycle with you anywhere. But I don't know if I can, because I haven't ridden a bicycle for 20 years.

Love to you and all the family

May XXX

09.06.08

Frowning mood

May. Sorry about your kettle, but glad it didn't burn the place down. I'm in a strange bad mood and I don't know why. It's not PMT. I feel really restless and anxious and am constantly in a mood with Justin. Partly it's his work – last month he was away for three weekends, and this month it is another three weekends – I never know if he'll be there or not. He'll pop up in the middle of a day unexpectedly and say, 'Look, here I am, I get loads of time off!' But that's not the same. Perhaps secretly I'm jealous that he drifts about like a free spirit. Also, I'm worried about my work as I haven't done any shifts for ages; there's just no work about and that makes me edgy.

Do we know yet which is better between Jordan and Lebanon? Such a pity you can't just make the application from within Iraq; it's yet more hassle, having to do it all in a third country.

I got to nursery today and Elsa was mixing some Rice Krispie cakes, and looking so at home. She had on a yellow dress and purple socks, with her fuzzy blonde hair all ringlety. She is like a little duckling. But more assertive: she punched me when I picked her up for a cuddle. Think I embarrassed her in front of her new friends. I'm just consumed with love for her at the moment in almost a jealous way; I'm sure that's not good.

My mind keeps jumping around from one thing to another, and this is a rubbish letter because of my weird mood.

I'll try to be cheerier in my next email.

Hugs

Bee XXX

Wooooooooooow can't believe it

Hi there, love

I just got an email from CARA telling me the documents are on their way . . . Oh BEEEEEEEE, I can't believe it.

You are not on your own. I am also in a terrible mood. I feel as if I am trying to squeeze myself out of a bottleneck. It happens, lovely Sis. Don't give it much thought. It is natural that when one thing goes wrong, other things tend to follow suit. Bad things seem rather contagious, but really it's the bad mood that reinforces a negative attitude to things (rubbish talk, isn't it?).

We are in the middle of the final exams. A new dean has been appointed recently and the man has come with a lot of zeal. I don't really know much about him, but I have noticed a couple of things that indicate his intention to make a difference at the college.

The first thing I noticed was that he tried to recover part of the long-lost dignity of the teachers. For the past five years payday has been a very tiresome event. No matter what title one held, we all had to stand in a queue and wait for an hour, or maybe two, to get our salary. This was not the case before the invasion, but that is how it is now.

By the way, we have two queues in Iraq – one for men and the other for women – so if you are number 7 in the women's queue then this means you have at least 14 people before you, in addition to those who push in because they occupy prominent posts or are friends with the accountant or just pure insolent.

The second thing he ordered was to install air conditioners in the classrooms where the final examinations are taking place. This is a great improvement, because you can't imagine how much students and teachers suffer from the heat during the exams. I remember when I was a student, I used to feel drops of sweat running down each side of my face, uniting at my chin and dropping down on to the answer sheet. So let's hope the dean can maintain his zeal.

I did not work on my translations this afternoon because of the very bad mood I was in. I had a series of rows with Ali and my mother. They just don't understand that I need to concentrate when I'm working. I hate being disturbed and called to see this or that, or to give my opinion on something. They even ask me to make them tea while I am working. Anyway, I screamed my head off and had a huge fit of tears. But it was effective because I am now writing to you with Ali sitting watching TV very quietly, the sound low, and all is perfectly harmonious.

I wonder why I had to make such a fuss to get this?

Hope your mood is better now.

May XXXX

10.06.08

Chirpy

Hello, love

Got myself out of that wretched mood, although it was a bad idea to watch the news last night. Everything disturbed me, from starving children covered in flies (STILL – how can this go on?) to dead dolphins and a badly researched item on kidnapping in Colombia. Well, I suppose it's good that I'm not doing any news shifts if everything makes me cry.

You and I were in a bad mood at the same time and had annoying husbands at the same time: you just have to laugh! I can't believe Ali asks you for tea when you're working. Wait till you hear this: on Sunday we'd had a lovely barbecue with the girls and it was sunny, everyone was happy. Then Justin asked me where his new CDs were. I was loading the dishwasher and said I didn't know. He asked again and told me to think about it; I said I still didn't know. He asked me twice more where they were, and I said I really didn't know, and to stop nagging me about it. He insisted: 'Well, just TRY to think where they might be!' I began to get really angry; I've got quite a short fuse and I didn't want to spoil everything by becoming a shrieking harridan. I stormed upstairs to start the girls' bath. He followed me and ASKED ME AGAIN if I REALLY didn't know where his CDs were. I stomped off to put Elsa to bed, ignoring him. He bathed the girls, and was putting them to bed when I came back downstairs.

Out of passing curiosity I looked at the heap of CDs that are always next to our stereo. There they were. He hadn't actually looked for them. When he came down I demanded to know why he hadn't looked for them himself. He often asks me where things are and goes mad, accusing me of throwing stuff away, only to find it in his paperwork heap later. I said, 'It's not the first time you've done this.' He smirked, saying, 'No, and it probably won't be the last.' Well, that was it! I flew out of the house, slamming the door as hard as I could, and went for a bike ride up by Kenwood House at the top of the Heath. Came back a bit calmer, but not completely calm.

HURRAY for your new dean. It's a mark of a country with a great cultural heritage if it respects its academics. God knows they don't get paid enough, so at the very least they should be held in high esteem. Just a few details like that can make people feel more valued; even without a pay rise it can 'buy' people's workplace satisfaction.

Elsa has started saying a few words: Mummy, Daddy, Era, Lolo (Eva and Zola), yes, no, mine, bee (for bees, flies, anything flying), boo (poo), Lo! (hello) and beez (please). She's also started flying into a rage if you thwart her. I had the cheek to cut her toast in two when we were on the Heath, and she cried as though I'd just pinched her really hard. Tears fell on to the front of her dress making large wet patches, and she sank down in despair. Luckily it blew over quickly; I was getting a bit annoyed by the sympathetic glances she was garnering. It brings a whole new level of drama into her life. She has a bit of a scream at bedtime now too. She used to nicely kiss everyone and say, 'Bye-bye,' but now she must have realized that the girls are still up doing stuff, and she's missing out.

Guess what, the girls both got replies from their letters to the Queen and the Prime Minister! Or rather, replies on their behalves – but even so, I was glad. The Queen's Lady-in-Waiting assured Eva that Her Majesty was delighted to hear about her chilli plant and her sisters, and Gordon Brown's representative thanked Zola for raising her concerns about traffic and added how much he values hearing from young people. They took the letters into school.

Take care, and write soon.

Bee XX

16.06.08

Headphones/a week's email

Dearest Bee

I am exhausted from cleaning. We are still getting the successive sandstorms that have been blowing every other day, or at least twice a week, varying from mild to fierce.

I have to set and mark the final examinations. I am dreading the thing, but I guess it is a must. As for my request to take a one-year sabbatical, I was told that the assistant dean did not approve, so I went to see him myself and then went and introduced myself to the new dean. The man was very kind and told me that if the sabbatical is part of my entitlement as a university teacher, he doesn't mind granting it. The request now has to go to the president of the university and it will take around two weeks.

Sunday. Finished marking papers. The dean has changed his mind and decided not to grant me a sabbatical after all. I guess all the boats will have to be burned. Just as well these harassments are taking place, so there will be no regrets. They tell me that someone has convinced him not to accept my request.

Monday. I just miss you so much and miss the lively emails you send. As you know, I have applied for the Jordanian visa and hopefully they will let us through, otherwise Lebanon will have to be plan B.

A funny thing took place during the exams. We were informed that some students were cheating by wearing headphones under their head covers and connecting them to their mobile phones. The head of department asked me to check the students' ears. It was so embarrassing; I had to stand in front of everyone and apologize, then inspect every girl's ears, apologizing once again. The girls who didn't wear head covers started to ask me to check their ears. I laughed out loud and said that their ears were clearly visible and there was no need for that. One student said, 'But we feel left out.' This was on the first day.

Today the head of department asked me to do it again but I refused and said I hated the whole thing, so she went to another examination hall. A male colleague told me that yesterday she asked all the male teachers to leave the room, closed the door and then asked the students to remove their head covers for her to check. Thank God there was no one with headphones among our students.

Hugs

May XX

I'm excited

Well, I'm excited for several reasons:

1) I'm playing some Colombian music loudly and it keeps making me leap up and do a quick dance then carry on with what I'm doing.

2) The oven is full of almond cakes, starting to smell good.

3) My oldest friend, Lucy, is visiting from Leeds, and last night we had a picnic right on top of Primrose Hill with Amy as the sun went down over London. (Lucy left her bag on the bus yesterday and has just gone off to collect it, so I'm sneaking in a quick email!)

4) The cakes are out. They're amazing! I've done one batch plain so I can put icing on them for the kids, and the other batch is grown-up cakes with lightly toasted flaked almonds on top. Oh, heavenly smell!

5) Can't think of a 5) but it's sunny outside and it's a good day, and I hope you're having one too.

Hugs

B XX

PS I can't even talk about the book any more. It's prohibited. I feel sick if anyone asks me about it; the suspense is getting too much.

Today's activities

Dearest Bee

You've been with me all day. I woke up at 6.30 a.m. without a clock and got up from the couch feeling all hot and sweaty. We sleep in the living room now, and Ali has a mattress on the carpet, because it is too hot to sleep upstairs.

Driving to college is something I enjoy most of the time, except when there are bombs or American convoys with their sign 'DEADLY FORCE KEEP AWAY', because I usually listen to the radio. They have all these songs which were popular in the 1980s and 1990s, mostly Lebanese and so optimistic, lively and full of love.

I reached college about 8.45 (the exam was at 9). The woman who cleans the department and makes coffee brought me my coffee, and I smoked a cigarette watching everyone hurrying to the examination hall. I felt so relaxed that I just couldn't be bothered to move before I finished my coffee and cigarette. The woman kept talking about her grandson, who wanted to enlist in one of the security forces, but I couldn't concentrate. I was thinking of you and imagining how we will land at Heathrow and whether you will come to meet us there or not and the girls etc. I noticed that the woman was waiting for the cup, so I gulped down the rest, took my keys and hurried to the exam hall.

It was 9.15 by then, but there were more than enough staff and my late arrival didn't make any difference. We were 5 teachers invigilating 28 students, which is a farce. 'We are not in a prison,' I thought. What was the point of bringing everyone in every day? We talked and gossiped and probably affected the students' concentration. But, guess why? The promised salary increase is already two days late.

The last student handed her notebook in at 11.15. I went to the shop we have at the college, and bought lovely hair things to send for the girls: some are butterflies and others are small teddies and trinkets shaped like feet, and two children's bracelets.

You know, Bee, that we dread having to fly from Baghdad airport. We have heard such nasty stories about people being seized and killed there. Ali is terrified and says he just can't take the risk. The problem with our people is that they seem to seek revenge on anyone, innocent or not. Although there is a clear religious text, which says that 'you must not hold one responsible for the crime of another', they never seem to understand.

I heard something today that may help clarify the picture for you a bit, so you can see how ignorant and misled the militias are. They were talking today about the ruins of Babylon. In the museum we used to have statues from ancient Babylon, some thousands of years old. When the Americans opened the gates of the museum and let the mob in to loot, some of them just didn't know how valuable these things were and looked at the small statues and asked what these dolls were. They smashed them and said it was better to make statues of the present-day clerics instead. IMAGINE! The museum curators tried to stick the pieces back together afterwards, with their tears flowing, but a lot of damage had been done to this irreplaceable heritage. The same applies to libraries and bookshops. These also experienced their share of vandalism. I don't know who and what makes the militias behave like that. They just don't listen to reason; they hate education and knowledge and pose a threat to everything civilized and cultured.

I remember my late husband telling me of a similar incident that took place back in the 1970s. The government established a school in one of the poor areas in Baghdad, and the inauguration was attended by the mayor and some prominent state officials of the time. Towards the end of the ceremony a crowd of residents marched towards the school with stones in their hands and started throwing them, breaking the school windows and shouting, 'We don't want schools. You can't force this on us.' I guess these were the parents of the present militias.

OK, lovely, there is a gorgeous Turkish series on TV so I'll finish off by saying I love you and hope you are feeling much better.

May XXX

20.06.08

Memories

Dearest Bee

I think we will eventually lose our minds. I noticed that while we were watching a film we've seen before, Ali and I had tears streaming down our cheeks. We have become so fragile I don't know what has come over us. But we are very happy because things are moving and we will hopefully be getting out of here in a matter of weeks. Plus my salary has doubled and things have been calm over the past two days.

But there still is something that is troubling me. I haven't talked to Ali about it but I've been turning it over in my mind. Maybe leaving a place and a country we have lived in, and loved, was the hidden reason for our tears. The UK has always been my dream of peaceful living, getting away from all the violence, harassment and annoyance. But aren't we still part of all that? Aren't the people killed over all these years our friends, relatives and fellow citizens?

How I will miss my things. They are not worth much if you add it all up, but they mean a lot to me. I looked at my *Encyclopaedia Britannica*. Oh Bee, I have the 1967 version, which was originally my father's. Every volume has his signature on it. I have cherished it and it has accompanied me throughout the years of my study. I also have a couple of mugs with my name inscribed on them. One was from my late husband while he was in Italy in the late 1970s, and the second is from Ali. There are two bottles among the things that I hold dear. One is 150 years old and belonged to my great-grandfather. The design painted on it has been done with gold water. The second is bohemian crimson and gold, and it belonged to my father. I've just remembered something. During the difficult years of the economic sanctions, previously well-off families tried to ease the economic hardship by selling the antiques inherited from their ancestors. The antiques trade flourished. It was common for the nouveau riche (embargo merchants) to buy portraits of Iraqi Ottoman Empire officials and place them in their homes as their own ancestors. I wonder who will appropriate my simple things if my house is taken over by the future nouveau-riche? Will my father's encyclopedia become somebody else's? But I think such people are never interested in books.

I guess all these things will be part of the past, like everything in this country. If you manage to become invisible and listen to a conversation between any two Iraqis, you will hear a great nostaligia for the past. I've always thought that if a person dwells too much on the past then that person can never move forward, but in this particular case I can't blame them, because the present is much worse.

Would you believe that I wasn't very happy when my salary was doubled? I don't really know why, but the first thing I thought about was that our bellies are being stuffed, while millions are displaced and others are starving. We deserve the pay rise, but others also deserve to live decently. The authorities should regard it as their duty to give all the unfortunate people in this country a decent salary. Oil is our national wealth, which belongs to each and every person holding this country's nationality, so what is the difference between government employees and other Iraqis?

My feelings are not yet clear because everything is still vague, but what I know for a fact is that I can't go on living like this, no matter how dear my career, furniture, books, china and house are to me.

Do write, Bumbo Bee. I miss you.

Love and lots of hugs to you all

May XX

25.06.08

Back again

May, so sorry I've been away for so long. Are you OK? Hope you didn't think I'd forgotten you. Each day flies by more quickly and I feel I'm doing everything at 100 miles an hour. Last week, after two days ill in bed, it was like stepping back into a river with the strong current pulling me along. I had a load of school Summer Fair stuff to chase and catch up on; the girls had class teas and assemblies; Elsa got ill and has been off nursery; my sister and her boyfriend came to stay; it was Eva's birthday; Justin was working on Sunday AGAIN. Even now I'm in the office but my colleagues are getting their appraisals done, so I'm single-handedly chasing annoying little stories interspersed with big miserable stuff about Zimbabwe.

There was a meeting this afternoon with the head of World Service and he announced the death of yet another language service. This time it was the Romanians. I made my point about losing regional expertise – you never get it back – and he said it's a shame but we have to make savings. I think the best bits of the BBC aren't quantifiable by market forces, because knowledge is priceless. I feel sad; I nearly had tears in my eyes as he rambled on about cost-cutting. World Service is an old-fashioned thing, and no one seems to know what to do with it.

I'm guessing you haven't heard back yet from Jordan about your visa applications. It should be this week, shouldn't it?

Better go.

Love to you, as always

Bee XX

27.06.08

Friday's motto is 'laziness'

Dearest

Thinking of you all the time. I hope you are well. The exams will be over soon. I have also asked for a two-month break from the news agency, starting on 1 July.

Driving to college today was awful. The 10- or 15-minute drive took almost 90 minutes. There was a traffic jam and many of the old cars overheated and made it worse. The reason behind this is that the secondary school examinations have started. There were these huge buses bringing the male students to the university complex (females sit their exams in their local schools). The government have announced that this is for security reasons. It was past 9.30 and the students were still trying to cross the bridge to get to the university complex. They were coming from various suburbs and the outskirts of Baghdad to sit their exams (equivalent to 'A' Levels).

You should see the poor kids, all hot and tired before the exams had even started. Then on the news we heard that another group had been taken to a deserted college, in another area of the capital, only to find that the place wasn't prepared for them. There was no water or electricity. When the minister of education visited them to inspect the process, the students tried to protest BUT his security guards shot at them and the exam was cancelled. CAN YOU BELIEVE THIS?

Laziness is my motto today. I've just washed some dishes, fried ready-made rolls filled with minced meat and vegetables, made salad and then sat and chatted with Ali. The examinations and my second job have made me so tired that I rarely have the energy or am in the mood to exchange ideas and chat with him. This makes him very lonely, and so today is dedicated to him. I am sneaking this email because he is having a nap.

Will make some tea and wake him up.

Hugs to you all

May XX

30.06.08

Some overdue news items!

May, dearest May

Does life get faster and faster? When we're kids we wait for ever for Christmas and birthdays to come. Part of the magic of youth is that constant yearning, and the feeling that life is happening somewhere else or sometime soon. But now it's the opposite; I just try to keep up with it all. (I don't mind much really, apart from when that means doing five laundries having just got back from the Glastonbury Festival last night).

Anyway, to fill you in on news from here: we've just got back from Glastonbury. You'll remember we went last year and it was mired in deep mud, like a scene from the First World War. This time it was sunny. Glastonbury is like a small city spread out over a very English valley. The scale is mad: 135,000 people camp there. Our part was very child-friendly; the kids made a bird box and did yoga. Further afield, a man in very small glittering underpants rode a bike through a sheet of flames. Lots of fat men in tutus looked like they'd been up all night. There were women dressed in Sellotape and sequins, and every kind of music possible. The girls all ran about in complete joy.

I was itching to go off on my own and explore, so after his presentation thing I told Justin I'd be gone for an hour, and left him looking grumpy. Got a beer, found some good music and pushed through the crowds. Suddenly my phone rang: Zola had got lost, could I come to collect her? (The person put her on the phone and she was crying. I'd labelled the kids with my phone number, so of course the call came to me.) By the time I'd sprinted all the way back to the other side of the festival, Justin had already found her and she was OK. But that gave me time to get myself into a state of towering indignation about how women never get a break, and men can make these mistakes because we ALWAYS pick up the slack for them.

I'm not just saying that Justin's selfish or that men are necessarily lazy, it's just that in almost all couples I know who have kids, the woman has the ultimate responsibility. But who is the woman's safety net? Maybe I overreacted because hearing Zola crying got me all upset. I gave Justin a row, then we ate some banana fritters at the Brixton Tea Party tent and everything was OK again.

Well anyway, this week it's the Summer Fair on Saturday and also my father is visiting until tomorrow.

LOVE YOU

Bee XX

02.07.08

Largest available suitcase

Dearest

It was so sweet of Eva and Zola to send some e-cards, we were really overjoyed to see them. I sometimes wish that I had never grown up. Life was so nice and simple. At Eva's age I used to travel in the summer holidays with my grandmother (God bless her soul). She used to wait till my exams were over, and we would go by tourist bus to Lebanon where she owned a small villa in the mountains.

I had friends there who waited for my arrival and we would go roaming around, climbing mountains and picking fruit. She never said no to anything I wanted or any amount of money I asked for. I felt like a princess. She was very religious and this was reflected when I used to fall ill; she would hold my hands and read from the Holy Quran and keep asking if I was any better. I realized how great she was when I finally lost her at the age of 15. All of a sudden I became an ordinary citizen. My mother is not like her. She is a very practical person who has mastered the art of hiding her feelings, and showing the exact opposite.

I don't know why I'm telling you all this. Let me cheer you up a bit. I've bought the largest suitcase to be found in our shops. I've packed our winter clothes in it because of your cold weather. So half the packing is already done. I also need to pack some sheets and towels and put our summer clothes in another suitcase, for Jordan or Lebanon. I've put the car up for sale and a man called this afternoon asking about it. He can't come to our area (he is probably a Shi'ite) so we have to arrange to meet in a neutral place. I will take someone with me because it's not safe to meet someone you don't really know.

You are a busy Bee these days.

Love

May XX

04.07.08

Mad 24 hours

May, I've just had the weirdest experience.

On Wednesday I was riding my bike with Amy to go for a swim, when suddenly my right arm went all floppy. It was a bit disorientating but we went for our swim anyway. It didn't improve, so when I got back I had a hot bath, but it was still floppy like a rubber arm. It was as if it didn't belong to my body and it kept bumping into me. I mentioned it to Justin on the phone and he said I should go to the hospital. I went to Accident and Emergency (A&E) thinking they'd look at me and send me away again. But they kept me in; I was waiting and wondering for hours and hours. They did reflex and nerve tests on me and it became clear that they thought I'd had some kind of stroke, or 'vascular event'.

In the end, they kept me in overnight, but I had to stay in A&E. People were screaming and moaning; the person in the next bed shat himself; there was a guy with a thing stuck up his nose and blood everywhere. Imagine strip lighting, chemical smells, beds on wheels. Patients were hobbling around in those hospital robes which make you look demented. I was fully dressed and compos mentis, and felt like screaming, 'I'm innocent, let me out!' Justin was working late and couldn't get to me until 11 p.m., by which time I was really frightened. He brought me some food and clothes for the night. Thank God I had a book to read, otherwise I'd have gone up the wall (I also used it to hide behind when the neighbouring patients started exchanging illness banter).

After a mostly sleepless night they came and did more tests. The hospital staff were wonderful, and my friend Talia works there and kept popping by. They sent me for an MRI scan of my brain to see if there was a blood clot or 'deviant' vein. I was strapped into a huge machine that made roaring and drilling noises, and was not allowed to move for 30 minutes. I tried to pretend that the noises were music and looked for repetitions in the sequences, then I recited some poetry in my head (thanks to that teacher who made me learn 'Spring and Fall: To a Young Child' off by heart, if she only knew), then I did some yoga breathing and pretended it was a nice excuse for a relaxing lie-down.

Hours passed as I waited in A&E for the results: they said the results would determine whether I'd have to stay another night or go home. I was anxious as I'd previously promised Zola that I'd take her to the cinema to see *Indiana Jones* (Justin had taken Eva on a work trip, and Zo felt left out). As the hours ticked by I got more and more distressed about not getting out of there, and letting Zola down. Finally, at 5 p.m. the results came back clear: no evidence of a blood clot or stroke, so I was allowed to go. But they still want to do more tests on me to find out why it happened.

I RAN home and was there in time to change my smelly hospital-y clothes and squirt on some perfume. I swept Zola up, we walked in the light rain and I marvelled at everything, sniffing the fresh air and dripping leaves and clean sky as though I'd just been let out of prison – after only 24 hours 'inside'! The precious, ordinary world was there all along.

Aren't bodies mysterious, all the things that are happening inside that you never think of? Really there is so much to be grateful for in any given moment. Hope I haven't worried you with my mad story; I'm sure I'll be fine now. They've asked me to take aspirin, and my arm stopped being floppy yesterday.

All my love

Bee XX

04.07.08

Slower pace

Oh dear, lovely sister

I never thought that I had so much love for you inside. I just never realized how strongly attached I've become to you. Reading your email had me in tears. I got so worried. I also had a strange feeling yesterday (which I kept dismissing) that something was not quite right. I kept opening and closing my email, and I so wanted to send you a message, but I kept telling myself that I was just being selfish and you were really busy.

Thank God you are OK now. I do think you have to slow down a bit. The beauty of life cannot really be captured without moving at a slower pace. There is always tomorrow to catch up and do things that need to be done.

Lovely Bee, I just don't know what to say in this particular case. I am at a loss for words, which is rather unusual.

Ali is also very sad and asks you to take care of yourself.

Love you always.

Hugs

MAY XX

11.07.08

Finally about to slow down

May, I'm back at last.

The Summer Fair was good. It rained in the morning, and fewer people came along, but in the end we made £3,500, which is more than I expected. Running the PA is all over now – it's someone else's two-year nightmare! You can feel glad now that you will never, ever get an email from me about school fairs again.

My mum was down for a visit and she came with me to the hospital for my next tests. They still don't know why my arm went floppy. They scanned my neck and took loads of blood. The nurse looked at my notes and said, 'Oh, we're going to leave you dried out, my dear.' After some lunch my mum and I went into town, but it was rainy and Oxford Street was a spiky mass of jostling umbrellas. That was a daft thing to do.

Very nervously I gave my mum the printout of our book so far. She read the whole thing and didn't seem to mind anything in it; in fact she kept laughing and exclaiming over parts of it. I found that reassuring. She left yesterday and I was sad; she enjoys the kids so much and it helped me to think about slowing down. For example, we collected Elsa from nursery and usually I'm hurrying her along exasperatedly, saying, 'Come on, come on!' But my mum was popping out from behind trees at Elsa and chasing her around lamp posts, both of them screaming with laughter. It took ages to get home, but it was so sweet.

All my love

Bee XXX

49-year-old toddler

Dearest Bee

Today I discovered that I am a 48.8-year-old baby. Or 'toddler' is more correct, I suppose (I can't bring myself to say 49). I will be competing with Elsa next thing I know. This afternoon Ali, seeing me so exhausted, asked me to lie down and close my eyes, and so I did. He started stroking my hair and singing nursery tunes but altering words to include my name. Then he started telling me a story about Father Christmas and how he came and took May on a ride with his sleigh and reindeer to the moon. Imagine, I really enjoyed the songs and found myself crying without even realizing it. After that I felt much better. Am I retreating to childhood? I don't know, but I felt good. So maybe Elsa and I will be attending nursery together when I get to the UK (hehee).

My editor at the news agency called and we agreed that my unpaid leave starts 16 July and runs till 1 Sept. If all goes well, we will be leaving before the end of this month, but I still have to be a bit cautious, as life has taught me to be.

Love you always

May

Lullaby

Hello, toddler. You and Elsa will have a fantastic time at nursery together! Dear Ali, that is lovely. I think he realized that you have been doing everything, and needed looking after for a change. You are lucky. In both our lives we need to slow down a little, take care and not get stressed about things. That's become very clear during the last week.

Rest assured that when you are in Jordan we will be right on your case; I will be calling you, and calling Kate too to see if she can get any extra information. I have no intention of letting this slip away from us, May. I don't want it to be like when you were in Damascus. I'm ashamed to admit that when you were in Damascus there was a stage when I just panicked and thought, 'Oh God, what have I got myself into? I can't help any more than this and it's an unwinnable situation.' I felt trapped. That's not your fault, May. You didn't do anything wrong; it was just my reaction. But this time will be different. I don't want you to feel vulnerable and cut off. We'll do the job properly.

Last night an odd thing happened. We'd put the girls to bed and they were writing in their notepads with pencils, in bed. As I tucked them in, I took their notepads and put a kiss mark on each, (I was wearing lipstick). They liked it and were amazed, as if I'd done a magic trick. Anyway, 20 minutes later there was a quiet tap on the door. I put on my cross face and said, 'WHAT?' And in crept the girls, both in tears, saying the lipstick print had made them think about how one day I'm going to die. I promised them I wouldn't die for ages: they'd be old ladies and probably sick of me by then (trying to make light of it) but they were still upset. Zola said, 'But everyone dies.' I put them to bed again and sang the 'Train Whistle Blowing' lullaby that they love.

The song brings a lump to my throat when I sing it to them. Like Ali's, it has a bit where I change the words to include their names (Scrappy is what we called Elsa when she was a bump).

Train whistle blowing, makes a sleepy noise,
Underneath their blankets go all the girls and boys.
Eva's at the engine, Zola rings the bell,
Scrappy swings the lantern, to show that all is well.

Rocking, rolling, riding, out along the bay,
All bound for Morningtown, many miles away.

Maybe it is raining, where our train will ride
But all the little passengers are snug and warm inside.
Somewhere there is sunshine, somewhere there is day,
Somewhere there is Morningtown, many miles away.

Rocking, rolling, riding, out along the bay,
All bound for Morningtown, many miles away.

Oh May, in the middle of writing that, it has made me think of you and Ali on your journey. My tears came plopping down on to the keyboard and I'm quite overcome.

I definitely have PMT.

I miss you.

B X

PS A naughty thing: Justin and I are having a weekend in NEW YORK! He suggested it because he's doing some filming, so his flight and hotel are covered, and I can just pay for a flight to join him for two days. New York is the best and most exciting city in the world and I can't wait.

21.07.08

Back from the Big Apple

MAY, hello there, how are you?

I missed the girls horribly when we were in New York. I kept noticing other people's children and getting a heavy feeling in my heart. Justin is still out there filming until Thursday. When I came through customs and out into the arrivals area, I couldn't stop thinking about you and Ali making the exact same journey.

New York was amazing, but I knew it would be. We didn't stop for a moment; you have to just drink in the excitement and the atmosphere at every turn. We ranged from the posh Upper East Side, the Met, and the newly returned Klimt portrait of Adele Bloch-Bauer (a blast of nostalgia from the early days with Justin when we went to Vienna) right down to Coney Island and the seaside fairground that hosts the world hot dog eating championships.

We ate a lot, but American portions are so grotesque that, greedy as we are, we were completely defeated and never once made it as far as dessert. The worst offender was a towering order of 'Deep-Fried Popcorn Prawns'.

Write soon.

Jetlagged hugs

B X

22.07.08

Sudden move!

May! Oh my goodness. What are you doing? You've just sent a text saying: 'We're flying to Beirut on Sunday. I'm fed up of waiting.' I was shocked and contacted Kate on her holidays to find out if this is the best way. I feel a bolt of nerves, or a kind of electricity, in my stomach. It's put us in a bit of a panic about what is going on.

B x

What's going on?

May, May, where are you now? After that flurry of texts, it's gone quiet at your end and I don't know what's going on, but I have a feeling you're going a bit nuts with all this waiting. It has, after all, taken years to get to this point. I understand that you are on leave from the translating job and the university is on holiday, so you don't want to waste this time. But I think you have to do what Kate says, as she's managed many cases like yours and I trust her.

Thinking back, the contrast between our lives could not be much starker than me swanning off to New York on a whim last week, just flying in there with no visa worries, for pure fun. Did you think that? Don't you resent it at times? I wouldn't blame you. I tell you about pleasures like the holiday in NY, in the knowledge that on the one hand it may cheer you up, but on the other it's like flaunting a freedom that you cannot enjoy, just because of where you were born. It is the wild lottery of nationality.

When we meet, I wonder what it'll be like. I'm a very transparent person, very open, and I can be argumentative and indiscreet. I know that you are much more private than me and reserved. You've told me yourself that if something offends you, you keep it all inside. I hope you will feel that you can tell me anything.

I'm very sleepy; it's humid and my eyes are itchy. Yesterday loads of flying ants took over the world; they were everywhere, horrible clumsy big ones bumping into each other and landing everywhere.

I wonder how they all do it on the same day. School has finished today, and they've all gone off to the paddling pool.

Have you had any rest yet?

Have to go now.

Bee XX

23.07.08

Did I mess up?

Dearest Bee

Oh, I think I've messed it all up. The visa people said we must wait two more weeks to hear whether we are allowed into Jordan, and there is a possibility that we may be refused because only 50 per cent of Iraqis who apply are accepted. So I panicked and thought we could try Beirut instead. I emailed Kate before I even sent you the text message, and waited. Since I got no response from anyone I thought it was quite alright to go to Beirut, and went ahead with the rest of the arrangements. I've paid for the tickets and hotel reservation for three days, sold the car and transferred the ownership to the buyer. Bee, what happens NOW? (Baghdad without a car is miserable.)

Don't think it was because of your NY trip. No, Bee, I think you know me by now. I've opened up my heart for you and told you the smallest details of my life so I am not reserved with you. It is really the time factor, and the hot prison we live in, that made me panic.

SHOULD I LOSE THE MONEY AND SIT AND WAIT FOR THE JORDANIAN VISA? OR CAN IT BE DONE FROM BEIRUT?

Waiting very much for your reply

May XXX

28.07.08

Back to 24-hour eating

Dearest Bee

Luckily, we got a refund for the tickets to Beirut and now there is nothing else to do. We are back to the phase of eating all day long. We have breakfast, then Turkish coffee and chocolates, then lunch, then tea with whatever is available, such as cheese and cream and jam or biscuits, then more tea, then fruit, then dinner, then tea, then fruit and so on until we fall asleep from lack of blood to our brains because it has all gone to our stomachs.

Yesterday we sat and watched TV series we have seen many times before. Imagine, I can even say parts of the dialogue before any of the characters do. It's so boring. We tried to amuse ourselves by imagining things and planning mischief (all imaginary of course).

For example, Ali dreamed of an imaginary court for human rights and how he would punish all those who stood against our marriage, sentencing each and every one of them to a hilarious punishment. We spent the whole afternoon joking and laughing like that. Well, I know it is silly but we have to keep our minds busy with some-thing, don't we? I've just finished the tea that precedes dinner and Ali is watching a series about the last king of Egypt, which I liter-ally know by heart, so I thought I would write to you instead and use the blessing of electricity.

I can't move without a car in this boiling weather, so it's best to stay home and shop from the nearby shops.

Will go now, lovely

May XXX

28.07.08

It's me again

Hello again, Bee

I had to tell you what just happened. I just heard banging on the outside gate (we don't have bells because they don't work without electricity) so I looked out of the window and there was a man on a bike. Ali went to see who he was, and he turned out to be the electricity man. He usually comes every two months to read the meter and hand us the electricity bill. We don't have the payment systems you have – things are paid cash, directly to the authorized person. I know this is not a practical way, but it's all we have.

A couple of months ago we received a warning from the electricity company requesting (ironically) an overdue payment. As we had already paid the man who brought the bill, and we have a receipt for the money, I went out and asked, 'How dare you request payment twice while we get no electricity?' The man just shook his head, saying that the other man had disappeared with all the cash he had collected and we simply have to pay again. And there is nothing we can do! The same applies for water bills. All this cash must seem strange to you. Banks are just for depositing money, and many people in Iraq don't even trust them, so they keep their cash at home or buy jewellery for their wives, which they can sell in times of need.

Anyway, I will go again now.

Love

May x

28.07.08

Late afternoon sun coming through the apple tree

Hello, poor bored May (though 24-hour eating is all we did in NYC and it was great, haha). It is a bit like Damascus all over again, isn't it? Please don't despair. I'll talk to Kate soon.

It couldn't be more different at this end. We are going on our summer holiday soon and so I have to get everything done beforehand. God, God, God, I want so much to believe in God so that I can pray for help to get over this last and final hurdle. We just need ONE MORE BIT OF LUCK to be on our side to get you and Ali through.

Our holiday starts very early on Saturday; we're catching an early (= cheap) Eurostar train to Paris and changing to get a train to Germany. We're spending a week in Freiburg. Do you remember my stoical old granny? She had a bad stroke two weeks ago and has been hospitalized. On the phone she sounds very depressed. She is fiercely independent and won't even let anyone else clean her house or help her in any way, so you can see how she would hate being incapacitated. After Germany we're going off to France for a week, sharing a holiday place with some friends.

I'll have my phone with me, so don't worry about me disappearing and losing touch. Hopefully, during this time, you'll both get to Jordan and set things in motion. We just need some movement; like you, I hate this hanging around. But we have to keep in mind the wise words of Kate, who remarked: 'After waiting this long a few more weeks is neither here nor there.' We have to try to be sensible (we're NOT, though, are we?).

Try not to go too mad. Have you dusted down the Snakes and Ladders board yet? Then you know things are really desperate, haha!

All my love and a big hug

B x

07.08.08

Ill-fated

Bee, oh Bee

What can I say? The visa papers have arrived from Jordan. Today is August 7th, but they have been here since the 4th, and no one bothered to tell us. I had called them on the 4th and 5th, but they denied the papers had arrived. Anyway, I went and got them, only to find out that they have written Ali's second name wrong, which means the papers have to go back to Jordan for correction.

I applied for the papers to be corrected, and the man at the document delivery company warned me that it would take at least a month to go and come back. I nearly collapsed. I tried asking him if there was any other way but he said absolutely not. The taxi was waiting for me outside and I was weeping behind my sunglasses. I dreaded reaching home. Ali called while I was on my way back and he sensed that there was something wrong. Finally, I arrived home and we both broke down in tears. Imagine, Bee, after all that waiting and suffering we have been met by this stupid obstacle. We kept looking at one another, tears just flowing.

Can this be true? Ali tells me to go on my own and just get out by myself, but I won't. Nothing in this life is worth us being apart. I am crying right now. Oh Bee, what has happened? Why are we so ill-fated? Do you know what Ali is doing now? He is talking to the visa letter, a mere piece of paper. He is shouting at the man who made this typing error, asking him if has any idea how miserable he has made one particular family by his carelessness, and whether or not he knows that his mistake might even separate this family for God knows how long. I'll go and stop him, and come back to you.

It is so heartbreaking. Ali held on to me like a child sobbing his heart out, asking me not to leave him on his own. This is the first time since we met that I've seen him like this – my poor big baby clutching on to me. Oh, I can't go on – I am in tears myself.

Sorry to disturb your holiday. I hope you don't read my email until you are back.

Love you

May XXX

08.08.08

OH NO!!

Oh May, what else can go wrong? It's just unbelievable. I am so sorry for you both. It's as though a new and unexpected obstacle manages to meet us at every single stage of the process.

I was thinking about you a lot last night, and starting to feel a sense of dread. I knew we were expecting a response any day now, and if you didn't text me it must be bad news. But even with that sense of dread, I wasn't prepared for something so pathetic and unnecessary. I can quite see how you and Ali must feel somehow cursed. BUT, May, I have always thought that a big load of bad luck means that the same amount of good luck is on its way, and so it means that you and Ali are due some really wonderful luck.

It is the last day of our holiday here in Germany and it's been mixed. This is a place of childhood memories for me, and I love to see the girls enjoying all the adventures that I had here when I was little. But it's horrible without Oma; she's still in hospital. We've visited her a few times and the last time I washed her hair and put it in curlers (nervously, I've never done this before). Her left leg is still partly paralysed; she seems to be making some progress, but she's in a wheelchair. It's been a few weeks now but my father hadn't yet spoken to a doctor, so when we were in the hospital I found a doctor to talk to us about how she is doing, how long it might take and so on. Tomorrow we leave for France, the Auvergne region, to share a house for a week with some friends.

OK, MAY, I'd better go now. Please tell me what happens next. Keeping all my fingers crossed.

Love to Ali

LOVE BEE XXXX

10.08.08

Learning more English

Dear Bee

Don't know anything yet about rectifying the spelling mistake, but will tell you as soon as I can.

As part of our renewed hope, mingled with the new obstacles created by the Jordanian clerk, Ali asked me a new question. He asked what the dirtiest English word was. And I was a bit reluctant, but then told him it was the 'F' word. Oh Bee, you should have listened to him practise! He began by repeating the sentences that he learned ages ago: 'Hello, Bee. How are you? I am so happy to meet you.' Then he moved on, saying: 'Bee! F . . . Jordan, F . . . President Bush.' I burst out laughing, telling him that he will be making a great impression. Then he asked if it would be more suitable to say this to Justin, because it was inappropriate to say it in front of a lady?

I just kept laughing and telling him it was bad to say that to anybody, but I was sure they would understand why he was saying it (hehee). I remember when he first learned to say his famous: 'Hi, Bee, how are you? I am so happy to "BEAT" you.' Then it changed to: 'I am so happy to "HEAT" you.' Finally he mastered the correct form: 'I am so happy to meet you.' I thought a bit of humour would ease the tension we are all going through.

OK, love, I will have to go now.

My kisses to you all and a big fat wish for you to have a gorgeous time in France

May XX

12.08.08

Plenty of time to reflect

Dearest Bee

Nothing, so far, about 'name correction'. So apart from eating, I have really plenty of time to fret, worry, curse and become angry, or reflect, just to feel alive. I haven't been out of the house since the day I went to get the visa papers. I feel choked.

I was listening to a popular song that talked about Iraq's plight and the wretched situation we have reached. A sentence starting with 'Before . . .' stopped me (meaning, of course, before the invasion) '. . . we never forgot our dead no matter how many years passed . . . whereas today we bury them in the morning and forget all about them by the afternoon.'

This moved me, and I began to reflect on all the deaths that have taken place and how we feel less and less affected. We used to criticize the West for being so very practical – how they would come back from the burial service and have drinks and a gathering that slowly changes into a party as alcohol begins to take its effect.

Now the traditions here are also changing, though not so dramatically. What the song says is true to some extent.

I've noticed that women no longer wear black for years and years in mourning for their husbands. Back in the 1970s, my mother was regarded as a bit unconventional because she wore black for only THREE years, while some of my uncles' wives never took it off, and others wore it till their elder sons got married. Taking it off is an indication that a new man now runs the household. Now most widows are fairly young, 18–20 (around 1.5 million women have been widowed since the invasion) and I've come to notice that a one-year maximum for wearing black has become very common. I've realized that the continuous wars and countless deaths are behind the changes – and this is true in all societies.

I think it was the First and Second World Wars that caused all the social changes in Europe, and now we are going through the same sort of change. But the difference lies in the terms 'invader' and 'invaded'. I dread the impact on our society because 1.5 million young widows means at least 3 million orphans, with no state to care for them or proper social security and education.

Well, back to the song, which also talks about not being able to distinguish thieves from authority because they intermingle (the song says they wear the same uniforms, hinting at the militias that have joined the government, police and armed forces.) I'll leave you at this point to make some tea. Hope you're enjoying your stay in France.

I miss you, my friend.

Love as always

May XXX

19.08.08

Back to sort-of-normal

May, I'm back.

But it's just that I can hardly bear to write to you. It's not your fault, but the words are too heavy. There's no lightness; I tend to hit a slough like this when we have repeated obstacles and no move-ment. I know I can't cheer you up, and I'm almost certain there's no good news from your end, just more waiting and desperation. I keep thinking that I should write to you, but I find it so hard to do. But anyway, I guess I'll just plod on and tell you the latest from this end, if that's what you want to hear.

We got back from our holidays two days ago. In the end, we had to flee the bad weather in France and return to Germany early. I just couldn't stand for Zola's birthday to be a rainy day stuck inside a cold house. So we drove the six hours back to Freiburg, where it was much warmer and we finally got some sun. Zola's birthday was brilliant. We went to Europa-Park, which is the German answer to Disneyland – only much more charming. Zo went on her first roller coaster. She began by crying with fear then suddenly started laughing halfway round, then declared it to be the best thing she'd ever done. We had hot dogs and a cake with her name on.

Elsa has a new habit: she does a huge loud burp, then looks around, grinning, for everyone's reaction. She did it in a quite elegant restaurant in France; we were surrounded by smartly dressed elderly couples, quietly eating their lunch. Elsa let out a roaring eructation, and there was a moment of hush. A few people looked our way and I can only imagine that they blamed Justin for it, for who would suspect a blonde little angel? Now known as 'Elsa the Belcher'. Eva learned to dive and spent hours diving with Justin. She also went head first down a slide into a swimming pool, and chipped off half of her front tooth – an adult tooth, not one of the baby ones. We'll have to get it fixed. But luckily it didn't hurt her, and though we were shocked we tried to make light of it, saying, 'It's perfect for drinking through a straw.'

It's feeling like autumn today. I'm at work now and just getting ready to leave. It's been quite a busy day and I love it.

How are you?

Hugs

Bee XX

Iraqi corpse obtains visa

Lovely friend

First of all, I am glad that you are back; and second, sorry I am making you feel bad; and third, I hope Oma recovers soon.

I know how you feel about writing. Yes, it is difficult in such circumstances. I've written several emails but didn't send them. I just recorded my feelings. I deleted some, saved others as drafts, then deleted these too. What can I say, and how can I describe it?

Putting it bluntly, I FEEL AWFUL.

I feel that my life is on the verge of collapse. The curtains will finally close on the most beautiful and strangest love story in the Middle East. There is an enormous emotional conflict between my heart and my brain. I usually follow my brain with no trouble at all. I normally cry for a couple of days, take a pill or two, have some extra sleep and then begin again, starting from scratch.

It is very difficult this time. I've been suffering for the past two months. I look at Ali and the tears just roll down my face; I can't seem to curb my emotions. I also catch him crying discreetly sometimes, and when we bring up the subject of having to separate, we just burst into tears. I really don't know what to do. If I wait much longer my visa might expire, and the Jordanians are so unpredictable. If I leave Ali behind, it is too hazardous for him to follow me on his own. I think this Jordanian clerk has destroyed us with his mistake.

I've just heard a heartbreaking story. It made me think again about just how deeply we Iraqis have been degraded by US democracy. We are like human garbage and wait to be accepted, after long delays, into the 'Holy Land of Jordan'.

I was moaning to one of my colleagues about the delays and spelling mistakes that had occurred during the visa process, and how I have reached the point of hating myself and cursing the day I was born. Out of sympathy she told me the most tragic story. She said that a young Iraqi physician, who had graduated top of his class, was threatened with assassination, so his family sent him to work in Libya. This summer he wanted to travel home to see his family during the holidays. This required having to apply for a Jordanian transit visa. After three months of waiting he was refused entry and the poor man had to stay where he was, forgetting all about the family reunion. But it seems that fate had other plans for him, because he was electrocuted and died in an accident. When his family applied for a visa in order to transport the body home for burial in Iraq, Jordan granted the corpse an entry visa without any delay.

Oh Bee, I am exhausted. I think I will wait another one or two days, then decide what to do.

May XXXX

21.08.08

The last day

Dearest Bee

Right. Today is the last day of waiting as, in a matter of hours, we will know if something can be done or not. If not, I think I will have to enter Jordan and wait for Ali there, in case my visa expires. I have to get things moving or else everything we've worked so hard for over the past two years will go down the drain. By Saturday, or Sunday at the latest, I think you will receive better news from my side. Don't worry – I won't let you down, I promise.

I did try to get things moving via Beirut, but you remember how strongly it was recommended that we wait for the Jordanian visa. Well, I can't say any more now, love. See you in another email (hopefully not from here).

Love you always

May

21.08.08

'The darkest hour is before dawn'

We just have to not go mad, that's all we can do. I called Kate yesterday; she was out of the office but I'll try again. I know you must feel that after all this you probably should have gone to Beirut when you had the chance, but let's just keep looking forward. In a way, it's reassuring still to have Beirut as Plan B, if Jordan proves utterly futile.

I feel that it's all going to be OK, you know, May. A great friend of mine said a lovely thing this week. It's my friend Terka, who takes a great interest in you. She's gone back to work after her recent maternity leave and her office is near here, so we met up for lunch. She asked about you and I was all despondent and angry. She said: 'They say the darkest hour is before dawn.' Well, it doesn't get much darker than this, does it, May? So she must have a point. I like to think so. We have to stay positive somehow, May. It's awful when we lose sight of what we're trying to achieve and how far we've come.

Righty-ho. Put a smile on your face and keep on breathing.

Love always

Bee XXX

21.08.08

Expect it to ease

Bee

Fate seems to be playing around with me. No news, so I decided to go to Jordan and try to speed up Ali's papers myself. Well, just listen to the outcome of my decision. I phoned the travel agency, wanting to book a flight on Saturday. Apparently all flights are full for Saturday, so Sunday's flights have been cancelled and pushed to Monday. This means Monday is already fully booked and I have to wait till Tuesday. CAN YOU BELIEVE THIS??

You are saying that we should try not to go mad. Well, I agree with you, but HOW can I stay sane with all this bloody madness? Anyway, I called Ban, my friend in Jordan who is working on speeding up Ali's papers, because I had also asked her to rent a small flat or a bedsit (prices have soared in Amman). I told her that I won't be arriving on Saturday or Sunday as planned. She was very kind and said: 'Let's just hope that Ali's papers will be ready by then.'

Oh, another thing, Jordan does not let you enter unless you have booked a return ticket, which means double the price – and no refund if you do not return.

I will try not to go mad for as long as I possibly can. Ali of course has already crossed the insanity bridge (hehee) and I only need a little longer, and one more single provocation, to enter the mental institution myself.

Well, lovely, that's all I have. Thank you for the comforting words; you really made my day. I am glad that you are back at work.

Love you always

May XXX

25.08.08

A madwoman

Dearest Bee

It has been more than 10 days since I first contacted my dear friend Ban. We call her at least twice a day, as if waiting for her to perform a miracle. The poor soul puts up with us, comforts us and asks us to be a bit more patient. I called her last thing yesterday afternoon, asking her if I should pay for the plane ticket, and she advised me to go ahead and make the booking, leaving Ali to follow on. I went to the travel agency to pay for the flight. The whole office now knows me by first name, and each and every one of them greeted me as I went in. I asked the man in charge what I should do, and he recommended that I take the risk and go by land to the border, together with Ali, and try to explain the issue to the officers there. He said it all depended on our powers of persuasion. I called Ali there and then, discussed it with him, and Ali agreed. I made reservations for the two of us by car for today, paid half the price and then bought some medicines we need on the way back home.

As I arrived at the house, Ban called and said that she has found someone at TNT Jordan (the company in charge of delivering the visa applications and the corrected papers). The man told her that the correction has been done and should have been sent. This news turned the plan upside down. We didn't know what to do. TNT Baghdad, on the other hand, denied receiving any papers. One of the TNT offices is not telling the truth, and unsurprisingly my suspicions are directed at the Baghdad branch.

Ban told us to postpone our departure till Thursday, and so I phoned the travel agency again and rearranged everything.

I will go now, my lovely. Say hello to all the family.

Hugs

May XXXX

25.08.08

Yorkshire hello

May, what does it all now mean? Will you fly to Jordan alone and try to sort it out, or will you both go by car to the border and try to explain? What does it depend on? I'm totally confused. Please don't cross over the bridge into lunacy; we need you to maintain a shred of sanity for just a while longer (but when you get to England you can be as mad as you like, haha). Keep in mind Terka's words about the darkest hour.

I'm at my mum's, which is heavenly. We came up on Friday afternoon; the girls were really good on the train. My mum collected us and the girls went into a whirlwind of shrieky joy to be here. They just run off down the garden laughing and screaming. The garden is all bushy and overgrown after all this rain and so you can hide away and make dens and pop out suddenly and eat plums and catch frogs. Zola fell in the pond but only got her legs wet.

Instead of trying to get anything done I have tried to do as little as possible. I finished *Middlemarch* (it's taken me all summer – it's huge and got better and better as I turned each page, so I was gripped late last night in bed waiting to see what would become of the heroine). And my mum has taught the girls to knit with some kids' knitting needles; there was a charming Victorian vignette where all four of us were knitting away. We were like a three-generational illustration of modest feminine virtue, or some such antiquity. Elsa mostly tags along with the bigger two but they have so much more freedom here; they go off on their own and even go out on their bikes.

OK, May, just a quick hello and I really, really hope things move soon.

Anything is better than being stuck.

Tell me what's happening.

Love from us all

B XX

27.08.09

On my way!

Dearest Bee

By the time you read this email, I should be on my way to the border on my own. I've decided to follow up Ali's papers from Jordan. I can't describe the tears and the heartbreaking look on Ali's face as I left. He was almost hysterical. He would turn away, then start sobbing and turn back to hug me. I tried my best not to show him how upset I was, but I couldn't help it and I started to cry involuntarily. I felt like I was going to die.

Anyway, these things must be done and someone has to take the initiative. May God never forgive the clerk responsible for the spelling mistake in Ali's visa and the Jordanians for their heartlessness and the invasion for causing all this . . .

Wish me luck, Sis.

May XXXXX

29.08.08

You're OUT!

MAY, when I got your text yesterday my heart beat faster. You're over the border and inside Jordan! How did you do it? I guess you explained at the border what is happening and they let you in, after all that. The feeling that something is finally moving makes me feel nervous and want to do something, but there's nothing I can do.

Over the last few weeks every time I thought of you I knew exactly where you were (at home with Ali) and what you were doing (both going mental) so there was a certainty in one way, though a horrible one.

But now you are out there, setting off like the youngest son in those Grimms' fairy tales, who goes off alone to try to save his family. I don't know who you're talking to or what you're actually doing. I just hope my weird theory of loads of bad luck meaning that good luck is just around the corner will prove true this time. Can I make any calls to Jordan or do anything to add pressure or help in any way?

Right now, it's the last day of our holidays. We're going out to take the girls pony-riding in about 10 minutes and it's a perfect sunny day with buttery late-summer sunshine. All the gentle sounds of the English countryside are around us: the distant bark of a dog, a lazy aeroplane sound, birdsong. It's most civilized and it's really been a perfect holiday for relaxing and just being happy.

Have to catch the 2 p.m. train back down to London and then it'll be back into the onward spin of catching up with life.

Let me know what happens. I really can't believe you're out of there. Oh please, please let it just WORK this time . . .

All my love and wishes

Bee XXXX

30.08.08

Quite an adventure

Dearest Bee, oh Bee . . .

It was quite an adventure. I will start from the very beginning. Tears of course and heartbreaking scenes and a sleepless night. Ali and I suffered quite a lot and feared that we might not see each other again, but I put on a brave face.

The taxi driver collected me at the crack of dawn, just after 5 a.m. I reached the travel agency around 5.30 and was greeted by a very nice person. I was surprised to discover that travel agencies co-operate with each other and exchange passengers, and so I was passed to another agency. The driver was old and grumpy and objected to my luggage, saying that he'd never seen such a large suitcase. Then he told me to empty some of its contents and leave them at the agency for my family to pick up. I screamed that I did not have a family and I would NOT empty my suitcase and he would have to put up with it or I wouldn't travel with him. The nice man at the original agency explained to him that I might be going for quite a long time, and the driver grumbled and accepted it but with very bad grace. There isn't really a big choice of drivers going to Jordan. I found out later that only 20 to 30 drivers in the whole country are allowed over the border into Jordan.

Before we set off he told us that if we carried any credentials dated post-2003, we'd better get out now, because Jordan won't accept them. Thank God I didn't change mine after we got married, because that would have presented another problem. Then he said that any documents belonging to other people, even if they were only photocopies, were not allowed, so I had to tear up Ali's photo-copied passport and other papers.

The journey was awful because there was a state of emergency. I had heard a vast explosion at 5 a.m. just before I left the house, and that must have been the cause. Then the awful driver didn't turn on the air conditioning until around 10 o'clock and I boiled from the heat. I sat next to a woman with her 13-year-old boy wearing safari shorts and a T-shirt, and a cap hiding his hair. The boy looked as normal as any boy his age.

To break the silence and to pass the time I started a chat with the mother. She told me she was going to Jordan for her son's surgery, and that he was already late because of the visa measures. The boy should have been operated on in April. Then she told me the boy's horrifying story. He had been in the car with his father when an exchange of fire broke out between the army and the National Guard on one side, and the armed militias on the other. She said that a bullet had penetrated the rear window and then the front seat, piercing the boy's skull and finally landing in the glove compartment of the car. As a result the boy's brain was exposed, and he was subsequently operated on several times. And now it was time for more surgery. She took the cap off the boy's head and I saw the most horrifying sight of my life. The boy's head was completely deformed.

Will write to you again to complete the story of how I managed to cross the border. Just wish me and Ali luck.

May XXXX

31.08.08

The frightful journey, continued

Dearest friend

I hope this email finds you well. A lot of things have happened; there has been such a complete change of environment and my newfound freedom is indescribable. I wear my denim jeans and walk endlessly and aimlessly through the streets of Amman, just trying to get my mind adjusted. The only problem is that there are no internet cafés locally and I have to go quite a distance to find one.

Sorry I couldn't finish the story yesterday. I had a lot of emails to send plus Ali was on the messenger with me (driving me crazy because I have to type in Arabic and I am not used to that).

My mother is taking care of Ali 'in her own way', and driving him crazy. He kept moaning about that. I know she means well, but her good intentions are getting on his nerves. He says she woke him up twice, just to check on him, bringing tea and cakes. But, well, that is my mum.

Let me tell you about the journey. As we arrived at the Jordanian border we were stopped at the first checkpoint. We had to take our luggage out of the car, and of course my HUGE suitcase. At this point I began to realize what had bothered the driver and why he'd been grumbling all the way. I also had two briefcases – one for documents and one with photos and photo albums. They searched them all, going through every single photograph and asking who the people in them were. I was extremely patient, fearing that they might just ban me from entering their country. Then I heard them murmur something, and when I looked they were examining an old photo of me in a bathing suit. I cursed Ali for putting it in with the rest. They used a knife to pierce the carrier bag holding Elsa's teddy and the girls' handbags.

After that we moved on to another checkpoint. They repeated the process, searched the luggage more thoroughly and sent the car to be X-rayed. An old blind woman who was with us was returned to Baghdad for holding a nationality card that was dated post-2003, despite her valid passport.

Then came the body search and the scrutiny of our personal belongings. We were directed to a bungalow where two women searched us and read every single bit of paper. I didn't know it would be that bad or I would have emptied unnecessary rubbish out of my handbag. There were all sorts of papers, phone numbers, students' marks, exam postponement requests, make-up, a perfume bottle, cigarettes etc. They opened the cigarette packs, broke one from each just to check, put on some of my perfume.

The worst part was when one of the women looked into the case of my reading glasses where my devoted Shi'ite friend had left a note for me after I was shot at last year. She said it would protect me from all kinds of evil, and I have kept it there ever since. The woman's face changed and she eyed me up and asked if I was a Shi'ite. I realized that my entry into Jordan was at stake. I pretended to be horrified, and asked, 'Have you ever heard of Shi'ites in

Salah-al-Din province?' She asked which part I was from, and the astonishing thing is that I answered quite fluently that I was from the heart of the province. And for the first time in my life I felt perfectly relaxed about lying. She let me go after a quick body search, but took away the piece of paper.

The fourth checkpoint was just as complicated. They searched and X-rayed the luggage, and sent us for another search. Two women repeated the whole process, but this time the briefcase was searched in minute detail. Every single piece of paper was read, if it was in Arabic, and examined, if it was in English. They sent my perfume and make-up to be X-rayed. I think it is just to make matters as complicated as possible. Then they asked me to take my clothes off. Oh God, Bee, I felt so embarrassed, but I did it. They did not touch me, and told me to put my clothes on again. After that I went back to the X-ray room. There I found my books and dictionaries on display together with my Arabic poetry and newspaper clips of some of my old writings and translations. They also asked about my MP3 player and requested to see its contents. I told them that I did not object, but in the end they left it alone. At this point I heard the first and only apology, from the man doing the X-rays, but I told him it was OK because they were merely doing their job.

The whole process took approximately four hours. After all that we went to the entry office and there was another kind of inspection. This time they asked for birth certificates and national city cards, along with passports. They checked them all. Thank God we didn't change our IDs after Ali and I were married or it would have been a disaster.

AT LAST we entered Jordan. The rest was easy, and I apologized to the driver and forgave him his grumpiness at having me as a passenger. By midnight I had arrived at the apartment rented by Ban. I felt exhausted, nervous but satisfied that at last I had taken the first step of my one-thousand-mile journey.

Will go now, lovely. It's a long way back. Write and tell me what you think.

Love you always

May XXXX

31.08.08

The difference could not be greater

May, I'm startled. It's such a jolt to have emails from you suddenly packed with events and shocking detail. It's as though you have gone from one extreme of experience to another, from near isolation to being shunted around by an assortment of people who all have power over you, one way or another. I don't know how you kept your patience throughout the four-hour search. And I can hardly bear to think about that boy with the damaged head. It's a different experience when I think about you now. I feel scared, but with a ripple of excitement, because you've started the journey.

Well, things over here couldn't be more normal and wholesome – the total opposite of your life. It was a tranquil break up in York and I also got a few runs in. (I'm trying to practise for a Women's 5 km Challenge thing next weekend; I got roped into doing it for a Colombian charity that I support.) I ran with Eva tootling alongside me on her bike asking constant long-winded questions.

Catching the train back from my mum's in York I had to use my steeliest resolve to get us four seats around a table. I tend to ask people to move for us (if they think about it, their alternative is to have my kids crawling all over them, haha), so the table was a life-saver as they could all draw and do writing. Elsa wriggled around on the floor and it all went quiet. Always a suspicious sign. When I looked down she'd found some dusty hairy old Maltesers left on the floor, and had a chocolate-smeared and very happy face. We pulled into King's Cross, all piled on a bus and finally got back home. There was no food in, so I made a load of pancakes and the girls declared I was the Best Mum In The World Ever.

OK, May, please tell me what happens next as I'm really on tenterhooks. Also, I don't actually know what you're doing about Ali. Can you rectify that spelling mistake and then he'll come to join you there, or are you submitting both applications yourself for the UK visas, or what? What is the plan?

Love you, May. Getting closer!

B XX

01.09.08

Ramadan

Dearest Bee

Today is the first day of Ramadan. Funny coincidence that last Ramadan I was in Syria, and this Ramadan in Jordan, while in between stuck in Baghdad. Maybe this month has something special for me. Ali, as you know, is still in Baghdad and I am really worried about him, but what consoles me is that he is fasting (I seem to have been the reason behind the religious neglect that came over him). He phoned this morning asking about recipes and how to make custard, jelly and some other type of sweets. I thought they were too fattening, but I didn't tell him. He can get as fat as he likes if it eases his frustration. I know that overeating is a sign of depression but WHO CAN BLAME AN IRAQI?

I lazed about all morning, then showered and came to the internet café. We have made another request for the correction to be made to Ali's visa, and hope it will speed things up, though I doubt it. I won't be seeing Ban much in Ramadan because it is a family occasion, and on top of that I don't fast and she does. So I will console myself by watching the enormous number of programmes prepared by Arab satellite channels, especially those of Al-Sharqiya because they criticize our government and the present situation in such a clever and hilarious way.

Kate has made it very clear that Ali has to be with me before applying for the UK visa. We have agreed to wait another 10 days for him to get here before giving up all hope of him obtaining the Jordanian visa.

OK, lovely, will have to go now.

Do write soon.

May XXX

02.09.08

A dark horse's memories

Dear Bee

You remember there were things I said I wanted to tell you, but I wasn't ready to talk about them then? Well, now, with the change of atmosphere, my memory seems sharper and I feel that I want to tell you about one of the most interesting encounters in my life, and that is my meeting with Saddam Hussein.

I had arrived back in Iraq after sitting my GCE exams in Glasgow and wanted to apply to university, but to my great shock I discovered how a mistake in filling out a form or a mistaken choice can leave a person stuck for life.

My own misjudgement, combined with family pressure, had persuaded me to study at the College of Science. However, I soon discovered that I wasn't suited to this kind of study, in part because the regime had issued a decree changing the language of scientific studies to Arabic, which I didn't have full command of at the time.

Used to British freedoms, I didn't think changing college was such a big issue. 'I will get a transfer to another college,' I thought. It never really occurred to me that choosing the wrong college was like entering into a Catholic marriage.

I filed a request with the Ministry of Higher Education for a transfer to the College of Arts, to study English. But I was informed that they did not have the authority to transfer a student from a scientific college to one that offered the humanities. Someone then told me to get a medical report saying that it was affecting my mental health, so I did. I tried my best to make it convincing: I gave the wrong answers to the silly questions on the form; I remember writing that TV scared me and I hated watching it. However, my efforts were in vain and it seemed there was no hope.

I learned that it was only Saddam Hussein's authority that could get me the transfer. Young as I was, I thought, 'God, do I need a vice-president to solve the problem?' Being determined, I thought, 'Why not?' Encouraged by his popularity with the Iraqi people at the time, I was convinced that he wouldn't let me down.

I obtained his phone number. It was normal for people to call him if they had a difficult problem – and they usually got what they wanted, no matter how tricky the situation might appear.

After some procrastination on my part, I finally picked up the phone and dialled his number.

'S.H. speaking,' was the answer on the other end.

His powerful masculine voice sent shivers down my spine. I was scared stiff but there was no going back now.

'Sir, this is the citizen M.W.'

'Are you a member of our party?'

'No, sir . . . I mean yes, sir . . . I have just applied to join.'

(Someone had told me to do so to make life easier.)

'Are you married?'

'Yes, sir.'

'Who is your husband?'

'It's F.W., sir. An engineer, sir.'

'Oh you (W's), you always marry relatives and near cousins.'

Knowing that this was not true, I tried to clarify: 'No, sir, not really. We . . .'

'Don't interrupt.'

'But, sir, it was . . .'

'I told you not to interrupt.'

'Sorry, sir.'

'What is your complaint?'

'Sir, it is educational.'

'OK, a date for an interview will be set. You will be contacted.'

He hung up.

I was left in a state of fear and shock. I scolded myself for my bad manners. I should not have interrupted him. But I was only 18 at the time and inexperienced. I just couldn't understand why I had to remain silent in the presence of my superiors if what they said was incorrect.

A few days later I was contacted and informed of the day of the interview. It was a very hot summer afternoon when I was driven to the Information Office at the presidential palace.

The procedures adopted for the meeting may easily be described as a horror film. I was not alone; many other people were also there to meet him on the same afternoon. We were all thoroughly searched. They took away watches, rings, handbags, cigarette boxes and lighters etc. We were then medically examined for skin disease and coughs. We were warned not to stay for more than three minutes and also not to kiss or shake hands with him. At this point I was so scared that I needed to go to the bathroom quite a few times. The guard taking me there did not breathe a word, which made it worse for me.

Saddam read my request, then eyed me from head to toe. Then he repeated his question about why the Witwits marry their relatives. Forgetting all about my previous experience with him, I tried to defend my case again. I was once again scolded and told not to interrupt, so I apologized. Then he looked at me and asked, 'Have you ever heard that I broke the law for any reason?' I politely answered, 'No, sir.'

Realizing that my request had been refused and the three minutes were over, I attempted to get up and take my leave. His voice froze me. 'Already bored?' he asked. 'People dream of meeting me, and you look bored.'

Nothing of the sort had crossed my mind. My expression was one of fear. But I apologized once more and was dismissed. When I got out, it was dawn. My family had been waiting for hours. Disappointed, I resigned myself to accept the fact that I was doomed and that no other university or college would take me in.

A few years later, I found out that I could apply to institutes that did not belong to the Ministry of Higher Education. These were called Training Centres, and students could take a three-year diploma course. This was in the early 1980s. By now, Saddam Hussein had become president and the Iraq–Iran war was raging.

I graduated top of the whole institute with an average of 96 per cent from the Petroleum Training Centre. Happy with my accomplishment, I wanted to continue my studies, but events conspired to prevent that. The top 10 graduates were expected to work for two years in the government services before applying for further study but, although I had graduated top, my name was not put forward for a post. The man in charge of appointing graduates offered me employment in the Beji Refinery. When I reminded him that I had the right to be appointed to government service, the man kept beating around the bush and hinting about a distant relative of my husband's who had been executed on a charge of opposing the regime.

My rebellious nature refused to believe this. My husband was serving at the front and I had worked very hard. I requested a second meeting with Saddam Hussein, and my request was rejected for the second time. At that point I realized that what I had heard from older members of my father's family was true – Saddam Hussein simply disliked our family. I never really found out why. I had kind of liked him, but that was how it went.

What a long email. I must go now, but I thought you might find it interesting.

May x

02.09.08

RE: A dark horse's memories

MAY! You are full of surprises. Of course I noticed that you didn't reply when I asked you to tell me more about meeting Saddam. I thought it made you uncomfortable, and now I see why. What a terrifying experience! It's hard for me to understand the whole cult of personality around this man; here in the UK the public generally loathe politicians, and anyone else in the public eye for that matter. But it makes me feel lucky to have the freedoms that we all take for granted.

Can't write much today as am at work, but will write more when this week's over and the kids are back at school etc.

Love always

B XX

08.09.08

Seems like ages

May, it seems like ages since I wrote but it's been the maddest few days. We had a big party at ours, then the next day was the Women's 5 km Challenge. It was like a student party – but without the cheap cider, haha – everyone was dancing about the place and the garden was full of candles. Some friends played guitar, percussion and accordion. I hardly spoke to anyone much, I was too busy dancing. Someone at the party told us a funny story afterwards; she'd gone upstairs to the toilet and there was a queue of about four people waiting. In the middle of the queue of rowdy partygoers was Zola, standing there all tousled and sleepy in her pyjamas. Apparently she waited her turn as if it was perfectly normal, went to the toilet then back into her room and shut the door without saying a word. (You'd think people would let her go to the front of the queue, seeing as it's her house!)

Only got three hours' sleep that night. Lucy had come down from Leeds for both the party and the run. We ate huge bowls of porridge for breakfast and then got a taxi, leaving Justin with the girls all shuffling through the party detritus of bottles and smelly rubbish. We found our group, registered and went for the warm-up. There were 15,000 women all getting ready to run, many in fancy dress. We took our places and there was an announcer on a massive tannoy saying stuff like, 'Well, fifteen thousand women in Lycra – oh, my dreams have come true!' TV and radio were there, and some Olympic heroines, including Christine Ohuruogu.

It was all buzzing, then after the starting gun was fired a strange quietness suddenly descended. Despite the crowds all around us, all you could hear was a light pattering noise: thousands of feet running. Lucy and I stuck together; at first everyone was overtaking us but at the end we got quicker and when I saw the finishing line I went mad and sprinted flat out with my head flung back. Justin was there with the girls (it was very sweet – being a women's race there were rows and rows of dads holding up cheering kids) and we got given 'goody bags' with a medal, food and drink. Got back home and had to vacuum up the broken glass so the girls could relax. The floor was sticky with bits of salami and stuff, so I mopped it too. By now I was kind of going into a trance of tiredness so I flopped on the sofa and watched some cartoons with the girls.

I can't really remember anything else that I've done, May. I'm still quite sleepy but I have Zola off school with tonsillitis, and now we have to go and get Eva from school. It's hard when one of them is ill but the other full of beans, as you can't really balance their needs. Whatever we do someone will think it's inadequate.

Oh God, Zo is screaming at Elsa and now they're both crying and I'm going to be late for Eva.

Sorry to rush.

Love you XXXXX

PS Still tickled at the thought of Saddam asking whether he was boring you!

09.09.08

Tension by phone

Dearest friend

All the details of the party sound lovely, but too tiring for me. Back in the 1970s I used to entertain and have a social life, but not since then. We actually stopped entertaining in the early 1980s when the Iraq–Iran war raged and soldiers filled the streets. And you know the rest. I imagine I would be out of place in such surroundings and wouldn't know how to behave.

The internet café here in Amman is run by Iraqis and I've got a discount through some sort of subscription. Amman is more expensive than Baghdad, but much better – its peaceful environment cannot be compared in any way to Baghdad's volatile and dusty atmosphere, yet we Iraqis seem to carry our pain with us wherever we go. It is, I think, ingrained in every fibre of our bodies and forms the nucleus of every cell. Even when I try to sweat it out, my efforts are in vain, and there is always that bitter taste at the back of my throat.

Ali is not making it any easier for me. I think the poor soul has gone insane. I can't really blame him BUT he blames me! He says I have deserted him but, Bee, I haven't. I don't want to, and never will, dream of doing anything like that. I will back him up till the end, and I'll be the happiest person on earth to see him back on his feet again. I keep telling him that it is only a matter of time, but it's no use. One moment he is convinced everything will work out, and then the next he turns against me and makes the atmosphere all tense between us. He threatens to go to Syria and reminds me of how he left his family for my sake, and then threatens to divorce me. I usually hang up when it gets out of control. Then he calls again, apologizing for everything and promising to wait for the spelling mistake to be corrected.

I know we stand at a crossroads; I've kept nothing secret from him and all he really needs is patience. I hate his attitude. I have never been mean to him, and you know how hard I have worked to keep him comfortable in every way possible. He can at least show support by being patient. He thinks I should sacrifice my dreams at the altar of his 'love' for me. And I can't do that. This is my life's accomplishment and our safe haven, and I will not back out even if it means the end.

I know he is tired but so am I, and the difference is that he is still young and can start afresh, while I can't. He should think about gaining skills and working hard to get qualified before the age of 40, just as I did. Oh Bee, I clung to the hard rock with bare fingers (figuratively speaking) at a time when the regime was cruel and the economic embargo at its worst. I used to study by candlelight and would sit up the whole night, not realizing how many hours had passed, till I heard the call to Morning Prayer at dawn announcing the start of a new day.

Well, Bee, this is what has been going on since I arrived. I've also met up with old friends, and when Ali found out he just flew off the handle and made me promise to stop seeing them.

Sorry for pouring all this out, but what are younger sisters for, eh? By the way, I slipped and bumped myself while showering this morning. Thank God nothing is broken, but my right leg hurts a bit.

Love you always.

Hugs

May XXXXXXXX

09.09.08

Huh, unreasonable men

Hello dearest

Well. May, my usual thoughts about Ali are supportive. Ali is all alone now, and his predicament is worse than yours was, because he has no contact with his family and it's more dangerous for him to go out. Also there is the background worry of him not working but being supported by you, which I suspect isn't easy for him. So generally I feel very sympathetic. I don't blame him for getting depressed, and it's natural that he will take it out on you up to a point.

But reading your email I am now quite cross with him. How dare he ask you not to see your friends? You would never ask him not to see his friends. And he really shouldn't threaten you like this. I think it's just his fear and paranoia coming out. You shouldn't promise not to see your friends; he can't ask that of you. You need your friends more than ever and he should appreciate that.

Maybe you are feeling a bit like I have felt these last few months. It's a helpless feeling; all you can say is: 'Be patient! Be patient!' But you know it just seems impossible from the other person's perspective. And like me you are doing all that you can, but it still doesn't seem to be enough. It must be so much harder to feel the difference when you're stuck in Baghdad and there's no sense of progress.

I don't know, May, but is there anyone I can call about the wretched spelling mistake? Will they speak English? Is there anything we can do at this end to try to speed things up a bit?

Dearest May, I hope you're feeling OK. Despite the fact that I'm a bit indignant that Ali doesn't want you to see your friends, I think that the best thing to do is to keep trying to reassure him. Basically, just keep doing what you're doing.

Take care.

Bee XX

10.09.08

Wish me luck for tomorrow

Dearest friend

Thank you. Your letter was very supportive. From the title of your email I knew that all you'd say was true.

While roaming around the city I came across a shop that sold T-shirts and I went in and bought one. It turned out to be too small so I had to go back to the shop. I changed it without trying the new T-shirt on and it also turned out to be too small, so I returned for the third day in a row. The shop owner was friendly and laughed; I then asked about men's T-shirts and he said, 'Just bring your husband in and we'll find suitable things for his size.'

I started telling him about Ali's problem, and how long it has taken. I was even a bit blunt, telling him that the visa people were not corrupt but lazy – which is worse, because with corruption you can pay for things to be done, but there is no cure for laziness. The man was very sympathetic and told me that he used to have a friend at the Ministry of the Interior. He advised me to ask for a meeting with the minister himself, and to explain how time is running out for me to take up my fellowship.

He said that it is easy to meet any senior official in Jordan, and even if you request to see the king in person, you may well be granted the opportunity. This view was supported by the taxi driver on my way back, and then by Ban when she came to see me this afternoon. I WILL GO to the ministry tomorrow and meet whoever is available, and hope it works.

Ramadan in Jordan is more decorative than in Iraq and Syria. It is more like Christmas. You see lights resembling a crescent and stars at almost every window in the place where I live. A taxi driver asked if I was fasting and I was too shy to say no, and so he advised me to cover my hair if I were fasting so that it would be 'accepted by God'. I did not argue and thanked him for being such a devout person.

In Jordan freedoms are respected. You see all sorts of people wearing all sorts of things. Some young women are half naked, others decently dressed, and some are covered from head to toe with even their faces covered. They all enjoy their freedoms and no one interferes. The other thing I noticed about Amman is that public transport is rare – unlike Damascus, which enjoys an almost perfect 24-hour system of public transport and is very cheap as well. Ban tells me that there is almost no middle class in Jordan; people are either filthy rich or strikingly poor. This I haven't seen, but I will keep my eyes open because it is rather interesting. I've also heard that salaries are inadequate and many people have two jobs or more.

Well, love, wish me all the luck you can for tomorrow. Maybe I'll make some progress.

By the way, if Justin is a Gemini it is really impossible to cure him of working all hours and being away. The wife of a Gemini friend succumbed to depression trying to get hold of her husband, who was always at work and enjoying it. She used to travel during summer with the children, while he would be away working on some case or another. OK, lovely, I'll go now. It is getting rather late and I will have to walk on my own for quite a distance (still phobic).

Love you always.

May XXX

12.09.08

Ministry visit

Dear Bee

I went to the ministry but didn't accomplish anything tangible. An official there couldn't spare me even five minutes of his time to explain, and the juniors said it was outside their authority. But I insist on carrying on with my battle for Ali. I did make a fool of myself at one point, when I failed to overcome my tears, but never mind.

As you know, the advice I got from the Jordanians to seek an audience with the minister indicated some kind of democracy, and the idea sounded attractive and presented an almost perfect solution to my problem. So I woke up before 7 a.m. and put on a new black and white top, a pair of black trousers with a formal handbag and matching shoes, and then climbed into a taxi. The building was small and humble; it lacked all the luxurious fittings and marble walls and floors of most government offices in Baghdad. Entering the building was relatively easy; I had expected very strict measures but there was nothing like that and the security people were nice and friendly. I approached the information desk, told the man that I wanted to meet the minister, and he directed me to an ordinary wooden door with a soldier standing at it. I went right up to the soldier and asked for a meeting; he said that work had not yet started and I would have to wait.

By 12.15 I had been waiting all morning and my feet were killing me. I asked the soldier, who was beginning to look a bit sympathetic, if there was any influential person behind that door other than the minister, and he pointed to a room and let me in. I went into that room, where an important-looking man (Faisel Beg) was sitting behind the desk reading through some papers. The man who couldn't spare me five minutes of his time the day before was also there. When the official had finished his reading, I told him my story in a hurry, trying to insert as much detail as I could. I choked, trying to suppress my tears.

Faisel Beg looked at the other man and said, 'Something has to be done about these spelling mistakes; there are too many.' Then he tore a piece of yellow paper from a notebook and wrote a few words to some employee in the other building requesting him to help me. The man who could not spare me the five minutes asked in a sharp tone, 'Who sent you here?' and I said, 'The people.' He repeated, 'NO, I mean which official recommended that you should come here?' and I said, 'No one. It was the taxi driver, the shop owner and other ordinary Jordanians.'

I took the yellow paper and went to the other building but the man I was referred to was on leave, so I returned to the minister's building again and this time the soldier let me in immediately. Faisel Beg was not really happy to see me again; he took the paper, wrote another name on it and grumbled that this was not his job. The other man was still there. I realized that this was futile, and decided to continue standing at the wooden door until someone let me see the minister.

When 'Mr Five Minutes' came out he saw that I was still standing there. He finally asked me what the problem was. My efforts to suppress my tears failed, and so I talked to him with tears dropping on to Ali's documents. I explained about the separation, the fellow-ship offer, and I don't remember what else. He looked at me and said, 'Can you give me till Sunday (the first working day of next week) because I have to run to the bank now?' He added that he is in charge of all corrections.

I told him another two or three days are nothing in comparison to the past three months of waiting. I got him to sign the back of Ali's passport copy to say that I should come back on Sunday, and then he left in a hurry. I didn't really catch his name, but it was either Saleh or Salah Beg.

I cried all the way back and burst into tears when Ali called and asked what had happened. The taxi driver, listening to the whole conversation, suggested that I go to the minister's house after breaking my fast and talk to his wife about my problem. This sounds absurd but I might just consider doing it if things don't work out through the proper channels.

You know, Bee, this drives me to say that before the invasion, Iraq was the only country that functioned properly, and maybe Saddam's policies were not that bad after all. Nowadays this is no longer applicable and the country is mired in corruption. But, Bee, don't you think that paying to get your rights is better than not getting them at all?

Anyway, this is what has happened. I will go on Sunday and see. I think I will do just what little Jimmy Osmond sang in the 1970s: 'I'm gonna knock on their door, ring on their bell, tap on their windows too.'

Will go now.

Love

May XXXXX

Well done, my tenacious friend

MAY, Magic May, I'm very, very impressed. You know, there's nothing wrong with crying if you feel like it, and sometimes it actually helps in those hopeless anonymous bureaucratic situations. I once cried in a small Colombian airport when they'd sold off my mum's and my tickets, and they miraculously got us new ones. Maybe it helps to get through to their humanity. I guess they have to develop a hard shell and not be moved by people's plights. I think it's very nice that the taxi driver and shop people are trying to help and offer you advice. The taxi driver is right, you know: you should go and talk to the minister's wife. If she has any compassion at all she must try to help you. After all, it's still Ramadan.

But it sounds like it's Mr Five Minutes who is the key: he can really help, so you should pursue him as much as you can. Do you think he really is the person in charge of such things? Can you check with another person inside the ministry building? Find out what his exact name is too, as it makes more impact when you ask for a person by name. Oh, I wish I could be there, May. I'd stand by you and help chase down these people. Between us we'd make it impossible to ignore you. I wish I was there.

It was very busy at work yesterday (9/11 anniversary so lots of 'War on Terror' stuff), which is why I didn't write. Three days' work might not sound much but I felt I'd missed a lot of the girls' first full week at school. So today I've gone to the other extreme: Super-Mum Overdrive. I went in and did cooking with Eva's class this morning, and then after school I'm taking the girls plus three friends to the circus. We go each year. It's strangely kitsch and old-fashioned, but the kids just love it. We've got ringside seats; I will just try to avoid eye contact with the clowns so as not to do any horrible parent participation. And try not to lose anyone.

Am planning a quiet weekend. I will think about you all day Sunday and hope that luck is on your side this time.

All my love and hugs and a new surge of hope and optimism (where does it keep coming from!?).

B XX

14.09.08

DONE

Bee

I succeeded. I did it, and sent the corrected paper via email to Ali. If all goes well, he should be with me Tuesday night. Oh Bee, I am so HAPPY. Can't describe how I feel. Happy, overjoyed perhaps? I do hope you have a stronger term for me to learn. I went as planned this morning and was there at 9 a.m. sharp. The man kept his word. I waved to him as he came into his office and he recognized me, took the papers and in a matter of 45 minutes it was all done.

I hereby declare my thanks to Mr Saleh al-Zaban, Deputy Head of the Department of Nationality and Foreigners, for the care and help he has shown over our case.

I phoned Ali as soon as I left the building, not really believing it myself.

There is one other obstacle, though, and that is crossing the border. Someone at the visa office told me that it might take about 10 days for Ali's name to get on the computer at the border, and it would be better if he came by plane. I told the man that it may be unsafe for Sunnis to use the airports, as there could be militias. I will only relax when I see Ali in front of me with all 130 kg of his net weight.

He's been calling me like mad every 20 minutes, asking whether to bring this or that, and telling me to get a haircut and highlights and prepare him a hearty meal because he has vowed to fast all the way into Jordan and will not break his fast until he reaches our little flat. I kept laughing and the tension just faded away. Oh Bee, thank God, it was getting so hard.

OK, now that I've told you all about the correction, let me tell you about the Jordanian pauper I was watching yesterday. A saddening scene caught my eye as I was walking back to the flat carrying all sorts of pastries and sweets (so I wouldn't lose weight, hehee). An old man holding three carrier bags and a stick stopped by the rubbish containers on the street and started poking into them with the stick. By the way, Amman is much cleaner than Baghdad and Damascus. I slowed down to see what he was doing. The carrier bags were transparent and revealed the contents. The first contained empty Coke cans, the second old shoes and the third had some material in it that looked like clothes.

As he poked into the rubbish he brought out a couple of things. They turned out to be a pair of men's trousers and a shirt. He examined them closely, turning them upside down and looking through them, then he made a face and put them back. All the sadness I felt for the old man couldn't prevent me from laughing secretly. I did not laugh at the pauper but at the man who had discarded these things. He must have been a miser and had worn them to a point that even this pauper couldn't make any use of them. Just imagine, crushed Coke cans were worth more to the pauper than these rags. I wonder what kind of person had owned them.

As I got back to the flat, closed the door and lit a cigarette, the doorbell rang. At the door was another pauper, but this time it was a very nice-looking young female. She asked for money; I gave her some and she went on her way. I wondered if this was the reason behind refusing Iraqis – Jordan seems to have no place for the US-created beggars of the twenty-first century.

In another development yesterday, four journalists from the very popular Iraqi satellite channel Al-Sharqiya were assassinated in the northern Iraqi city of Mosul. This brings the number of Sharqiya journalists killed to 10. So much for democracy. There have been many similar events, but the saddening aspect in this particular case is that these journalists were not covering a military or a political event, but filming a Ramadan programme entitled *Your Fast-Breaking Meal Is On Us*. They visited poor families, cooked them hearty fast-breaking meals and donated a sum of $2,000 to each family they visited. So what objective can there be behind killing the poor journalists, other than to shut them up for attempting to expose how poverty has spread among the populace in 'filthy-rich Iraq'. This is my analysis, though proper analysts point fingers of accusation at all the religious sects in the country because all of them reject the secular attitude of the TV channel. Whichever is right, I see an organized scheme to silence 'messengers of reality' in Iraq, because even in the considerably stable region of Kurdistan statistics reveal that over 60 journalists have been silenced using various means.

What do you think, Bee? OK, lovely, will go now, so tired.

May XXX

14.09.08

MR 5-MINS SAVES THE DAY

WHAT DO I THINK!!? What do I THINK?!! May, I can hardly think at all – after the news about overcoming the 'Spelling Mistake of Despair' and Ali's joyful response, the rest of your email was a load of letters dancing about before my eyes and I had to read it all again about four times to make any sense of it. I just don't know what to say, May! And then a strange feeling came over me. You carried on talking about journalists and people being killed in Iraq, and do you know what? To my shame, I didn't care as much. I know it's wrong; so many lives will be lived like yours, but with no way out. Your story has loomed large over all of this tragedy, and now that you are almost out and the sun is shining at last, it is very hard to remember all that you're leaving behind . . .

It's late now and I'm sitting with Justin; the girls are all in bed and we'll probably get an early night too. Everyone's a bit tired. It's been a day of Enforced Family Bonding. We all picked apples from the tree together and went out together and did everything together; it's been sweet. I think Eva has become a little clingy since she went back to school. She keeps saying things such as she wants Daddy to be with her all the time, or kissing me again and again, so I think she just wants a bit of reassurance.

We had a funny scene today. We'd all gone up into Hampstead to the photo developing shop. Justin had ordered some prints (Elsa's birthday and some other baby photos) and we were so looking forward to seeing them. But the quality wasn't great, and they'd been badly cropped. Justin began to remonstrate with the poor woman at the till, saying, 'It's RUBBISH! It's USELESS!' and so on, in a loud voice. There was a queue of people behind him rolling their eyes and sighing. The woman looked upset; I felt mortified and tried to stop Justin from being rude. Then guess what happened? Eva and Zola were behaving beautifully but it was your little minx Elsa (out for the first time with no nappy on), who did a big wee on the floor.

I just looked down and saw a big puddle in the middle of the shop, and she was gazing dreamily at it. I said Justin *please* can you sort this out another day!!! and fixed him with my 'Meaningful Stare' that's supposed to signal that it's vital he cooperates. It worked and we left. At the door was a man with a small dog, so hopefully they'll blame the puddle on the dog.

So now it's Sunday, and Tuesday is so very soon. Ali must be leaping about the place; I bet he can't sit still. I think the bad luck has run out now, May.

YIPPEEEEE!!!!!

All my love

Bee XXX

More thoughtful but still got butterflies

Morning, dearest May! Monday morning now, which means Ali is coming tomorrow. Oh, let this be the time that our luck has finally changed.

I read your email again in a calmer way today and felt bad for having said I wasn't as interested in what happened to those Al-Sharqiya journalists. On Thursday when I was at work there was an NUJ (National Union of Journalists) meeting up in the newsroom. In the middle of a tirade about executive bonuses, in walked Alan Johnston, the guy who had been kidnapped by the Palestinians and paraded in a suicide bomber's vest. You remember, they kept him for months. We did vigils and so on at the BBC; and once, on an early shift, there was an appeal on the programme for his safety, and I was unable to contain my tears. Felt very silly as everyone assumed I was a friend of his, which I'm not; I just found it horrible. You're not supposed to show emotions in a newsroom, God forbid. Well, anyway, so he walks into the newsroom meeting all quiet and thin, and I had to suppress the urge to leap up and give him a massive hug. (I completely ignored him instead.)

So, in a roundabout fashion, it brings me back to your email about those journalists who were doing a light programme that was meant to be fun, cooking people's meals, and it got them killed. I don't even think that they were, as you say, exposing poverty or acting as messengers of the truth, and yet that didn't help them. I don't think journalists should consider themselves messengers of the truth, it has a too-glorious ring to it. The best way is simply to present the facts as you see them. World Service does this better than anyone as there are strict codes on the use of adjectives, value judgements and subjective language (famously, the word 'terrorist' is not used unless it is quoting someone else). This can make it harder, I guess, to make people care about stories, but it beats the alternative.

Well, anyway, I can officially tell you that I've gone off the idea of having another baby. Justin is appalled that I'm insisting on contraception again (poor man). I think it was a combination of him being away a lot, out-growing our house, and thinking about how the girls' lives are moving along at such a pace I can hardly keep up. You'll remember how, the first few months we tried, I became really upset, but then over the summer each time I got a period it came as more of a relief. So I'm now putting it on hold. When I explained this, Justin went into a tailspin, saying let's buy a house let's buy a house right NOW (after he'd just spent 20 minutes telling me why it's the wrong time to buy and we'll have to wait a year or so). But that's where I'm up to in my mind. So luckily you won't have as many Aunty May babysitting duties to do, HAHA! (Although an old college friend of mine has just got pregnant with her fourth. She is as sick as a dog, so it hasn't made me jealous yet . . .)

Just got butterflies when I thought about you and Ali meeting tomorrow in Jordan. At last we have something to celebrate. A step forward was so long overdue, wasn't it? How many more turns and twists of the rollercoaster . . . ?

Big hugs

Bee XX

15.09.08

Can't say how I feel

Dearest Bee

Can't say what I feel or how I feel. Maybe it is something like sitting right in the middle of Elsa's puddle (hehee). It is like one long nightmarish dream. There are only two more steps to go. The first is for Ali to cross the border safely, and then the major step of the British Embassy. I dread the last more than the first, but I don't think any of it will be worse than the previous steps.

Oh, Elsa's puddle made me laugh! The little baby must have enjoyed the freedom of going out without a nappy so she simply and naturally answered the call of nature. You were embarrassed, but I don't think she was. As I was thinking about Aunty May babysitting, a car playing music just like your ice-cream vans passed by (but in Jordan they sell gas bottles) and immediately I thought of green parks, ponds and feeding ducks. Though I expect, if I come, it will be autumn by then, and the colours will be all golden and brown, with leaves falling everywhere.

An old friend of mine has just called and asked me to come to Futoor – the fast-breaking meal (though I am not fasting). When I tried to refuse, she told me not to be silly because Ali might not let me see them when he comes. It will be a shame if he insists on not meeting them. They are a very nice, broadminded and highly educated couple, and they have always been on my side. But what she says is quite possible, so I will go for the Futoor right after sending your email.

Ban suggested that we celebrate, and so last night we ate sweets and drank tea. It is not a problem for her, as she is nice and slim. I don't really mind being fat just now; I will probably go on a diet when everything is settled. But, between you and me, my trousers have gone up a size . . . OK, lovely Sis, will write again (hopefully) after Ali's arrival.

Hugs to you all and a big special one for Elsa

May XXX

16.09.08

Bad-luck plague

May, we are just plagued by bad luck. We were out for dinner last night, and just as we left I looked at my phone. There was the message from you saying Ali's driver's mother has died (I hope it wasn't anything violent). Can he find a different driver, or is he using the same one as you did? You couldn't make it up! It's like the turn of the screw; at every junction there are more excruciating and unnecessary delays and obstacles. But I'm sticking to my theory that the more bad luck we overcome, the better. It can only mean that we wear it all out for the final push when you and Ali go to the British Embassy. That's when we really need luck to finally change sides and work in our favour. Can you believe how superstitious I've become? It's enough to send anyone bonkers.

Hope Ali isn't taking it too badly. Just a few more days.

Elsa went to nursery this morning with no nappy, wearing knickers. She joyfully weed on her key worker, Bridie, and again on me when I picked her up. She thinks it's funny. I'm not backing down this time, though.

What are the timing deadlines for your UK visa applications? Is your job/university still on hold? How long do we have?

Can't bear the tension rising.

Hugs

Bee XX

16.09.08

Frustrated

Dearest one

It seems we are haunted by bad luck. It is actually Ali who has suffered most. Being a woman is easier where transport and travel are concerned. Ali can't hop in with any driver haphazardly, as I did. He is coming with a Sunni driver. As I mentioned, only 20 or 30 cars are allowed to enter Jordan from the whole of Iraq, so drivers are really scarce. I hope your theory is right about bad luck because I will explode from desperation.

My job is being held open for me until 6 October. Ali is depressed but quieter this time, which means he is very sad. He sends you all his love and thanks you for your care.

Ban just called; she's at my flat. Will have to rush, love.

May xxx

17.09.08

Hopes and fears

Dearest Bee

Tomorrow is the big day (I hope). Ali should be leaving Baghdad at dawn, and I hope nothing happens till he crosses the border. He feels awful and phones almost every hour telling me that he has sealed the windows, taken the rubbish out and emptied the fridge and the deep freeze. Funnily enough, I don't feel anything towards the house and haven't missed it until now. I think it is the new spirit of hope that has started to grow inside me. I do hope all goes well and there are no more disappointments.

Ban came before fast-breaking yesterday and I had to rush. It is good that she doesn't live very far away. Taxis are available all the time, except at fast-breaking time and at 10 p.m. when it is time for a very popular Syrian soap opera. Almost everyone in the Arab world watches it, as do Ali and I. He is only permitted to phone me during the commercials. The soap opera is set in a neighbourhood in Damascus during the French occupation of Syria. It shows the old Arab traditions and how people lived at a time when the roles of the sexes were separate, and women had no say in the world of men. A time of heroic men and chivalry.

I saw you and Zo in a dream. I dozed off on the couch this morning and found myself at your house. You welcomed me and we hugged and talked, but your face kept changing; at first it was yours, then it became the face of a colleague. Then Zo came in and I hugged her hard and remembered that I had forgotten the children's presents. I told you not to worry, saying Ali is coming tomorrow and he will bring them along. Then Ali's phone woke me up at around 10 a.m. He told me that the driver had stopped by our house and told him to get ready to leave tomorrow at 4.30 a.m.

Bee, do you think there will come a day when we will have tea together and look back at this present time and laugh? Will it really become the past? I do hope so. You know, I started thinking about the girls growing up, then going to college and eventually getting married etc. But when I wondered if I could make a success out of my life, I got scared.

I bet you are as scared as I am about the same thing: have you thought how we will look and behave at our first meeting? Say, for example, we meet at the airport or the air terminal. Will you get dressed up, or will you regard me as family and look your normal self? I was thinking that I will not do anything unusual to myself but keep my look as it is. You already know the real May, so why bother camouflaging reality? We have loved each other and our families without seeing one another. Do you think we need to worry about first impressions?

OK, lovely, will have to go now.

Love you for ever and a day

May xx

19.09.08

Locked up and sent back like a criminal

Dearest sister

Talking about dragons spitting fire and spaceships kidnapping children would be more believable than all this misfortune. I can't quite see anything more humiliating, except being raped by gangsters and the forces of occupation.

All our hopes of a reunion were shattered. I woke up at 7 a.m. and called Ali, but his phone was off. I realized he must be passing through Anbar province where there is no coverage. I started cleaning the house and made a list of what I was going to give him for his fast-breaking meal. He had decided to fast all the way to Amman; this was to be his way of showing gratitude to God for saving him from the misery of being imprisoned in our home for the past 11 months.

At 10 a.m. he called, telling me that he was at the Iraqi border. You should have heard how happy he sounded and how he chuckled like a baby, teasing me about how I looked and asking whether I had gone and highlighted my hair or was I too stingy to spend money. By 10.30 he was heading towards the Jordanian border. I couldn't believe that they were driving at the speed of a rocket and that it was all going so well.

At 11 a.m. he called saying that he was at the final entry clearance office, but things did not look good. I just thought that this was part of his usual exaggeration and asked him to be patient. But at 1.15 p.m. he called again, screaming hysterically that they were not letting him enter, and I screamed back that this was impossible. The Intelligence officer at the border had told him that the spelling mistake hadn't been corrected. I told him to hang on while I went to the Ministry of the Interior to see what was wrong. The correction had been made on Sunday so there had been enough days in between to get everything sorted out.

I didn't think of anything and just grabbed my handbag and the documents file. I was wearing jeans and a T-shirt, and I sped out without wearing my wedding ring or watch or anything. I knew that on Thursdays office hours end at 2 p.m. so I took a taxi and sped to the Ministry of the Interior. I was there at 1.45 p.m. Most of the employees had left. I went straight to the desk where the correction had been made. The young man behind the counter remembered me. He checked his computer and his colleague did the same, and they assured me that the correction had indeed been made.

I told them that my husband was stuck at the border and they said it must be Intelligence who had not yet corrected their computer. I asked for Mr Zaban and he was there at the end of the big hall. I went right up to him and he said the same, adding that he could do nothing. Then, probably in an attempt to get rid of me, he told me to go to the Borders and Residency Office and described the location. I went out, not really seeing very clearly because of my tears, and took a taxi. It was after 2 p.m. but I thought that there has to be someone in charge at these important offices. The taxi driver was very kind. Seeing the state I was in, he came into the office with me and asked for some names he knew. The young officers on duty checked their computers and showed me that Ali's name HAD BEEN corrected. They also phoned the border and confirmed this correction, but the border police told them that the problem was not with them but with the Intelligence officer who wasn't convinced and wanted to see the correction on his own computer.

They apologized, saying that they could not interfere with Intelligence. The taxi driver suggested taking me to the home of the Minister of the Interior, Mr Eid al-Fayez. I was desperate and he was God's gift to me in my hour of need.

Ali kept calling and I kept asking him to be patient, but he said they had locked him in a car like a prisoner and were about to take him back to the Iraqi border. There had been a couple with him; the man was allowed entry but the wife was rejected because of a spelling mistake. The man couldn't leave his wife in the middle of the desert, and so he had to return with her. It seems to have become a sort of policy practised against Iraqi families requesting visas.

The minister's house turned out to be several blocks away from where I live and the driver waited for me, but the guards told me that they didn't know when he would be back, and I should return the next day at 7 a.m. to see him. It did cross my mind that the next day was Friday but, in the middle of all the tension and the self-pity I was feeling, I did not ask and instead convinced myself that surely the minister would be at home on Friday.

Ban came in the afternoon and suggested that I should go to the Intelligence office on Sunday and try to correct the spelling mistake. I really don't know how long I can keep up the struggle, Bee. Ali keeps telling me to return to Baghdad, but something inside makes me totally reject the mere thought. I can't tell him, of course — not when he is in such a bad state.

By 9 p.m. Ali was back home in Baghdad again. Thank God he arrived safely. Do you remember, Bee, when in my 'Apology to Hemingway' I said that they keep defeating you until you'll gladly want to destroy yourself? We have never ceased to struggle. It is as if we are living under constant punishment, lasting from the cradle to the grave. Is such a life really worth living? Where are our rights as individuals? Why do other countries assume that we have no feelings?

May xx

19.09.08

The last straw

Dearest. I couldn't sleep all night. I put my MP3 player on and listened to songs downloaded for me by Ali. I was afraid to sleep in case I was late.

I went out at 6.45 a.m. this morning. Amman was still asleep. The streets were empty and all the shops were closed. By 7 a.m. I was at the minister's gate. The same guard was still there and when I approached him he apologized, telling me that the minister does not receive people on Fridays and Saturdays and that he had forgotten to tell me. I tried to insist just a little bit and he said I should come again on Sunday and he will do his best to help me see the minister. I stood there for about 10 minutes, trying to decide what to do; I just couldn't stand the idea of being sent away because I knew that I might die from humiliation.

So, I will try my luck on Sunday. Seeing the minister will be the last attempt on my part, because if the minister can't solve the problem, who can? And if I don't get to see him, I will go to the Intelligence office as a final option. I just can't bear it any longer.

Funny how degradation in my life has taken several forms, but all have led to painful feelings and anger. My late husband squandered his salary on drink and I was forced to ask my mother for pocket money and to buy food. My mother saved my face in front of others, but never once did she forget to lecture me on the duties of a husband, making me hate myself.

Now in this marriage I am begging officials in a foreign country to help my husband, shedding tears and making a scene of myself.

The phase in between wasn't any better. I struggled with my in-laws, who thought their late son had left me money, and hinted at wanting their share. They also demanded a fancy funeral. When I told them that I had no money, they did not believe me. They arranged a fancy ceremony for him, then came to me demanding that I pay for it. One of them told me to sell the furniture and the fridge and give them the money.

I asked them to select either the Moslem way or the secular way. If they were devoted Moslems then the wife (where there are no children) would get a quarter of the inheritance plus her dowry and have nothing further to do with her in-laws. And if they wanted the secular way, then the wife would be in charge of the full inheritance but also the debts. They wanted the best of both, but the poor man had only his car, a worthless piece of land, and $10 in his wallet. My car was an old 1976 Renault 12 model, given to me by my mother to get away when his drinking got out of hand.

I don't know why I am telling you this, but no one believed me at the time. Even my only brother, whom I loved and almost worshipped, told my mother that I was hiding the money and denying my in-laws their legal rights, while in fact I was in debt for my husband's hospital expenses.

You talked on the phone to me about being strong. How much strength do you think I have left?

This Jordanian dilemma is the last straw. I know it is nobody's fault, but I can't stop blaming Ali and myself for getting married. Now we are stranded all alone in the Arab world, which believes in strength through numbers rather than acting as individuals. And so I feel obliged to go to any length to save Ali and my wretched self.

Ali just called and, after a lot of screaming on both our parts, we came to a final conclusion: if the meeting fails and the Intelligence office does not correct his name by Monday morning, then I will apply for the UK visa on my own and he will go to Syria. Otherwise, I will have to return home and buy a car with what is left of our money and resume my old life.

OK, lovely Bee, I will go because I need to sleep.

See you in another email.

May xxxx

19.09.08

Wretched

Dear May

Yesterday everything changed in an hour. I was high on optimism, and when I met a friend for lunch we chatted in the sunshine about how Ali is on his way and you could be here within three weeks. Then I heard your message on my phone. It had a strong physical effect on my body. I just drooped, my energy seeped away and I felt like a deflated balloon dragging along the ground.

I got home and, after calling you, I still felt horrible, even though it was some kind of relief that the reason he has been sent back is a clerical error and not anything more sinister. At the very least, this means it is worth trying again. You were right to go round to the minister's house, even though it may have seemed ridiculous. The situation has become so incredible that nothing you could do would seem out of place. I was completely convinced that we had it all in the bag; those last two obstacles (spelling mistake, then the driver's mother dying) made me irrationally confident that we were smoothing the way ahead. I felt so buoyant. Yet, since talking to you, it's all ebbed away.

I haven't cheered up since. Justin cooked me a lovely dinner but I felt miserable and couldn't really listen to what he was saying. In fact I felt ill; I was cold and very shivery. In the end, I went to bed with an extra duvet and woke this morning still feeling exhausted. I feel a bit dazed, but reading your emails has made me think that you're still moving; there is still something to be done, we just have to carry on and for the hundredth time tell ourselves not to give up.

I worry about Ali more than ever. Can anything else go wrong? As a teenager I loved Nietzsche and relished his notion: 'That which does not kill us makes us stronger.' Nowadays you often hear it from celebrities complaining about their drugs problems or being hassled by photographers, so I've rather gone off it. But yesterday I thought NO, he's just wrong, there's no way this is making Ali stronger. What if it does irreparable damage? Enough is enough. Optimism has become faltering and vulnerable. I'm just sorry, May. You must be exhausted.

Please try to stay strong and keep going. Sunday morning is our last chance. Do you have access to a printer? I thought I could write a letter of support that you can take with you. Would it be any use? Let me know.

Yours

Bee XX

20.09.08

The minister

Dearest Bee

Thank you for the idea. I don't think it would do any damage, so why not try and write the letter? I've been told that his English is good, so why not? I will be at the internet café for another two hours. If you have the time, write now. If you don't, just text me when you can.

Love you so. By the way, I feel awful too.

May XXXxxx

PS His name is Eid al-Fayez (His Excellency, I think, is the usual form of address).

20.09.08

Letter

May, SORRY it's a bit later on. I was out with the girls, and when we got back Elsa burned her hand on a halogen lamp and it took all my attention. They've only just gone to bed and I've opened my emails now. Here's the letter; I hope you can find a way to print it out. I'm worried about it not being signed, as I remember that was an issue when I wrote to the embassy in Syria.

But let's hope and pray . . .

All my love

Bee XX

20 September 2008

To His Excellency Eid al-Fayez

Re: Entry papers for the husband of May Witwit

Dear Sir

I write as a close friend and supporter of May Witwit. I am a journalist at the BBC World Service and we became friends through my work. We have since collaborated on a book to be published by Penguin, and May has been invited to do a PhD at the University of Bedfordshire.

May is in transit through Jordan, on her way to live in the UK on a student visa which includes her husband Ali. May is not only an outstanding scholar and original writer, but also an extremely special and beloved person who really deserves to reach her full potential in life.

It seems extraordinary that something as apparently trivial as a spelling mistake could threaten her hopes for the future. The fact that Ali was sent back from the Jordanian border has had a devastating impact on their emotional wellbeing. From London I can barely imagine the anguish May is enduring, having tried so hard to bring her husband safely in, only to have him rejected as the result of a minor error.

I write to you in the earnest hope that you may be able to help. I ask you from the heart to intervene in any way you see fit, and I appeal to your sense of justice.

I apologize for writing to you in such a direct fashion, but if it lies within your power to help May and Ali, I beg you to do so.

Yours most sincerely

Bee Rowlatt

23.09.08

Ali

Dearest Bee

Surprise, surprise . . . Ali has just crossed the border and is on his way to me.

I will tell you what I did, and to what lengths I went. Although they allowed him to enter Jordan, they have taken away his passport and told him to report to Intelligence next week.

I don't know what is going to happen, but it is better than being stuck in the inferno without hope. He is supposed to arrive in Amman within four hours. This has given me renewed energy. I feel recharged after the dreadful days, including today. Only now do I feel that I am alive.

Oh Bee, wish him luck so he will arrive safely. I've bought lots and lots of Iraqi food to feed my chubby one. I am happy, happy and again very happy. Thanks to Mr Saleh al-Zaban, by the way. It was his efforts that did it, and I will never forget him for the rest of my life. He really deserves to be promoted for all the patience he showed in putting up with me. I will send you lots of details as soon as Ali arrives and gets settled.

Bee, I can't believe it. Are we really in motion??

Love you for ever and a day

May xxx

Five-year-old child sent back from the border

Dearest Bee

This is a short one. Ali's passport was taken at the border so that his name could be corrected, and he has been given a date to go to the Intelligence office. Ali sends you his love and wanted to call you this morning. It was 7 a.m. our time, which means 4 or 5 in the morning your time, so I talked him out of it (for your sake, hehee). Plus all that he has learned are a few words in addition to his famous early phrases.

We woke up at 7 a.m. today not really believing it. We kept pinching each other to make sure. This is our first outing together in the local neighbourhood. We walked to the internet café. The man at the café greeted Ali and asked, 'Is he the one all the fuss was about?' and I said he was. Ali couldn't believe that everyone knew about him (even the janitor of the building greeted him and asked me if I am happy now). He laughed, saying that he has become famous because of my blabbermouth. Well, Bee, I cannot be blamed, can I? I mean, the issue deserved all this publicity.

Oh, before I forget: do you know what Ali saw at the border yesterday? What I am about to tell you is probably hard to believe, but Ali swears to God that it is true. An Iraqi woman at the border was granted entry to Jordan while her five-year-old daughter wasn't. The child cried, fearing that her mother would leave her there. Of course, as any mother (or any person, for that matter) would do in a similar situation, the woman took her child and returned to Baghdad. How would you assess such a situation? I will not comment at all.

By the way, how is Elsa's hand? I hope she is better, the poor baby. Love you, dearest sister. Also, have you heard anything about that problem with your arm? Do tell me. That gave me such a scare.

Must go now.

May XXXX

Reunited and it feels so good!

May. I can't believe you're both there, together again. I feel so happy and strangely light; that last setback really had me worried and full of fear. Well, now I feel like anything I say is insignificant in the light of what you've just been through, so I don't really know how to write to you after such an upheaval.

I guess the next step will be that you both submit the application forms together for the UK visa? It seems as though the Jordanians have been lovely, and I think it's very sweet that they welcomed Ali in your neighbourhood and knew who he was. The story of the mother being told to leave her five-year-old child behind is disturbing, but authorities here are also strict about people travelling with children. Even a newborn baby needs its own passport, they can't just be added to the parent's passport.

When Eva had just been born I flew to visit my German family, and landed over on the Swiss side of the border. At the time my passport had my old name on it, and Eva's had Rowlatt. The Swiss immigration man coldly asked me how I could prove she was my baby. It was horrible; he had a twitching little officious moustache and I felt like crying. I became agitated and emptied my whole bag on to his desk, scattering it with various cards and ID, some with my new name and some with my old. In the end, he believed me. Just the other night I had a nightmare about losing Zola on a crowded beach. It is the deepest fear there is, so I feel very sorry for that mother on the Jordanian border.

I'm at work and really hungry; my tummy keeps on gurgling loudly and I keep turning the radio up. The girls are all well but a bit tired; the weather is really changing here, it's a lot colder and grey and we all feel like hibernating. Eva and Zola are looking a little tired now that the school routine has settled in, but Elsa is having a great time. She has made sudden progress at her potty training. (About time – last week she weed on the sofa twice and I got furious even though you're not supposed to.)

I can't bear the suspense.

Loads of love and a big hug to Ali

Bee x

25.09.08

At the minister's gate

Dear Bee

So here's how it happened. I returned to the minister's gate on the Sunday, as arranged with the guard. The alarm clock had gone off at 5.30 a.m. and I dragged myself out of bed. I looked exhausted. I went out after the usual morning rituals and, trying hard to cover my drooping features under make-up, I was at the minister's gate by 6.45 a.m. The guard greeted me in a friendly manner. He pulled out a chair and made me sit down near his cubicle on the pavement and told me to wait for the minister's secretary.

When the guards changed at 8.00 a.m. I was worried as the gruff new guard asked me what I was doing there. I told him that 'I depended on God and His Excellency in my appeal' (a traditional phrase used by Arabs when they badly need something from someone), but even then he was a bit rough, thinking I wanted a residency permit or something. He told me that this was a private residence and not an office, and if I wanted anything I should go to the office. I had to cry out, 'For God's sake, I am a university teacher and have a fellowship in the UK, but my husband was turned back at the border.' His features relaxed and his tone changed, and eventually he showed me into a small living room in the official residence.

The room was beautiful in its mixture of western and eastern furniture. I found it enchanting to see a fireplace with a mantelpiece taking up one wall with two Victorian model chairs. The other wall had a picture representing some Indian legend. There was an elephant and on top of that elephant was a tiger and some other animals, each one on top of the other, till the lamb was on top of them all. I liked it so much and kept thinking that this is probably how the world operates.

I didn't dare move, not even to have a look at the photos on the mantelpiece, I was so nervous. Then there was the clatter of spoons and saucers and I remembered that this is a home, and the sounds of a home always afford a sense of security.

Soon the minister's secretary came in, and when I explained my situation he phoned the Ministry and told them to help me. He advised me to hurry to the Ministry to get the job done.

Of course I thanked him, and almost ran to get there as fast as possible. When I arrived at the Ministry I recognized all the people I had seen last Thursday and they all seemed very willing to help, but I was left waiting and then moved and then told to see someone else and then left waiting again until I finally went to the office of Mr Murtadha, the gentleman I had originally seen at the minister's house, and he repeated that he was following up my case.

So that was the end of my Sunday. That evening Ban came and, while we sat and talked, I felt an urge to go and read your letter to the minister. I told her about it and she agreed to come with me to the internet café where I printed it out with no particular reason or definite plan. I just thought I would take it with me on my next visit to his house if all else failed.

Ali called and I burst into tears. He kept asking me if I was going to desert him. This irritated me more than ever because I still had hope and dreaded thinking about having to make such an awful choice. I screamed at him to give me a break and to let me think about tomorrow. I hung up and burst into tears again. I didn't know what to do or what to think. I took Valium and slept.

On Monday I got to the Ministry of the Interior early. Only a few employees had arrived and I watched them coming in one by one, so that by 9 a.m. the office was like a beehive.

At 10 a.m. there was a rush in the hall and the senior employees were running towards the entrance. Suddenly there were a lot of men both in civilian clothes and in uniform. I concentrated hard, trying to find out what was going on, and there was His Excellency the Minister making a tour and inspecting performance. A woman approached him and complained about some matter and he listened to her attentively. I realized that I must also make a move, so I jumped up, took your letter out and just stood before him. I didn't know what to do next. He looked up at me and said, 'Speak up, daughter,' so I handed him your letter, saying that it was from a BBC journalist and friend to His Excellency. He pulled the letter out and read it. He turned to his office director, Omar Beg al-Mufti, who walks by his side wherever he goes, and told him to grant my husband entry to Jordan. Mr Zaban, who was also there, told the minister that he was following up my case and the minister said, 'OK, Saleh, see that it is done.'

This is the whole story, Bee, and I think your letter helped in speeding up the process. Thank you, love, it was great. Well, so much emailing has made me hungry so I will run home and have something to eat. By the way, it rained today on our way to the internet café, and of course Ali and I are not equipped for rain because it is rare in Iraq. We were drenched and got a taxi to the place, even though it is only a 10-minute walk.

OK, love, see you in another email.

May xx

Wonderful news

Extraordinary May!

Most of all I want to know what it was like when Ali arrived. Did he come to your flat or did you go to meet him? And I have to know what happens next. Tell me when you are going to the UK Embassy and what will happen. We only have that one hurdle left.

I'm on day two of five days in a row at work and it's great, but I miss the girls. Justin's mum has bought tickets to see the Royal Ballet's *Swan Lake* in October, and we're in a state of excitement. I got the storybook out of the library and we've read it every day (Elsa gasps at the pictures and pulls a bad face for the sorcerer and his evil daughter Odile). We viewed clips of the ballet itself and listened to the music online, so the girls will recognize the score and some of the steps when we go.

Anyway, I have to get sorted to leave the office in a few minutes. We just had the Pakistani High Commissioner in the studio talking about his country's relations with the US (looks like it'll be the next Iraq, the way they're going . . .).

All my love and hugs to you and Ali

Bee XXXX

Readjusting in Amman

Dearest Bumbo Bee

I will tell you about Ali's arrival. I remained worried even after he had crossed the border, because they had taken away his passport. I kept calling him every half an hour just to comfort myself.

Although deep down I knew that it was OK, the numerous setbacks had made me sort of paranoid. In Amman he called asking for the exact location of the flat, so I talked to the taxi driver and described the way. He was at the main entrance of the building within a short time. I ran down the steps and into the street. He had one suitcase with him and a carrier bag full of kebab despite the fact that I had already told him that I had bought lots and lots of food.

The meeting was very emotional and passionate. I had already made tea, and I prepared the food while he showered. We talked endlessly about the whole thing and how we had suffered. Later on Mr Zaban called to check if all had gone well, and we thanked him and promised to visit him at the office to thank him personally.

The next day, as I told you earlier, I stopped Ali from calling you at 5 a.m. your time! We had breakfast, then we went out and walked for hours. He bought a pair of shoes, because he couldn't do that in Baghdad. We didn't have anything to eat while we were out because it is Ramadan and all the cafés are closed. We returned to our flat, ate some of the enormous amount of leftovers and had tea, intending to go out after fast-breaking time.

Ban called saying she was coming over and we were delighted. We haven't entertained for years. I felt that life was gradually returning to normal. We had tea then some ice cream, and she went home around 10 p.m. and we went for a walk. Ali still fears going out at night, but he is gradually adjusting and I think our stay in Amman will be like a rehabilitation process, enabling us to adjust after all the tension and fear of Baghdad.

Kate had sent an email saying that she would be in Amman on Thursday night and so I sent her my new number and she called. Another delightful event. We exchanged calls on Friday and decided to meet (AT LAST). She took a taxi and came over to our flat, then we went out for dinner. We talked an awful lot about you, wishing that you were with us, and saying how great it would have been. I really missed you at that point. I operated as an interpreter while Kate and Ali talked. He said his famous phrases and then he moved on to sign language, using some other English words he has picked up during the past year. In general they communicated very well. So I have no fear that you will also communicate perfectly.

Ali should be able to pick up his passport on Monday if nothing else happens, then there will be a five-day holiday because of the post-Ramadan feast. This is supposed to end by Sunday. After that we will go to the UK Embassy. So this will be Monday 6 October, or Tuesday. These are the latest events, but I will write to you in my next email to complete the minister's episode. I can't wait to see you, Bee. I really want things to move very fast, but you can see how slowly things are going.

Love you always, and I wish you a great time at the *Swan Lake* ballet.

May xxx

27.09.08

Golden day

May, you are great. Well done with everything. You've been brilliant to keep it together. I feel really happy reading your email; it sounds like things are going so right and, although you say they're moving slowly, just think where we were a week ago. I think it's coming along perfectly. But I've learned to be a little more cautious now, so we can't take anything for granted. Yesterday at work I wrote to a friend's brother, who is very senior in the Foreign Office, asking if there was any way I could call his colleagues in Jordan and find out who it's best for you to talk to and so on. I guess it's worth just asking, isn't it?

I'm happy that Ali has bought some shoes – at last, some good news and stories of minor pleasant everyday events. The small happinesses are so precious. Today is the perfect autumn day; it started all misty and cold and I went for a run while J took the girls swimming. I ran up through the Heath as the mists were lifting. Rays of sun came through the trees, cobwebs were silver. It was almost like an ancient landscape, all lit up. I felt as if I was in a spell. I've never seen it looking so beautiful. I thought about how much I love Justin and the kids, and felt lucky.

Have to go now; we're having friends for a big lunch here soon. I might just drag the table out into the garden and catch the last of the autumn golden warmth while we eat.

Many hugs, to add to all those other ones we've emailed each other!!!!

Bee XX

30.09.08

Hello from the drizzle

May. So much is happening at your end that it seems to move on every day. I can't believe you're not in Iraq any more, and I bet you can't either. Today in the news the Iraqi government announced that the Eid holiday will last six days, instead of three. Made me laugh, as I remembered you getting annoyed at how they used to chop and change the holidays and festivals. Is everything OK about your jobs back in Iraq, and getting the extra time you need for the visa applications? I keep on asking you about the next stage: you must tell me what's going on! And what are you both doing every day now that you can relax together?

I haven't had a very relaxing time. Taking on a chunk of full-time work seemed like a great idea, but it's really too much to combine with three kids, and now I can't wait for a break. I've really missed them. Justin's away in Ireland, so I've had to be super organized in the mornings. This morning Zola needed a packed lunch for a school trip, Eva had to practise her violin and Elsa was demanding to be read *Swan Lake*. Zo had spellings to practise and wanted her hair put in plaits instead of bunches, but then screamed when I brushed it. Then Elsa wanted her hair done too. Zo argued about what shoes to wear, Eva wouldn't put her violin away and Elsa got covered in jam. I cleaned her and ran upstairs to brush my teeth. She began to scream, so I ran back down and caught Eva running away looking guilty; she wouldn't tell me what she'd done. This was on top of trying to make breakfast when we'd run out of porridge, and get myself ready to come in to do a day's work in some kind of respectable state. By the time I got them all to school/ nursery I felt like having a lie-down. Instead of cycling to work I caught the bus, then spent the whole journey trying to contact the doctor in charge of the various tests they did after that incident with my arm. No one seems to be in charge of it, and they don't know what to do.

Work is quite crazy with the economic meltdown. Bush just looks like a tired old man. There seems to be a certain strain of glee around the world about the heart of capitalism being hit so hard, but it does always hit the poorest in the end. I don't feel any glee about it. Hard to get a tangible feel for what it all really means, though.

It's cold and raining outside. Thank God I didn't come to work on my bike . . . OK, dear May, I'd better go now.

Enjoy the last week in Jordan. (Fingers and everything crossed!)

Bee X

02.10.08

Eid in Amman

Dearest Sis

It sounds like you are going through a very busy time. It's good, though. I know it can be hard for you with my lovely nieces, but it's good for you to have a change of scenery every now and then. Work is great – the only annoying thing about it is having to pull yourself out of bed in the morning. This, I know, I will have to retrain myself to do when I come over to the UK. But watch out for 'May the Bulldozer' after that . . .

By the way, I'd love it if you were free for a couple of days so that we can talk endlessly about us and move on from electronic and technological contact into a face-to-face tangible relationship.

Let me tell you about the Intelligence meeting with Ali. We woke up very early, having been unable to sleep. I knew that the offices didn't open until 9 a.m. but we were there at 8.15. The guard at the gate said that we were early. Ali had asked me the day before to go with him, because he said that I was a better talker (hehee, I think it's a polite way of saying a blabbermouth).

Anyway, a guard came out asking everyone the reason for their visit. When he asked Ali, Ali showed him the piece of paper he had been given at the border. He turned to me and asked, 'And you, Madam?' I replied that I was only accompanying my husband. He said that it was not permitted and I would either have to wait outside or go home. I knew that this was going to happen, but I couldn't tell Ali the night before because he was so depressed after all that had taken place. Ali was not in a position to object, and so to save time I took a taxi and went to the health centre to collect the results of his tests (a Jordanian requirement).

By 1.30 p.m. Ali was back, jumping, kissing his passport and waving it in the air. They gave it back to him without any trouble.

We were so happy and I called Kate and Ban telling them the good news. We went out for a long walk. It was great exercise but we compensated for the calories we'd burned by having ice cream and orange juice at an elegant café. Amman was crowded that night because it was the night before the Feast (Eid) and Ramadan was over. People thronged the streets and shops. There were traffic jams, and long queues at the baklava shops. People were buying new clothes and the cafés were full of giggling girls with their shopping bags.

We arrived back at our flat very late, exhausted, but very happy. This was one of the few nights in my life when I slept comfortably and soundly.

We spent all day Wednesday at home. Ban came to see us and I cooked lunch. I hadn't cooked at all until Ali came and had begun to enjoy being a lazy singleton! Anyway, we stayed home because the shops were closed. Today is the third day of the Feast and everything is back to normal. The internet café is open at last and here I am writing to you.

As for my leave from work: well, I am not really sure. I sent a medical report and asked for leave but I don't yet know the result. On Sunday morning we are supposed to get Ali a permit to stay for as long as they will grant him (I was granted three months) and then we will head to the UK visa section, which is not, as I had been told, at the embassy. Wc will get the forms, fill them out at home and take them back on Monday. I really don't want to rush filling them out. After that, I don't know how things will turn out.

OK, love, this is our news. Will write again as soon as we are on the move.

Take care of your health, Bee.

Love you for ever

May xx

03.10.08

Your arm

Lovely Bee

How are you? I don't know why the mention of your test results got me worried about you. Are you OK, love?

Ali and I walked for two hours yesterday, but we've spent the whole day today at home. Ali hates going out. Ban came over and we talked endlessly about anything and everything that has happened or is likely to happen. We also remembered the days when we were new at work and trying so hard to learn from our seniors. She left about an hour ago. I picked up a book that I was reading and tried to continue, ignoring the urge to go out. The book is written by an Iraqi lady whose mother was Scottish. Her book is a fictional account of the days of the economic embargo.

You know, Bee, I just love going out, no matter where or when, but Ali just loves watching TV. Anyway, when Ali saw the book in my hands he immediately said let's go out for a walk. I just threw the book aside, changed and went out. I told him I was worried about your arm so we've come to the internet café to write to you before continuing our walk. Please just drop me a line about your health.

Love you always

May xx

03.10.08

Good feeling . . .

Hello, lovely. Please don't worry about my health. The tests came back inconclusive on my weird arm thing. Guess that means it's OK. Not thinking about it any more.

Last night I woke at 4 a.m., which is unusual, and then as I lay there I started to think about you. I can't remember the last time I had a long period of time to let my mind wander without dozens of distractions. I lay awake for two hours, thinking and thinking about you and all we've done and what will happen and what to do next. I thought about how frustrating and bitter some of it has been; some of those bad times seemed to go on for ages. Recently, with all the new developments and good news, I've found it a bit hard to write to you about my daily life. On top of the problem of no spare time I also have the feeling, once again, that it all seems so trivial in the light of things that are happening. Last night I was writing a letter to you in my head that would've been the longest letter ever (can't remember half of it now); I got all excited and couldn't settle down to go back to sleep.

I don't know how long the flight from Amman to London is, but we will be there to meet you and Ali at the airport. A while back you asked about what we would look like when we finally met each other, and what that first moment will be like. It will be so funny! Don't worry about making a special effort or looking nice, as I will be my usual scruffy self. When I'm not working I'm lucky if I get the time to put any make-up on at all – and if I do, the girls laugh at me and ask me why I'm doing it (apart from Elsa, who demands to wear some). Sometimes I'll see myself in a shop window and think, 'Oh dear, you really needed a few more minutes!' But anyway, we have been practising a little phrase in Arabic to say to Ali when we meet him. I was taught it by a Syrian mum at the girls' school; she has been testing my pronunciation when we go to collect the kids.

At 6 a.m. I put the radio on to get the latest on the debate between the vice-presidential candidates, and that was when I finally fell back to sleep. Some of my thoughts were about your arrival; it could be so soon now. I want your first experiences in the UK to be friendly ones, so I think it will be best if you and Ali stay here for a little while, and then I can come to Luton with you and help you with finding a flat. This morning I asked Justin's parents if they could lend you their spare room just for a short while, and they agreed. We don't have room, but they are just up the road from us. So when you arrive we will take you there. There's only one problem: you absolutely cannot smoke there, not even leaning out of the window! They both hate it and Justin's mum gets asthma. I gave her my word that you wouldn't smoke there; you'll have to go somewhere away from the house. (Can you do it? I know you both love to smoke.)

Later in the morning, over a cup of tea, Justin was saying that the credit crunch means that rents are going down, which is good news for you. Even so, I think you'll get a shock when you see the prices of things. Anyway, I called the Middle East desk of the Foreign and Commonwealth Office and asked if I can send a letter of support. The man was very nice, so I emailed him a letter about your fellowship and so on, with your and Ali's details enclosed. I've asked him to forward them to whoever will be processing your visas. I did this on the advice of the other guy I know who works at the Foreign Office. Well, it can't hurt, can it? And it feels good to be able to do something constructive.

It's a very cold autumn. I swam in the pond on Wednesday; it was windy and there were brown leaves all over the water that we had to swim through. It was a gaspy 14 degrees. The cold is worse than last year when we made it to 1st November. I feel we have to beat that this year, but ouch ouch, oh I don't know, it's going to be a tough one. Perhaps you'll join us for the last one of the year . . . ? HAHAAA!

The girls are all in bed, tired at the end of the week, and I'm tired too. Justin is on his way home.

The world is OK, May.

B XX

05.10.08

More delays

Dearest

Thank God your arm is OK, but please do not exhaust yourself in any way.

Today is Sunday and time for filling out the forms. We went to the World Bridge visa section of the UK Embassy. We received the forms and were on our way back to fill them out at home. We stopped at a café for some tea and cakes. When I started looking through the papers I discovered that there were things which I couldn't really handle without consulting someone.

So we returned to the area near the visa building. There was a man, surrounded by people, sitting at the terrace of the Burger King snack bar. He was filling out forms for people. I listened first to what he was saying to them, and then decided to consult him. He looked at our papers and said that mine were OK, but they lacked an accommodation address.

As for Ali, the man said he will be refused a visa unless his name (as it appears in his passport) is mentioned in CARA's letter in a context that shows they really know that he is coming and staying with me and sharing the fund. Otherwise, he warned, I will be granted a visa but Ali will be rejected or required to produce a bank statement of his own showing a substantial amount of money. I called Kate, but it is Sunday, and then I called you and couldn't reach you, so I came to the internet café to tell you all about it. I will also write to Kate and see what she advises. More delays, I'm afraid.

OK, love, will have to write to Kate and then go home.

Love you always

May xxx

Butterflies . . . and thinking about dates

HELLOOOOOOOOOOOOOOOOOOOOOOOOO!!!!!!

Oh, I'm starting to get funny butterflies, May, when I think about it now. I'm trying, oh trying, to keep it all a bit squashed down, but it could be so soon. To think back on those long emails of despair and all you've been through, to be now making these last few arrangements . . . BUT, stop it! I have to remember how many times I've got myself all deranged and happy about developments, only to have yet another problem thrown our way.

I called the Foreign Office again today, and got through to a different woman. She said she'd seen the email I sent, and she confirmed that it had been forwarded to the Jordan office. It will be fabulous to have you close by. The girls can show you their favourite places (they each have secret dens near the duck pond). Please stop buying them presents or you won't fit on to the plane! You really don't need to. I'm guessing they will probably be a bit shy when they first meet you and Ali (apart from Elsa, who sings and dances for anyone). I'd guess Zola will be more adventurous and climb all over Ali, whereas Eva usually takes the longest to be comfortable with new people, but is very loyal.

When we have an arrival date for you, I'll book a day of flat-hunting in Luton. I was talking to my mum last night on the phone and she said Luton is quite ugly. I hope you won't mind it. I'm sure there are some nice bits, and if we don't find the perfect place straight away there will be time later to look again.

I've been moping around with a bout of nearly-flu. Wearing big sloppy clothes and hardly leaving the house. I'm not quite ill enough to be 'Officially Sick', but I feel rubbish and tired. J.'s been away filming; once again the dragging of my wretched self to school in the mornings with three moppets in tow is a pitiful sight to behold. I just wish the cough/cold whatever it is would just arrive properly so I can get over it, instead of lurking malevolently. I've even thought I should just go and swim in the Pond (it's down to 12 degrees now) by way of a 'kill or cure'! But at least the girls are all fine.

I'm blathering. One more cup of tea and then I might venture out into the autumn wind . . .

Hugs

B XX

08.10.08

A retrograde planet may have caused the delay

Dearest

Your email is a very cheerful one; I love it. You know, Bee, it is a feeling of love that began way back that makes me remember the girls whenever I see children's things. Of course I can't buy what I like for them, but there are sometimes small things that just catch my eye. They are your children, Sis, and I love them just for being so. After meeting them, I guess each will have her own special place in my heart and mind. From your descriptions each one seems to have very special qualities.

We are still waiting for CARA's letter of support to take to the embassy. I was expecting it today, but it seems that these horoscope things might after all be right (hehee) because they say at this particular time there is a retrograde (I can't remember which) planet and this, they say, causes delays in communication and also faults in electrical appliances and computers. Retrograde or not, I think all these delays will drive me nuts sooner than expected. Or maybe the state is long overdue? I'm not quite sure really.

I so much want to get settled and live normally. By the way, did I tell you that we are back once more to using plastic plates (just like in Syria)? I really hate eating off plastic. The plates just don't feel clean, no matter how hard you wash them. OK, lovely, will go now. Please thank Mrs Rowlatt for her kindness and tell her that I look forward to meeting her.

Love you always

May xxx

10.10.08

??? ?!!

May, May, May, is CARA's letter there? Have you been to the embassy? What's happening?

I'm like a jumping bean . . .

B x

13.10.08

Any news?

May, I'm sitting here with a load of dye on my hair. I thought I'd better cover up the greys in time for my birthday on Wednesday. That's no way to start a new year, is it? And there's a big stew on the cooker. Elsa is a bit ill and is doing jigsaws, with her rattling cough and puffy eyes. At least her temperature's gone down a bit.

On Saturday evening I was so looking forward to our favourite programme: *Strictly Come Dancing*. A load of famous people are paired with professional dancers, and have to learn various ballroom dances. Every week they try out a new one, perform it, and one person is voted off by the judges and the audience. The costumes are fabulous, glittering sequiny confections; the girls and I always argue over who gets which dress (Elsa likes the colourful ones, Zola likes the tarty ones, Eva likes all of them despite the fact that she's recently decided she wants to be a boy). It's the high point of the week. Anyway, we were only one dance in when Elsa was suddenly repeatedly sick, all over herself, me and the surrounding furniture. Poor miserable baby; she's never been sick before, so you can imagine how weird it must be to throw up if you don't know what's happening. I had to wash her, all our clothes and the carpet etc., and by the time I sat down again *Strictly* had just finished.

Eva and Zola both had their first ever sleepovers last week. It was so exciting. Eva was invited to stay at her friend's house, and so I invited one of Zola's friends to ours. Zo and her friend Gracie were up giggling and building nests until very late and had a 'midnight feast' of crisps and raisins at about 9 p.m. Eva's sleepover was a bit of an eye-opener for her: it turns out her friend is allowed to watch TV, eat limitless sweets and chewing gum, AND there's 'no bedtime' !!?? (Mine only watch TV on weekends/holidays.) It really made me wonder how strict and mean I am in comparison to other mums. I always thought I was a bit stricter, but maybe I'm a LOT stricter, my poor hapless children! Justin and I were both brought up in a similar way and I guess we just carried it on with our own.

Anyway, I'd better get this stuff washed off my head.

Goodbye, May. Please, please let there be no more delays!

Love

Bee XX

13.10.08

Bedtime rules

Dearest Bee

The letter has not yet arrived, but we were phoned by FedEx in Jordan this morning and informed that it is on its way.

Your bedtime rules reminded me of the rules we had when we were children. We were the only children in the family who were sent to bed at 7 p.m. All the other children never had this rule. My mother and father had both agreed that it was the right thing. I hated having to go to sleep so early and I used to hide near the staircase and listen to the TV programmes without their knowledge. My mother says that they sometimes noticed me but ignored me so as not to embarrass me or themselves. She says that I was always disobedient, and it was no use trying to force me.

You know, I've just remembered something about our bedtime story ritual. As a practical person my mother didn't see the point in sitting near each one of us to read an individual bedtime story. She used technology to solve the problem, bought a tape recorder and recorded three hours of bedtime stories in her own voice. She put the recorder in the corridor where all of us could hear, and let it play till we were fast asleep, so we had her voice while she was somewhere else.

I tried to argue with her about it when we grew older, but she insisted that it was valuable time which she could use to do other things. I still think that it was not a very wise thing to do, because what a child needs more than the story is the comfort of touching his mum and feeling her warmth. We were allowed to stay up till 8.30 on Thursdays because Friday was our weekend and there was no school. In the summer holidays we were allowed to stay up till 9.00 because the sun doesn't set until late. Anyway, I hated all these rules. They became less strict after my father's death, and I broke away from them as soon as I got the chance.

These childhood memories are so important, and they instill a certain attitude towards life, so I think parents should be really careful in applying their rules. I believe it is a good thing to allow children to mix with others and see other people's lifestyles, as long as these people are trustworthy. We were never allowed to stay overnight anywhere. Even in my forties I had to put up with some harsh words from my brother when I told him that I would be staying the night with a friend whose daughter was having an operation.

By the way, Bee, why did you use the word 'Goodbye' in your last email? I've not seen it before in your emails!!!!

I will have to go now.

Love you for ever

May xxx

14.10.08

Bad stuff and good stuff

May! Is the letter there? Is the letter there? Is the letter there yet?????? Will you text me when it comes, and also tell me when you're going to the embassy so that I can . . . well, I'm not sure what I'll do, but I want to know anyway so I can at least think about you at the right moment.

You know, it's so funny that you noticed me saying 'Goodbye, May' at the end of the last email. Reading back, it looks very final. It's just a silly thing: I find it really hard to end these emails at the moment, because I keep thinking each one might be the last one. It feels very different from the old days of writing to you. Back then was a bit like writing to someone in prison – trying to keep your spirits up but not knowing if you'd ever get out. Now, as we get closer and closer to the end, there's a different reason for writing. It's become more of a countdown. So now, when I sign off, I get a momentous feeling and that's why I went all pompous on you. Hope it didn't scare you, haha!

Some mad news from this end. Last week as I was going to bed (J. was out), I looked out of the window and saw a couple fighting in the street. The man shouted, 'I've never even heard of her!' then he punched the woman in the face. He punched her again, and she crumpled. As she fell, he brought his leg back, like a footballer taking a penalty, and kicked her. I began to shake and called the police. The man ran away, then returned. The woman was lying on the ground crying out for her dad. I was on the phone, peeping out of the window and giving a description of the man, when the police arrived. They were amazing: they chased him; he attacked them; they got him to the ground and everyone was screaming. Suddenly the whole street was full of flashing blue lights. There were cop cars and vans and ambulances everywhere. An officer came to our house and took a statement from me. It took almost an hour.

BUT THEN . . . the policeman's walkie-talkie buzzed and it was his colleague, who was with the girlfriend. I listened to what he was saying: she'd sustained severe injuries, and was in hospital. She had given a statement too, but hers was: 'I fell over. He was helping me. Leave him alone, he's my boyfriend.' I could not believe my ears. So even though she won't press charges, they want me to testify in court and I have agreed. I know you saw much worse than this from your house in Baghdad. It's very hard to shake off the fear and disgust afterwards, isn't it?

Anyway, poor Elsa is still ill. Last night I was up with her until 3 a.m. because every time I put her to bed she cried and cried and cried.

I think she did more crying than in the whole of her life to date. Every time I picked her up she pressed her little face into me; I think she just wanted the company. In the end she gave up, and we both got some sleep. But she's not much better today: swollen face, streaming nose, not eating, and occasional temperature. I'm a bit zombified too. It just makes me sad.

OK, dearest, I'm going to try to say goodbye in a normal and non-sensational way, but have got a bit self-conscious about it now . . .

er . . .

. . . bye then!

B XX

14.10.08

Happy birthday

Dearest

Well done, my brave sister. I think, if the police keep your identity hidden, this brute must be punished. Why for God's sake do women cover up for these animals? Don't say it is out of love because there cannot be any love in such a situation. I've seen similar things, but in Iraq 'decent women' are afraid to contact the police because of the old traditional way of thinking which maintains that only women of ill repute go to police stations. This reminds me that there are still a lot of men who feel uncomfortable if anyone finds out their wife's name. In similar situations the woman usually runs to her family. The issue is then handed to male members of the family to deal with: father, brothers and even cousins gather and teach that bastard a lesson. I don't mean to generalize, but that is one of the popular solutions.

Before the invasion women had the legal right to sue an abusive husband, jail him and then divorce him, but women didn't make use of this right because of the social rules. Women are now gradually losing their rights under the post-invasion laws, and one day they may have no legal status. There have been attempts to cancel the legal rights women have worked so hard to gain over the past century, and to make the subjugation of women official.

Tomorrow is your birthday and our day for going to the visa section: yes, the letter HAS arrived! So, lovely Sis, have a very happy thirty-seventh birthday. I will celebrate with you from Jordan and wish you all the best for the next 100 years.

A big cuddle for Elsa

May xxxx

16.10.08

WE DID IT!

Well, it's just the best birthday present ever. Yesterday was stressful enough with you submitting your papers and sending me texts asking about letters etc., but today was the final step. The big thumbs up, or down! I sent you a text message of support this morning, trying to be optimistic. But then it dawned on me at the same moment that this time I really have no Plan B; there was nowhere to go if the embassy rejected your visa applications, nothing to say.

So when the phone rang and I heard Ali shouting, I had a huge adrenalin rush, and actually it's still subsiding. My legs have gone wobbly and that stomach-churning feeling is still there. I texted all my mates saying simply 'May & Ali got their visas' and floods of texts came back. A lot of people have had to listen to me rambling on about this and have become interested in you. There is so much love and support for you both.

So then I sat down to write this letter, as I want to remember this moment, this sunny autumn day, the day after my birthday, when we FINALLY BEAT THE BAD LUCK!!

We did it!

Bee X

17.10.08

We are coming

Dearest Bee

WE DID IT, yes we did. I can't describe how Ali and I feel. When you called in the afternoon we were having lunch at a café, and were too scared to finish because we knew we would have to go and collect the results of our visa applications. At 5 p.m. we moved, got a taxi and went to World Bridge. They wouldn't let us both in, so I went in alone. The man handed me two envelopes and when I asked him about the results he said he didn't know. I opened the first envelope and there was my passport. It involuntarily opened at a page with a stamp that had my photo and the words 'Entry Clearance'. Then I had to sit down and open Ali's envelope. I just couldn't believe my eyes. His had the same thing. I went out and found him waiting, his face pale.

I played my last trick on him. I changed my face to look sad, and turned to face him. He tried hard to ask and when he managed at last to say, 'May, what are the results?' I burst out laughing and shouted, 'Congratulations! We made it!' The security guards at the door were all looking at us, and they laughed when Ali explained to them what I'd done.

After that we called you and Kate, then took a taxi and went to a travel agency and booked a flight with Royal Jordanian for Sunday 19 October. We should be in Heathrow by 3.45 p.m. your time. Bee, I am so happy. A whole new life is opening up before us. I thanked God. I have prayed to Him since the first day I came to Jordan and God has answered my prayers. Now you and I will meet face to face and talk and have our cup of tea together. I can't wait for Sunday.

Numerous hugs and kisses to you all

May xxxxx

17.10.08

The last email ever

Can't believe you tricked Ali like that, poor thing. It's unbelievable, isn't it, May? What a birthday present — for both of us! Well,

I've been imagining these words for so long, May, and now at last I can say them:

SEE YOU AT THE AIRPORT ON SUNDAY.

Love and hugs

Bee XX

Acknowledgements

May: special thanks to Charles and Penelope Rowlatt, Helen Späth, Bee and Justin Rowlatt, Kate Robertson, Professor Akkar and Lucy from CARA, Dr Jim Franklin, Professor James Crabbe, Professor Alexis Weedon, University Vice-Chancellor Professor Les Ebden, Ms Christine Ross and Miss Johannah Flaherty from the University of Bedfordshire, Venetia Butterfield and Jenny Dean from Penguin, Mr Adrian Sington from Westpark Pictures for their unlimited support. My thanks also extend to my friend Ban Dhayi for putting up with me during the Amman ordeal, and deep gratitude goes to my best friend, Maysoon, who nominated me for the BBC interview in the first place. I also thank everyone whom I have yet to meet for the help and support extended through my friend and beloved sister, Bee.

Bee: my thanks and love to my mum, Helen, and to Dave, and to Penelope, Charles and all the Rowlatts. Helen and Penelope in particular stepped up in the darkest hour, and I can never thank them enough. Justin was unfailingly generous and upbeat throughout, although just wait until he actually reads it (only kidding!). Many people have been supportive, but special thanks go to Lucy Potter, Amy Neil, Terka Acton, Vicki Harrison-Neves, Talia Barry, Nicola Baird, Tina Andersson, Donna Walmsley, Andy North, Kate Utley and Ian Simpson, and to Emilio Echeverri. Also, we owe pretty much everything to the following people: Adrian Sington for his patience, advice and support throughout the endless hysterics; the fabulous Venetia Butterfield and Jenny Dean at Penguin; and finally Kate Robertson and everyone at CARA for the despair-defying work that they do every day.

The Council for Assisting Refugee Academics (CARA) was established in 1933 in response to the persecution of academics across Europe under fascist regimes. A good number of those it helped went on to become the most distinguished academics of their time, including eighteen who became Nobel Laureates. This important work continues today, and in 2008 CARA assisted academics that fled from over thirty countries. Among these were a geologist escaping the dictatorship in Eritrea, an HIV activist running from government oppression in Cameroon, an education lecturer imprisoned in the Democratic Republic of Congo, a female lecturer sentenced to death in Libya for challenging the ideology of Colonel Gaddafi and a university professor from Afghanistan who was threatened with death. For further details go to *www.academic-refugees.org*.